Frank H. Peters

The Nicomachean Ethics of Aristotle

Frank H. Peters

The Nicomachean Ethics of Aristotle

ISBN/EAN: 9783337042899

Printed in Europe, USA, Canada, Australia, Japan

Cover: Foto ©Thomas Meinert / pixelio.de

More available books at **www.hansebooks.com**

THE NICOMACHEAN ETHICS OF ARISTOTLE

THE

NICOMACHEAN ETHICS

OF

ARISTOTLE

TRANSLATED BY

F. H. PETERS, M.A.

FELLOW OF UNIVERSITY COLLEGE, OXFORD

FOURTEENTH EDITION

Revised and adapted to Bywater's Text

LONDON

KEGAN PAUL, TRENCH, TRUBNER & CO., LTD.

BROADWAY HOUSE, 68–74, CARTER LANE, E.C.

Printed in Great Britain by Butler & Tanner Ltd., *Frome and London*

PREFACE TO THE FIFTH EDITION.

MANY more or less important alterations have been made in this translation, which was first published in 1881, as new editions have from time to time been called for. The present edition in particular has been revised throughout, and brought into accordance with Bywater's text (Oxford, 1890),* which is coming to be recognized, not in Oxford only, as the received text of the Nicomachean Ethics. I wish gratefully to acknowledge the debt which, in common with all lovers of Aristotle, I owe to Mr. Bywater, both for his edition and for his "Contributions to the Textual Criticism of the Nicomachean Ethics" (Oxford, 1892).

To Mr. Stewart also I wish to express my gratitude, not only for much assistance derived from his admirable "Notes on the Nicomachean Ethics" (Oxford, 1892), but also for much kindly and helpful criticism in that work and in a review of my first edition (*Mind*, July, 1881). My old friends Mr.

* In the few passages where this text is not followed, the reading adopted is indicated in a note.

A. C. Bradley and Mr. J. Cook Wilson (Professors now at Glasgow and Oxford respectively) will allow me to repeat my thanks for the valuable help they gave me when the first edition was passing through the press. To Mr. F. H. Hall of Oriel, and Mr. L. A. Selby Bigge of my own College, I am indebted for some corrections in a subsequent edition. To other translators and commentators I am also under many obligations, which I can only acknowledge in general terms.

When I have inserted in the text explanatory words of my own, I have enclosed them in square brackets thus [ ]. A short Index of leading terms and proper names has been added to this edition (in preparing which I have found Mr. Bywater's Index of the greatest service). This Index makes no pretension to completeness or anything approaching to completeness (except in regard to proper names). Its aim is merely, in conjunction with the Table of Contents, to help the reader to find the more important passages bearing on the questions in which he may be specially interested.

F. H. PETERS.

OXFORD, *May*, 1893.

CONSPECTUS.

	BOOK
Of the good or the end	I.
Of moral virtue in general	II.
Of the will	III. 1–5.
Of the several moral virtues and vices ...	III. 6–end of V.
Of the intellectual virtues	VI.
Of forms of moral character other than virtue or vice	VII. 1–10.
First account of pleasure	VII. 11–end.
Of friendship or love	VIII. and IX.
Second account of pleasure	X. 1–5.
Conclusion	X. 6–end.

TABLE OF CONTENTS.

BOOK I.

THE END.

CHAP.		PAGE
1.	In all he does man seeks some good as end or means ...	1
2.	*The* end is *the* good; our subject is this and its science, Politics	2
3.	Exactness not permitted by subject, nor to be expected by student, who needs experience and training	3
4.	Men agree that the good is happiness, but differ as to what this is. We must reason from facts accepted without question by the man of trained character	5
5.	The good cannot be pleasure, as some hold, nor honour, nor virtue	6
6.	Various arguments to show against the Platonists that there cannot be one universal good: even if there were it would not help us here	8
7.	The good is the final end, and happiness is this. To find it we ask, What is man's function? Resulting definition of happiness...	12
8.	This view harmonizes various current views	18
9.	Is happiness acquired, or the gift of Gods or chance? ...	22
10.	Can no man be called happy during life?	23
11.	Cannot the fortunes of survivors affect the dead?	27
12.	Happiness as absolute end is above praise	28
13.	Division of the faculties and resulting division of the virtues	30

BOOK II.

MORAL VIRTUE.

CHAP.		PAGE
1.	Moral virtue is acquired by the repetition of the corresponding acts	34
2.	These acts must be such as reason prescribes; they cannot be defined exactly, but must be neither too much nor too little	36
3.	Virtue is in various ways concerned with pleasure and pain	38
4.	The conditions of virtuous action as distinct from artistic production	41
5.	Virtue not an emotion, nor a faculty, but a trained faculty or habit	42
6.	Viz. the habit of choosing the mean	43
7.	This must be applied to the several virtues	48
8.	The two vicious extremes are opposed to one another and to the intermediate virtue	52
9.	The mean is hard to hit, and is a matter of perception not of reasoning	55

BOOK III.

CHAPTERS 1–5. THE WILL.

1.	An act is involuntary when done (*a*) under compulsion, or (*b*) through ignorance: (*a*) means not originated by doer, (*b*) means through ignorance of the circumstances: voluntary, then, means originated with knowledge of circumstances	58
2.	Purpose, a mode of will, means choice after deliberation ...	66
3.	We deliberate on what we can do—not on ends, but means	68
4.	We wish for the end, the real or apparent good	72
5.	Virtue and vice are alike voluntary: our acts are our own; for we are punished for them: ignorance is no excuse when due to negligence: if this be our character, we have made it by repeated acts: even bodily vices are blamable when thus formed. We cannot plead that our	

PAGE

notion of good depends on our nature; for (1) vice would still be as voluntary as virtue, (2) we help to make ourselves what we are 74

CHAPTERS 6–12. THE SEVERAL MORAL VIRTUES AND VICES.

6. Of courage and the opposite vices 80
7. Of courage—*continued* 82
8. Of courage improperly so called 85
9. How courage involves both pain and pleasure 89
10. Of temperance 91
11. Of temperance—*continued* 93
12 How profligacy is more voluntary than cowardice 96

BOOK IV.

THE SAME—*Continued.*

1. Of liberality 99
2. Of magnificence 108
3. Of high-mindedness 113
4. Of a similar virtue in smaller matters 120
5. Of gentleness 122
6. Of agreeableness 125
7. Of truthfulness 127
8. Of wittiness 131
9. Of the feeling of shame 133

BOOK V.

THE SAME—*Concluded.* JUSTICE.

1. Preliminary. Two senses of justice distinguished. Of justice (1) = obedience to law, = complete virtue ... 136
2. Of justice (2) = fairness, how related to justice (1). What is just in distribution distinguished from what is just in correction 140

CHAP. PAGE

3. Of what is just in distribution, and its rule of geometrical proportion 144
4. Of what is just in correction, and its rule of arithmetical proportion 147
5. Simple requital is not identical with what is just, but proportionate requital is what is just in exchange; and this is effected by means of money. We can now give a general definition of justice (2) 152
6. (It is possible to act unjustly without being unjust.) That which is just in the strict sense is between citizens only, for it implies law 160
7. It is in part natural, in part conventional 163
8. The internal conditions of a just or unjust action, and of a just or unjust agent 165
9. Sundry questions about doing and suffering injustice ... 169
10. Of equity 174
11. Can a man wrong himself? 176

BOOK VI.

THE INTELLECTUAL VIRTUES.

1. Must be studied because (*a*) reason prescribes the mean, (*b*) they are a part of human excellence. The intellect is (1) scientific, (2) calculative: we want the virtue of each 180
2. The function of the intellect, both in practice and speculation, is to attain truth 182
3. Of the five modes of attaining truth: (1) of demonstrative science of things unalterable 184
4. Of knowledge of things alterable, viz. (2) of art in what we make 185
5. And (3) of prudence in what we do, the virtue of the calculative intellect 186
6. (4) Of intuitive reason as the basis of demonstrative science 189
7. (5) Of wisdom as the union of science and intuitive reason. Comparison of the two intellectual virtues, wisdom and prudence 190
8. Prudence compared with statesmanship and other forms of knowledge 192

CHAP. PAGE

9. Of deliberation 195
10. Of intelligence 198
11. Of judgment. Of reason or intuitive perception as the basis of the practical intellect 199
12. Of the uses of wisdom and prudence. How prudence is related to cleverness 202
13. How prudence is related to moral virtue 205

BOOK VII.

CHAPTERS 1–10. CHARACTERS OTHER THAN VIRTUE AND VICE.

1. Of continence and incontinence, heroic virtue and brutality. Of method. Statement of opinions about continence 208
2. Statement of difficulties as to how one can know right and do wrong 210
3. Solution: to know has many senses; in what sense such a man knows 214
4. Of incontinence in the strict and in the metaphorical sense 220
5. Of incontinence in respect of brutal or morbid appetites ... 224
6. Incontinence in anger less blamed than in appetite ... 227
7. Incontinence yields to pleasure, softness to pain. Two kinds of incontinence, the hasty and the weak ... 230
8. Incontinence compared with vice and virtue 233
9. Continence and incontinence not identical with keeping and breaking a resolution 235
10. Prudence is not, but cleverness is, compatible with incontinence 237

CHAPTERS 11–14. PLEASURE.

11. We must now discuss pleasure. Opinions about it ... 239
12. Answers to arguments against goodness of pleasure. Ambiguity of good and pleasant. Pleasure not a transition, but unimpeded activity 240
13. Pleasure is good, and the pleasure that consists in the highest activity is *the* good. All admit that happiness is pleasant. Bodily pleasures not the only pleasures 243
14. Of the bodily pleasures, and the distinction between naturally and accidentally pleasant 246

BOOK VIII.

FRIENDSHIP OR LOVE.

CHAP		PAGE
1.	Uses of friendship. Differences of opinion about it ...	251
2.	Three motives of friendship. Friendship defined	253
3.	Three kinds of friendship corresponding to the three motives. Perfect friendship is that whose motive is the good	255
4.	The others are imperfect copies of this	258
5.	Intercourse necessary to the maintenance of friendship ...	260
6.	Impossible to have many true friends	262
7.	Of friendship between unequal persons, and its rule of proportion. Limits within which this is possible	265
8.	Of loving and being loved	267
9.	Every society has its own form of friendship as of justice. All societies are summed up in civil society	269
10.	Of the three forms of constitution	271
11.	Of the corresponding forms of friendship	274
12.	Of the friendship of kinsmen and comrades	276
13.	Of the terms of interchange and quarrels hence arising in equal friendships	279
14.	Of the same in unequal friendships	283

BOOK IX.

FRIENDSHIP OR LOVE—*Continued.*

CHAP		PAGE
1.	Of the rule of proportion in dissimilar friendships	286
2.	Of the conflict of duties	289
3.	Of the dissolution of friendships	292
4.	A man's relation to his friend like his relation to himself	294
5.	Friendship and good-will	297
6.	Friendship and unanimity	299
7.	Why benefactors love more than they are loved	300
8.	In what sense it is right to love one's self	303
9.	Why a happy man needs friends	307
10.	Of the proper number of friends	312
11.	Friends needed both in prosperity and adversity	314
12.	Friendship is realized in living together	316

BOOK X.

Chapters 1–5. PLEASURE.

CHAP. PAGE

1. Reasons for discussing pleasure 318
2. Arguments of Eudoxus that pleasure is the good 319
3. Argument that it is not a quality; that it is not determined; that it is a motion or coming into being. Pleasures differ in kind 322
4. Pleasure defined: its relation to activity 325
5. Pleasures differ according to the activities. The standard is the good man 330

Chapters 6–9. CONCLUSION.

6. Happiness not amusement, but life 335
7. Of the speculative life as happiness in the highest sense ... 337
8. Of the practical life as happiness in a lower sense, and of the relation between the two. Prosperity, how far needed 341
9. How is the end to be realized? 346

THE NICOMACHEAN ETHICS OF ARISTOTLE.

BOOK I.

THE END.

1 1. EVERY art and every kind of inquiry, and likewise every act and purpose, seems to aim at some good: and so it has been well said that the good is that at which everything aims.

In all he does man seeks some good as end or means.

2 But a difference is observable among these aims or ends. What is aimed at is sometimes the exercise of a faculty, sometimes a certain result beyond that exercise. And where there is an end beyond the act, there the result is better than the exercise of the faculty.

3 Now since there are many kinds of actions and many arts and sciences, it follows that there are many ends also; *e.g.* health is the end of medicine, ships of shipbuilding, victory of the art of war, and wealth of economy.

4 But when several of these are subordinated to

some one art or science,—as the making of bridles and other trappings to the art of horsemanship, and this in turn, along with all else that the soldier does, to the art of war, and so on,*—then the end of the master-art is always more desired than the ends of the subordinate
arts, since these are pursued for its sake. And this is 5
equally true whether the end in view be the mere exercise of a faculty or something beyond that, as in the above instances.

The end is THE *good; our subject is this and its science Politics.*

2. If then in what we do there be some end which 1
we wish for on its own account, choosing all the others as means to this, but not every end without exception as a means to something else (for so we should go on *ad infinitum*, and desire would be left void and objectless),—this evidently will be the good or the
best of all things. And surely from a practical point 2
of view it much concerns us to know this good; for then, like archers shooting at a definite mark, we shall be more likely to attain what we want.

If this be so, we must try to indicate roughly what 3
it is, and first of all to which of the arts or sciences it belongs.

It would seem to belong to the supreme art or 4
science, that one which most of all deserves the name of master-art or master-science.

Now Politics † seems to answer to this description. 5

* Reading τὸν αὐτὸν δὲ.

† To Aristotle Politics is a much wider term than to us; it covers the whole field of human life, since man is essentially social (7, 6); it has to determine (1) what is the good?—the question of this treatise (§ 9)—and (2) what can law do to promote this good?—the question of the sequel, which is specially called "The Politics:" *cf.* X. 9.

For it prescribes which of the sciences a state needs, and which each man shall study, and up to what point; and to it we see subordinated even the highest arts, such as economy, rhetoric, and the art of war.

Since then it makes use of the other practical sciences, and since it further ordains what men are to do and from what to refrain, its end must include the ends of the others, and must be the proper good of man.

For though this good is the same for the individual and the state, yet the good of the state seems a grander and more perfect thing both to attain and to secure; and glad as one would be to do this service for a single individual, to do it for a people and for a number of states is nobler and more divine.

This then is the aim of the present inquiry, which is a sort of political inquiry.*

Exactness not permitted by subject nor to be expected by student, who needs experience and training.

3. We must be content if we can attain to so much precision in our statement as the subject before us admits of; for the same degree of accuracy is no more to be expected in all kinds of reasoning than in all kinds of handicraft.

Now the things that are noble and just (with which Politics deals) are so various and so uncertain, that some think these are merely conventional and not natural distinctions.

There is a similar uncertainty also about what is good, because good things often do people harm: men have before now been ruined by wealth, and have lost their lives through courage.

Our subject, then, and our data being of this

* *i.e.* covers a part of the ground only: see preceding note.

nature, we must be content if we can indicate the truth roughly and in outline, and if, in dealing with matters that are not amenable to immutable laws, and reasoning from premises that are but probable, we can arrive at probable conclusions.*

The reader, on his part, should take each of my statements in the same spirit; for it is the mark of an educated man to require, in each kind of inquiry, just so much exactness as the subject admits of: it is equally absurd to accept probable reasoning from a mathematician, and to demand scientific proof from an orator.

But each man can form a judgment about what he 5
knows, and is called "a good judge" of that—of any special matter when he has received a special education therein, "a good judge" (without any qualifying epithet) when he has received a universal education And hence a young man is not qualified to be a student of Politics; for he lacks experience of the affairs of life, which form the data and the subject-matter of Politics.

Further, since he is apt to be swayed by his 6
feelings, he will derive no benefit from a study whose aim is not speculative but practical.

But in this respect young in character counts the 7
same as young in years; for the young man's disqualification is not a matter of time, but is due to the fact that feeling rules his life and directs all his desires. Men of this character turn the knowledge

* The expression τὰ ὡς ἐπὶ τὸ πολύ covers both (1) what is generally though not universally true, and (2) what is probable though not certain.

they get to no account in practice, as we see with those we call incontinent; but those who direct their desires and actions by reason will gain much profit from the knowledge of these matters.

So much then by way of preface as to the student, and the spirit in which he must accept what we say, and the object which we propose to ourselves.

4. Since—to resume—all knowledge and all purpose aims at some good, what is this which we say is the aim of Politics; or, in other words, what is the highest of all realizable goods? *Men agree that the good is happiness, but differ as to what this is.*

As to its name, I suppose nearly all men are agreed; for the masses and the men of culture alike declare that it is happiness, and hold that to "live well" or to "do well" is the same as to be "happy."

But they differ as to what this happiness is, and the masses do not give the same account of it as the philosophers.

The former take it to be something palpable and plain, as pleasure or wealth or fame; one man holds it to be this, and another that, and often the same man is of different minds at different times,—after sickness it is health, and in poverty it is wealth; while when they are impressed with the consciousness of their ignorance, they admire most those who say grand things that are above their comprehension.

Some philosophers, on the other hand, have thought that, beside these several good things, there is an "absolute" good which is the cause of their goodness.

As it would hardly be worth while to review all the opinions that have been held, we will confine ourselves to those which are most popular, or which seem to have some foundation in reason.

We must reason from facts accepted without question by the man of trained character.

But we must not omit to notice the distinction 5
that is drawn between the method of proceeding from your starting-points or principles, and the method of working up to them. Plato used with fitness to raise this question, and to ask whether the right way is from or to your starting-points, as in the race-course you may run from the judges to the boundary, or *vice versâ.*

Well, we must start from what is known.

But "what is known" may mean two things: "what is known to us," which is one thing, or "what is known" simply, which is another.

I think it is safe to say that *we* must start from what is known to *us.*

And on this account nothing but a good moral 6
training can qualify a man to study what is noble
and just—in a word, to study questions of Politics.
For the undemonstrated fact is here the starting- 7
point, and if this undemonstrated fact be sufficiently evident to a man, he will not require a "reason why." Now the man who has had a good moral training either has already arrived at starting-points or principles of action, or will easily accept them when pointed out. But he who neither has them nor will accept them may hear what Hesiod says *—

> "The best is he who of himself doth know;
> Good too is he who listens to the wise;
> But he who neither knows himself nor heeds
> The words of others, is a useless man."

The good cannot be pleasure, nor honour, nor virtue.

5. Let us now take up the discussion at the point 1
from which we digressed.

* "Works and Days," 291-295.

It seems that men not unreasonably take their notions of the good or happiness from the lives actually led, and that the masses who are the least refined suppose it to be pleasure, which is the reason why they aim at nothing higher than the life of enjoyment.

For the most conspicuous kinds of life are three: this life of enjoyment, the life of the statesman, and, thirdly, the contemplative life.

The mass of men show themselves utterly slavish in their preference for the life of brute beasts, but their views receive consideration because many of those in high places have the tastes of Sardanapalus.

Men of refinement with a practical turn prefer honour; for I suppose we may say that honour is the aim of the statesman's life.

But this seems too superficial to be the good we are seeking: for it appears to depend upon those who give rather than upon those who receive it; while we have a presentiment that the good is something that is peculiarly a man's own and can scarce be taken away from him.

Moreover, these men seem to pursue honour in order that they may be assured of their own excellence,—at least, they wish to be honoured by men of sense, and by those who know them, and on the ground of their virtue or excellence. It is plain, then, that in their view, at any rate, virtue or excellence is better than honour; and perhaps we should take this to be the end of the statesman's life, rather than honour.

But virtue or excellence also appears too incomplete to be what we want; for it seems that a man might have virtue and yet be asleep or be inactive all his life, and, moreover, might meet with the greatest disasters and misfortunes; and no one would maintain that such a man is happy, except for argument's sake. But we will not dwell on these matters now, for they are sufficiently discussed in the popular treatises.

The third kind of life is the life of contemplation: 7
we will treat of it further on.*

As for the money-making life, it is something 8
quite contrary to nature; and wealth evidently is not the good of which we are in search, for it is merely useful as a means to something else. So we might rather take pleasure and virtue or excellence to be ends than wealth; for they are chosen on their own account. But it seems that not even they are the end, though much breath has been wasted in attempts to show that they are.

Various arguments to show against the Platonists that there cannot be one universal good.

6. Dismissing these views, then, we have now to 1
consider the "universal good," and to state the difficulties which it presents; though such an inquiry is not a pleasant task in view of our friendship for the authors of the doctrine of ideas. But we venture to think that this is the right course, and that in the interests of truth we ought to sacrifice even what is nearest to us, especially as we call ourselves philosophers. Both are dear to us, but it is a sacred duty to give the preference to truth.

In the first place, the authors of this theory them- 2
selves did not assert a common idea in the case of things of which one is prior to the other; and for this

* *Cf.* VI. 7, 12, and X. 7, 8.

reason they did not hold one common idea of numbers. Now the predicate good is applied to substances and also to qualities and relations. But that which has independent existence, what we call "substance," is logically prior to that which is relative; for the latter is an offshoot as it were, or [in logical language] an accident of a thing or substance. So [by their own showing] there cannot be one common idea of these goods.

Secondly, the term good is used in as many different ways as the term "is" or "being:" we apply the term to substances or independent existences, as God, reason; to qualities, as the virtues; to quantity, as the moderate or due amount; to relatives, as the useful; to time, as opportunity; to place, as habitation, and so on. It is evident, therefore, that the word good cannot stand for one and the same notion in all these various applications; for if it did, the term could not be applied in all the categories, but in one only.

Thirdly, if the notion were one, since there is but one science of all the things that come under one idea, there would be but one science of all goods; but as it is, there are many sciences even of the goods that come under one category; as, for instance, the science which deals with opportunity in war is strategy, but in disease is medicine; and the science of the due amount in the matter of food is medicine, but in the matter of exercise is the science of gymnastic.

Fourthly, one might ask what they mean by the "absolute:" in "absolute man" and "man" the word "man" has one and the same sense; for in respect of manhood there will be no difference between them;

and if so, neither will there be any difference in respect of goodness between "absolute good" and "good."

Fifthly, they do not make the good any more good 6
by making it eternal; a white thing that lasts a long while is no whiter than what lasts but a day.

There seems to be more plausibility in the doctrine 7
of the Pythagoreans, who [in their table of opposites] place the one on the same side with the good things [instead of reducing all goods to unity]; and even Speusippus * seems to follow them in this.

However, these points may be reserved for another 8
occasion; but objection may be taken to what I have said on the ground that the Platonists do not speak in this way of all goods indiscriminately, but hold that those that are pursued and welcomed on their own account are called good by reference to one common form or type, while those things that tend to produce or preserve these goods, or to prevent their opposites, are called good only as means to these, and in a different sense.

It is evident that there will thus be two classes of 9
goods: one good in themselves, the other good as means to the former. Let us separate then from the things that are merely useful those that are good in themselves, and inquire if they are called good by reference to one common idea or type.

Now what kind of things would one call "good 1
in themselves"?

Surely those things that we pursue even apart from their consequences, such as wisdom and sight

* Plato's nephew and successor.

and certain pleasures and certain honours; for although we sometimes pursue these things as means, no one could refuse to rank them among the things that are good in themselves.

If these be excluded, nothing is good in itself except the idea; and then the type or form will be meaningless.*

11 If however, these are ranked among the things that are good in themselves, then it must be shown that the goodness of all of them can be defined in the same terms, as white has the same meaning when applied to snow and to white lead.

But, in fact, we have to give a separate and different account of the goodness of honour and wisdom and pleasure.

Good, then, is not a term that is applied to all these things alike in the same sense or with reference to one common idea or form.

12 But how then do these things come to be called good? for they do not appear to have received the same name by chance merely. Perhaps it is because they all proceed from one source, or all conduce to one end; or perhaps it is rather in virtue of some analogy, just as we call the reason the eye of the soul because it bears the same relation to the soul that the eye does to the body, and so on.

13 But we may dismiss these questions at present; for to discuss them in detail belongs more properly to another branch of philosophy.

And for the same reason we may dismiss the *Even if there*

* For there is no meaning in a form which is a form of nothing, in a universal which has no particulars under it.

were, it would not help us here. further consideration of the idea; for even granting that this term good, which is applied to all these different things, has one and the same meaning throughout, or that there is an absolute good apart from these particulars, it is evident that this good will not be anything that man can realize or attain: but it is a good of this kind that we are now seeking.

It might, perhaps, be thought that it would never- 14
theless be well to make ourselves acquainted with this universal good, with a view to the goods that are attainable and realizable. With this for a pattern, it may be said, we shall more readily discern our own good, and discerning achieve it.

There certainly is some plausibility in this argu- 15
ment, but it seems to be at variance with the existing sciences; for though they are all aiming at some good and striving to make up their deficiencies, they neglect to inquire about this universal good. And yet it is scarce likely that the professors of the several arts and sciences should not know, nor even look for, what would help them so much.

And indeed I am at a loss to know how the weaver 16
or the carpenter would be furthered in his art by a knowledge of this absolute good, or how a man would be rendered more able to heal the sick or to command an army by contemplation of the pure form or idea. For it seems to me that the physician does not even seek for health in this abstract way, but seeks for the health of man, or rather of some particular man, for it is individuals that he has to heal.

The good is 7. Leaving these matters, then, let us return once 1 more to the question, what this good can be of which we are in search. *the final end and happiness is this.*

It seems to be different in different kinds of action and in different arts,—one thing in medicine and another in war, and so on. What then is the good in each of these cases? Surely that for the sake of which all else is done. And that in medicine is health, in war is victory, in building is a house,—a different thing in each different case, but always, in whatever we do and in whatever we choose, the end. For it is always for the sake of the end that all else is done.

If then there be one end of all that man does, this end will be the realizable good,—or these ends, if there be more than one.

By this generalization our argument is brought to the same point as before.* This point we must try to explain more clearly.

We see that there are many ends. But some of these are chosen only as means, as wealth, flutes, and the whole class of instruments. And so it is plain that not all ends are final.

But the best of all things must, we conceive, be something final.

If then there be only one final end, this will be what we are seeking,—or if there be more than one, then the most final of them.

Now that which is pursued as an end in itself is more final than that which is pursued as means to something else, and that which is never chosen as means than that which is chosen both as an end in itself and as means, and that is strictly final which

* 2, 1. See Stewart.

is always chosen as an end in itself and never as
means.

Happiness seems more than anything else to answer 5
to this description: for we always choose it for itself,
and never for the sake of something else; while honour
and pleasure and reason, and all virtue or excellence,
we choose partly indeed for themselves (for, apart from
any result, we should choose each of them), but partly
also for the sake of happiness, supposing that they will
help to make us happy. But no one chooses happiness
for the sake of these things, or as a means to anything
else at all.

We seem to be led to the same conclusion when we 6
start from the notion of self-sufficiency.

The final good is thought to be self-sufficing [or
all-sufficing]. In applying this term we do not regard
a man as an individual leading a solitary life, but we
also take account of parents, children, wife, and, in
short, friends and fellow-citizens generally, since man
is naturally a social being. Some limit must indeed 7
be set to this; for if you go on to parents and descendants and friends of friends, you will never come to a
stop. But this we will consider further on: for the
present we will take self-sufficing to mean what by
itself makes life desirable and in want of nothing.
And happiness is believed to answer to this description.

And further, happiness is believed to be the most 8
desirable thing in the world, and that not merely as
one among other good things: if it were merely one
among other good things [so that other things could
be added to it], it is plain that the addition of the least

of other goods must make it more desirable; for the addition becomes a surplus of good, and of two goods the greater is always more desirable.

Thus it seems that happiness is something final and self-sufficing, and is the end of all that man does.

9 But perhaps the reader thinks that though no one will dispute the statement that happiness is the best thing in the world, yet a still more precise definition of it is needed. *To find it we ask, What is man's function?*

10 This will best be gained, I think, by asking, What is the function of man? For as the goodness and the excellence of a piper or a sculptor, or the practiser of any art, and generally of those who have any function or business to do, lies in that function, so man's good would seem to lie in his function, if he has one.

11 But can we suppose that, while a carpenter and a cobbler has a function and a business of his own, man has no business and no function assigned him by nature? Nay, surely as his several members, eye and hand and foot, plainly have each his own function, so we must suppose that man also has some function over and above all these.

12 What then is it?

Life evidently he has in common even with the plants, but we want that which is peculiar to him. We must exclude, therefore, the life of mere nutrition and growth.

Next to this comes the life of sense; but this too he plainly shares with horses and cattle and all kinds of animals.

13 There remains then the life whereby he acts—the

life of his rational nature,* with its two sides or divisions, one rational as obeying reason, the other rational as having and exercising reason.

But as this expression is ambiguous,† we must be understood to mean thereby the life that consists in the exercise of the faculties; for this seems to be more properly entitled to the name.

The function of man, then, is exercise of his vital 14
faculties [or soul] on one side in obedience to reason, and on the other side with reason.

But what is called the function of a man of any profession and the function of a man who is good in that profession are generically the same, *e.g.* of a harper and of a good harper; and this holds in all cases without exception, only that in the case of the latter his superior excellence at his work is added; for we say a harper's function is to harp, and a good harper's to harp well.

(Man's function then being, as we say, a kind of
life—that is to say, exercise of his faculties and
action of various kinds with reason—the good man's
function is to do this well and beautifully [or nobly].
But the function of anything is done well when it 15
is done in accordance with the proper excellence of
that thing.) ‡

* πρακτική τις τοῦ λόγον ἔχοντος. Aristotle frequently uses the terms πρᾶξις, πρακτός, πρακτικός in this wide sense, covering all that man does, *i.e.* all that part of man's life that is within the control of his will, or that is consciously directed to an end, including therefore speculation as well as action.

† For it might mean either the mere possession of the vital faculties, or their exercise.

‡ This paragraph seems to be a repetition (I would rather say a re-writing) of the previous paragraph. See note on VII. 3, 2.

If this be so the result is that the good of man is exercise of his faculties in accordance with excellence or virtue, or, if there be more than one, in accordance with the best and most complete virtue.* *Resulting definition of happiness.*

16 But there must also be a full term of years for this exercise; † for one swallow or one fine day does not make a spring, nor does one day or any small space of time make a blessed or happy man.

17 This, then, may be taken as a rough outline of the good; for this, I think, is the proper method,—first to sketch the outline, and then to fill in the details. But it would seem that, the outline once fairly drawn, any one can carry on the work and fit in the several items which time reveals to us or helps us to find. And this indeed is the way in which the arts and sciences have grown; for it requires no extraordinary genius to fill up the gaps.

18 We must bear in mind, however, what was said above, and not demand the same degree of accuracy in all branches of study, but in each case so much as the subject-matter admits of and as is proper to that kind
19 of inquiry. The carpenter and the geometer both look for the right angle, but in different ways: the former only wants such an approximation to it as his work requires, but the latter wants to know what constitutes a right angle, or what is its special quality; his aim is to find out the truth. And so in other cases we must follow the same course, lest we spend more

* This "best and most complete excellence or virtue" is the trained faculty for philosophic speculation, and the contemplative life is man's highest happiness. *Cf.* X. 7, 1.

† *Cf.* 9, 11.

time on what is immaterial than on the real business in hand.

Nor must we in all cases alike demand the reason 20
why; sometimes it is enough if the undemonstrated fact be fairly pointed out, as in the case of the starting-points or principles of a science. Undemonstrated facts always form the first step or starting-point of
a science; and these starting-points or principles are 21
arrived at some in one way, some in another—some by induction, others by perception, others again by
some kind of training. But in each case we must try 22
to apprehend them in the proper way, and do our
best to define them clearly; for they have great in- 23
fluence upon the subsequent course of an inquiry. A good start is more than half the race, I think, and our starting-point or principle, once found, clears up a number of our difficulties.

This view harmonizes various current views.

8. We must not be satisfied, then, with examining 1
this starting-point or principle of ours as a conclusion from our data, but must also view it in its relation to current opinions on the subject; for all experience harmonizes with a true principle, but a false one is soon found to be incompatible with the facts.

Now, good things have been divided into three 2
classes, external goods on the one hand, and on the other goods of the soul and goods of the body; and the goods of the soul are commonly said to be goods in the fullest sense, and more good than any other.

But "actions and exercises of the vital faculties or soul" may be said to be "of the soul." So our account is confirmed by this opinion, which is both of long standing and approved by all who busy themselves with philosophy.

3 But, indeed, we secure the support of this opinion by the mere statement that certain actions and exercises are the end; for this implies that it is to be ranked among the goods of the soul, and not among external goods.

4 Our account, again, is in harmony with the common saying that the happy man lives well and does well; for we may say that happiness, according to us, is a living well and doing well.

5 And, indeed, all the characteristics that men expect to find in happiness seem to belong to happiness as we define it.

6 Some hold it to be virtue or excellence, some prudence, others a kind of wisdom; others, again, hold it to be all or some of these, with the addition of pleasure, either as an ingredient or as a necessary accompaniment; and some even include external prosperity in their account of it.

7 Now, some of these views have the support of many voices and of old authority; others have few voices, but those of weight; but it is probable that neither the one side nor the other is entirely wrong, but that in some one point at least, if not in most, they are both right.

8 First, then, the view that happiness is excellence or a kind of excellence harmonizes with our account; for "exercise of faculties in accordance with excellence" belongs to excellence.

9 But I think we may say that it makes no small difference whether the good be conceived as the mere

possession of something, or as its use—as a mere habit or trained faculty, or as the exercise of that faculty. For the habit or faculty may be present, and yet issue in no good result, as when a man is asleep, or in any other way hindered from his function; but with its exercise this is not possible, for it must show itself in acts and in good acts. And as at the Olympic games it is not the fairest and strongest who receive the crown, but those who contend (for among these are the victors), so in life, too, the winners are those who not only have all the excellences, but manifest these in deed.

And, further, the life of these men is in itself 10
pleasant. For pleasure is an affection of the soul, and each man takes pleasure in that which he is said to love,—he who loves horses in horses, he who loves sight-seeing in sight-seeing, and in the same way he who loves justice in acts of justice, and generally the lover of excellence or virtue in virtuous acts or the manifestation of excellence.

And while with most men there is a perpetual 11
conflict between the several things in which they find pleasure, since these are not naturally pleasant, those who love what is noble take pleasure in that which is naturally pleasant. For the manifestations of excellence are naturally pleasant, so that they are both pleasant to them and pleasant in themselves.

Their life, then, does not need pleasure to be added 12
to it as an appendage, but contains pleasure in itself.

Indeed, in addition to what we have said, a man is not good at all unless he takes pleasure in noble deeds. No one would call a man just who did not take pleasure in doing justice, nor generous who took no pleasure in acts of generosity, and so on.

13 If this be so, the manifestations of excellence will be pleasant in themselves. But they are also both good and noble, and that in the highest degree—at least, if the good man's judgment about them is right, for this is his judgment.

14 Happiness, then, is at once the best and noblest and pleasantest thing in the world, and these are not separated, as the Delian inscription would have them to be:—

> "What is most just is noblest, health is best,
> Pleasantest is to get your heart's desire."

For all these characteristics are united in the best exercises of our faculties; and these, or some one of them that is better than all the others, we identify with happiness.

15 But nevertheless happiness plainly requires external goods too, as we said; for it is impossible, or at least not easy, to act nobly without some furniture of fortune. There are many things that can only be done through instruments, so to speak, such as friends
16 and wealth and political influence: and there are some things whose absence takes the bloom off our happiness, as good birth, the blessing of children, personal beauty; for a man is not very likely to be happy if he is very ugly in person, or of low birth, or alone in the world, or childless, and perhaps still less if he has worthless children or friends, or has lost good ones that he had.

17 As we said, then, happiness seems to stand in need of this kind of prosperity; and so some identify it

with good fortune, just as others identify it with excellence.

Is happiness acquired, or the gift of Gods or of chance?

9. This has led people to ask whether happiness 1
is attained by learning, or the formation of habits, or any other kind of training, or comes by some divine dispensation or even by chance.

Well, if the Gods do give gifts to men, happiness 2
is likely to be among the number, more likely, indeed, than anything else, in proportion as it is better than all other human things.

This belongs more properly to another branch of in- 3
quiry; but we may say that even if it is not heaven-sent, but comes as a consequence of virtue or some kind of learning or training, still it seems to be one of the most divine things in the world; for the prize and aim of virtue would appear to be better than anything else and something divine and blessed.

Again, if it is thus acquired it will be widely 4
accessible; for it will then be in the power of all except those who have lost the capacity for excellence to acquire it by study and diligence.

And if it be better that men should attain happi- 5
ness in this way rather than by chance, it is reasonable to suppose that it is so, since in the sphere of nature
all things are arranged in the best possible way, and 6
likewise in the sphere of art, and of each mode of causation, and most of all in the sphere of the noblest mode of causation. And indeed it would be too absurd to leave what is noblest and fairest to the dispensation of chance.

But our definition itself clears up the difficulty;* 7

* *Cf. supra*, 7. 21.

for happiness was defined as a certain kind of exercise of the vital faculties in accordance with excellence or virtue. And of the remaining goods [other than happiness itself], some must be present as necessary conditions, while others are aids and useful instruments
8 to happiness. And this agrees with what we said at starting. We then laid down that the end of the art political is the best of all ends; but the chief business of that art is to make the citizens of a certain character
9 —that is, good and apt to do what is noble. It is not without reason, then, that we do not call an ox, or a horse, or any brute happy; for none of them is able to share in this kind of activity.

10 For the same reason also a child is not happy; he is as yet, because of his age, unable to do such things. If we ever call a child happy, it is because we hope he will do them. For, as we said, happiness requires not only perfect excellence or virtue,
11 but also a full term of years for its exercise. For our circumstances are liable to many changes and to all sorts of chances, and it is possible that he who is now most prosperous will in his old age meet with great disasters, as is told of Priam in the tales of Troy; and a man who is thus used by fortune and comes to a miserable end cannot be called happy.

1 **10.** Are we, then, to call no man happy as long as *Can no man be called happy during life?*
he lives, but to wait for the end, as Solon said?

2 And, supposing we have to allow this, do we mean that he actually is happy after he is dead? Surely that is absurd, especially for us who say that happiness is a kind of activity or life.

But if we do not call the dead man happy, and if 3
Solon meant not this, but that only then could we safely apply the term to a man, as being now beyond the reach of evil and calamity, then here too we find some ground for objection. For it is thought that both good and evil may in some sort befall a dead man (just as they may befall a living man, although he is unconscious of them), *e.g.* honours rendered to him, or the reverse of these, and again the prosperity or the misfortune of his children and all his descendants.

But this, too, has its difficulties; for after a man 4
has lived happily to a good old age, and ended as he lived, it is possible that many changes may befall him in the persons of his descendants, and that some of them may turn out good and meet with the good fortune they deserve, and others the reverse. It is evident too that the degree in which the descendants are related to their ancestors may vary to any extent.
And it would be a strange thing if the dead man were 5
to change with these changes and become happy and miserable by turns. But it would also be strange to suppose that the dead are not affected at all, even for a limited time, by the fortunes of their posterity.

But let us return to our former question; for its 6
solution will, perhaps, clear up this other difficulty.

The saying of Solon may mean that we ought to 7
look for the end and then call a man happy, not because he now is, but because he once was happy.

But surely it is strange that when he is happy we should refuse to say what is true of him, because we do not like to apply the term to living men in view of the changes to which they are liable, and because we hold happiness to be something that endures and is little liable to change, while the fortunes of one and the same man often undergo many revolutions: for, it is argued, it is plain that, if we follow the changes of fortune, we shall call the same man happy and miserable many times over, making the happy man "a sort of chameleon and one who rests on no sound foundation."

We reply that it cannot be right thus to follow fortune. For it is not in this that our weal or woe lies; but, as we said, though good fortune is needed to complete man's life, yet it is the excellent employment of his powers that constitutes his happiness, as the reverse of this constitutes his misery.

But the discussion of this difficulty leads to a further confirmation of our account. For nothing human is so constant as the excellent exercise of our faculties. The sciences themselves seem to be less abiding. And the highest of these exercises * are the most abiding, because the happy are occupied with them most of all and most continuously (for this seems to be the reason why we do not forget how to do them †).

The happy man, then, as we define him, will have this required property of permanence, and all through life will preserve his character; for he will be occupied continually, or with the least possible interruption, in

* The "highest exercise of our faculties" is, of course, philosophic contemplation, as above, I. 7, 15; *cf.* X. 7, 1.

† We may forget scientific truths that we have known more easily than we lose the habit of scientific thinking or of virtuous action; *cf.* X. 7, 2; VI. 5, 8.

excellent deeds and excellent speculations; and, whatever his fortune be, he will take it in the noblest fashion, and bear himself always and in all things suitably, since he is truly good and "foursquare without a flaw."

But the dispensations of fortune are many, some 12
great, some small. The small ones, whether good or evil, plainly are of no weight in the scale; but the great ones, when numerous, will make life happier if they be good; for they help to give a grace to life themselves, and their use is noble and good; but, if they be evil, will enfeeble and spoil happiness; for they bring pain, and often impede the exercise of our faculties.

But nevertheless true worth shines out even here, in the calm endurance of many great misfortunes, not through insensibility, but through nobility and greatness of soul. And if it is what a man does that deter- 13
mines the character of his life, as we said, then no happy man will become miserable; for he will never do what is hateful and base. For we hold that the man who is truly good and wise will bear with dignity whatever fortune sends, and will always make the best of his circumstances, as a good general will turn the forces at his command to the best account, and a good shoemaker will make the best shoe that can be made out of a given piece of leather, and so on with all other crafts.

If this be so, the happy man will never become 14
miserable, though he will not be truly happy if he meets with the fate of Priam.

But yet he is not unstable and lightly changed: he

will not be moved from his happiness easily, nor by any ordinary misfortunes, but only by many heavy ones; and after such, he will not recover his happiness again in a short time, but if at all, only in a considerable period, which has a certain completeness, and in which he attains to great and noble things.

15 We shall meet all objections, then, if we say that a happy man is "one who exercises his faculties in accordance with perfect excellence, being duly furnished with external goods, not for any chance time, but for a full term of years:" to which perhaps we should add, "and who shall continue to live so, and shall die as he lived," since the future is veiled to us, but happiness we take to be the end and in all ways perfectly final or complete.

16 If this be so, we may say that those living men are blessed or perfectly happy who both have and shall continue to have these characteristics, but happy as men only.

1 **11.** Passing now from this question to that of the *Cannot the fortunes of survivors affect the dead?*
fortunes of descendants and of friends generally, the doctrine that they do not affect the departed at all seems too cold and too much opposed to popular
2 opinion. But as the things that happen to them are many and differ in all sorts of ways, and some come home to them more and some less, so that to discuss them all separately would be a long, indeed an endless task, it will perhaps be enough to speak of them in general terms and in outline merely.

3 Now, as of the misfortunes that happen to a man's self, some have a certain weight and influence on his life, while others are of less moment, so is it also with

what happens to any of his friends. And, again, it 4
always makes much more difference whether those who are affected by an occurrence are alive or dead than it does whether a terrible crime in a tragedy be enacted on the stage or merely supposed to have
already taken place. We must therefore take these 5
differences into account, and still more, perhaps, the fact that it is a doubtful question whether the dead are at all accessible to good and ill. For it appears that even if anything that happens, whether good or evil, does come home to them, yet it is something unsubstantial and slight to them if not in itself; or if not that, yet at any rate its influence is not of that magnitude or nature that it can make happy those who are not, or take away their happiness from those that are.

It seems then—to conclude—that the prosperity, 6
and likewise the adversity, of friends does affect the dead, but not in such a way or to such an extent as to make the happy unhappy, or to do anything of the kind.

Happiness as absolute end is above praise.

12. These points being settled, we may now inquire 1
whether happiness is to be ranked among the goods that we praise, or rather among those that we revere; for it is plainly not a mere potentiality, but an actual good.

What we praise seems always to be praised 2
as being of a certain quality and having a certain relation to something. For instance, we praise the just and the courageous man, and generally the good man, and excellence or virtue, because of what they do or produce; and we praise also the strong or the swift-

footed man, and so on, because he has a certain gift or faculty in relation to some good and admirable thing.

3 This is evident if we consider the praises bestowed on the Gods. The Gods are thereby made ridiculous by being made relative to man; and this happens because, as we said, a thing can only be praised in relation to something else.

4 If, then, praise be proper to such things as we mentioned, it is evident that to the best things is due, not praise, but something greater and better, as our usage shows; for the Gods we call blessed and happy, and "blessed" is the term we apply to the most godlike men.

And so with good things: no one praises happiness as he praises justice, but calls it blessed, as something better and more divine.

5 On these grounds Eudoxus is thought to have
based a strong argument for the claims of pleasure to
the first prize: for he maintained that the fact that it
is not praised, though it is a good thing, shows that it
is higher than the goods we praise, as God and the
good are higher; for these are the standards by refer-
6 ence to which we judge all other things,—giving praise
to excellence or virtue, since it makes us apt to do
what is noble, and passing encomiums on the results
of virtue, whether these be bodily or psychical.

7 But to refine on these points belongs more properly to those who have made a study of the subject of encomiums; for us it is plain from what has been said that happiness is one of the goods which we revere and count as final.

And this further seems to follow from the fact that 8
it is a starting-point or principle: for everything we do is always done for its sake; but the principle and cause of all good we hold to be something divine and worthy of reverence.

Division of the faculties and resulting division of the virtues.

13. Since happiness is an exercise of the vital 1
faculties in accordance with perfect virtue or excellence, we will now inquire about virtue or excellence; for this will probably help us in our inquiry about happiness.

And indeed the true statesman seems to be espe- 2
cially concerned with virtue, for he wishes to make the citizens good and obedient to the laws. Of this 3
we have an example in the Cretan and the Lacedæmonian lawgivers, and any others who have resembled them. But if the inquiry belongs to Politics or the 4
science of the state, it is plain that it will be in accordance with our original purpose to pursue it.

The virtue or excellence that we are to consider is, 5
of course, the excellence of man; for it is the good of man and the happiness of man that we started to seek. And by the excellence of man I mean excel- 6
lence not of body, but of soul; for happiness we take to be an activity of the soul.

If this be so, then it is evident that the statesman 7
must have some knowledge of the soul, just as the man who is to heal the eye or the whole body must have some knowledge of them, and that the more in proportion as the science of the state is higher and better than medicine. But all educated physicians take much pains to know about the body.

As statesmen [or students of Politics], then we 8

must inquire into the nature of the soul, but in so doing we must keep our special purpose in view and go only so far as that requires; for to go into minuter detail would be too laborious for the present undertaking.

9 Now, there are certain doctrines about the soul which are stated elsewhere with sufficient precision, and these we will adopt.

Two parts of the soul are distinguished, an irrational and a rational part.

10 Whether these are separated as are the parts of the body or any divisible thing, or whether they are only distinguishable in thought but in fact inseparable, like concave and convex in the circumference of a circle, makes no difference for our present purpose.

11 Of the irrational part, again, one division seems to be common to all things that live, and to be possessed by plants—I mean that which causes nutrition and growth; for we must assume that all things that take nourishment have a faculty of this kind, even when they are embryos, and have the same faculty when they are full grown; at least, this is more reasonable than to suppose that they then have a different one.

12 The excellence of this faculty, then, is plainly one that man shares with other beings, and not specifically human.

And this is confirmed by the fact that in sleep this part of the soul, or this faculty, is thought to be most active, while the good and the bad man are undistinguishable when they are asleep (whence the saying that for half their lives there is no differ-
13 ence between the happy and the miserable; which

indeed is what we should expect; for sleep is the cessation of the soul from those functions in respect of which it is called good or bad), except that they are to some slight extent roused by what goes on in their bodies, with the result that the dreams of the good man are better than those of ordinary people.

However, we need not pursue this further, and may 14
dismiss the nutritive principle, since it has no place in the excellence of man.

But there seems to be another vital principle that 15
is irrational, and yet in some way partakes of reason. In the case of the continent and of the incontinent man alike we praise the reason or the rational part, for it exhorts them rightly and urges them to do what is best; but there is plainly present in them another principle besides the rational one, which fights and
struggles against the reason. For just as a paralyzed 16
limb, when you will to move it to the right, moves on the contrary to the left, so is it with the soul; the incontinent man's impulses run counter to his reason. Only whereas we see the refractory member in the case of the body, we do not see it in the case of the soul. But we must nevertheless, I think, hold that in the soul too there is something beside the reason, which opposes and runs counter to it (though in what sense it is distinct from the reason does not matter here).

It seems, however, to partake of reason also, as we 17
said: at least, in the continent man it submits to the reason; while in the temperate and courageous man we may say it is still more obedient; for in him it is altogether in harmony with the reason.

The irrational part, then, it appears, is twofold. 18

There is the vegetative faculty, which has no share of reason; and the faculty of appetite or of desire in general, which in a manner partakes of reason or is rational as listening to reason and submitting to its sway,—rational in the sense in which we speak of rational obedience to father or friends, not in the sense in which we speak of rational apprehension of mathematical truths. But all advice and all rebuke and exhortation testify that the irrational part is in some way amenable to reason.

19 If then we like to say that this part, too, has a share of reason, the rational part also will have two divisions: one rational in the strict sense as possessing reason in itself, the other rational as listening to reason as a man listens to his father.

20 Now, on this division of the faculties is based the division of excellence; for we speak of intellectual excellences and of moral excellences; wisdom and understanding and prudence we call intellectual, liberality and temperance we call moral virtues or excellences. When we are speaking of a man's moral character we do not say that he is wise or intelligent, but that he is gentle or temperate. But we praise the wise man, too, for his habit of mind or trained faculty; and a habit or trained faculty that is praiseworthy is what we call an excellence or virtue.

BOOK II.

MORAL VIRTUE.

Moral virtue is acquired by the repetition of the corresponding acts.

1. EXCELLENCE, then, being of these two kinds, intellectual and moral, intellectual excellence owes its birth and growth mainly to instruction, and so requires time and experience, while moral excellence is the result of habit or custom (ἔθος), and has accordingly in our language received a name formed by a slight change from ἔθος.* 1

From this it is plain that none of the moral excellences or virtues is implanted in us by nature; for that which is by nature cannot be altered by training. For instance, a stone naturally tends to fall downwards, and you could not train it to rise upwards, though you tried to do so by throwing it up ten thousand times, nor could you train fire to move downwards, nor accustom anything which naturally behaves in one way to behave in any other way. 2

The virtues,† then, come neither by nature nor 3

* ἔθος, custom; ἦθος, character; ἠθικὴ ἀρετή, moral excellence: we have no similar sequence, but the Latin *mos, mores*, from which "morality" comes, covers both ἔθος and ἦθος.

† It is with the moral virtues that this and the three following books are exclusively concerned, the discussion of the intellectual virtues being postponed to Book VI. ἀρεταί is often used in these books, without any epithet, for "moral virtues," and perhaps is so used here.

against nature, but nature gives the capacity for acquiring them, and this is developed by training.

Again, where we do things by nature we get the power first, and put this power forth in act afterwards: as we plainly see in the case of the senses; for it is not by constantly seeing and hearing that we acquire those faculties, but, on the contrary, we had the power first and then used it, instead of acquiring the power by the use. But the virtues we acquire by doing the acts as is the case with the arts too. We learn an art by doing that which we wish to do when we have learned it; we become builders by building, and harpers by harping. And so by doing just acts we become just, and by doing acts of temperance and courage we become temperate and courageous.

This is attested, too, by what occurs in states; for the legislators make their citizens good by training; *i.e.* this is the wish of all legislators, and those who do not succeed in this miss their aim, and it is this that distinguishes a good from a bad constitution.

Again, both the moral virtues and the corresponding vices result from and are formed by the same acts; and this is the case with the arts also. It is by harping that good harpers and bad harpers alike are produced: and so with builders and the rest; by building well they will become good builders, and bad builders by building badly. Indeed, if it were not so, they would not want anybody to teach them, but would all be born either good or bad at their trades. And it is just the same with the virtues also. It is by our conduct in our intercourse with other men that we become just or unjust, and by acting in circumstances of danger, and training ourselves to feel fear or confidence, that we become courageous or cowardly. So, too, with our animal appetites and the passion of anger; for by behaving in this way or in that on the occasions with which these passions are concerned, some become temperate and gentle, and others profligate and ill-tempered. In a word, acts of any kind produce habits or characters of the same kind.

Hence we ought to make sure that our acts be of 8
a certain kind; for the resulting character varies as they vary. It makes no small difference, therefore, whether a man be trained from his youth up in this way or in that, but a great difference, or rather all the difference.

These acts must be such as reason prescribes; they can't be defined exactly, but must be neither too much nor too little.

2. But our present inquiry has not, like the rest, 1
a merely speculative aim; we are not inquiring merely in order to know what excellence or virtue is, but in order to become good; for otherwise it would profit us nothing. We must ask therefore about these acts, and see of what kind they are to be; for, as we said, it is they that determine our habits or character.

First of all, then, that they must be in accordance 2
with right reason is a common characteristic of them, which we shall here take for granted, reserving for future discussion * the question what this right reason is, and how it is related to the other excellences.

But let it be understood, before we go on, that all 3
reasoning on matters of practice must be in outline merely, and not scientifically exact: for, as we said at

* In Book VI.

starting, the kind of reasoning to be demanded varies with the subject in hand; and in practical matters and questions of expediency there are no invariable laws, any more than in questions of health.

4 And if our general conclusions are thus inexact, still more inexact is all reasoning about particular cases; for these fall under no system of scientifically established rules or traditional maxims, but the agent must always consider for himself what the special occasion requires, just as in medicine or navigation.

5 But though this is the case we must try to render what help we can.

6 First of all, then, we must observe that, in matters of this sort, to fall short and to exceed are alike fatal. This is plain (to illustrate what we cannot see by what we can see) in the case of strength and health. Too much and too little exercise alike destroy strength, and to take too much meat and drink, or to take too little, is equally ruinous to health, but the fitting amount produces and increases and preserves them.
7 Just so, then, is it with temperance also, and courage, and the other virtues. The man who shuns and fears everything and never makes a stand, becomes a coward; while the man who fears nothing at all, but will face anything, becomes foolhardy. So, too, the man who takes his fill of any kind of pleasure, and abstains from none, is a profligate, but the man who shuns all (like him whom we call a "boor") is devoid of sensibility.* Thus temperance and courage

* These two, the "boor" (ἀγροῖκος) and he who lacks sensibility (ἀναίσθητος), are afterwards distinguished: *cf.* II. 7, 3 and 13.

are destroyed both by excess and defect, but preserved by moderation.

But habits or types of character are not only pro- 8
duced and preserved and destroyed by the same occasions and the same means, but they will also manifest themselves in the same circumstances. This is the case with palpable things like strength. Strength is produced by taking plenty of nourishment and doing plenty of hard work, and the strong man, in turn, has
the greatest capacity for these. And the case is the 9
same with the virtues: by abstaining from pleasure we become temperate, and when we have become temperate we are best able to abstain. And so with courage: by habituating ourselves to despise danger, and to face it, we become courageous; and when we have become courageous, we are best able to face danger.

Virtue is in various ways concerned with pleasure and pain.

3. The pleasure or pain that accompanies the acts 1
must be taken as a test of the formed habit or character. He who abstains from the pleasures of the body and rejoices in the abstinence is temperate, while he who is vexed at having to abstain is profligate; and again, he who faces danger with pleasure, or, at any rate, without pain, is courageous, but he to whom this is painful is a coward.

For moral virtue or excellence is closely concerned with pleasure and pain. It is pleasure that moves us to do what is base, and pain that moves us
to refrain from what is noble. And therefore, as 2
Plato says, man needs to be so trained from his youth up as to find pleasure and pain in the right objects. This is what sound education means.

3 Another reason why virtue has to do with pleasure and pain, is that it has to do with actions and passions or affections; but every affection and every act is accompanied by pleasure or pain.

4 The fact is further attested by the employment of pleasure and pain in correction; they have a kind of curative property, and a cure is effected by administering the opposite of the disease.

5 Again, as we said before, every type of character [or habit or formed faculty] is essentially relative to, and concerned with, those things that form it for good or for ill; but it is through pleasure and pain that bad characters are formed—that is to say, through pursuing and avoiding the wrong pleasures and pains, or pursuing and avoiding them at the wrong time, or in the wrong manner, or in any other of the various ways of going wrong that may be distinguished.

And hence some people go so far as to define the virtues as a kind of impassive or neutral state of mind. But they err in stating this absolutely, instead of qualifying it by the addition of the right and wrong manner, time, etc.

6 We may lay down, therefore, that this kind of excellence [*i.e.* moral excellence] makes us do what is best in matters of pleasure and pain, while vice or
7 badness has the contrary effect. But the following considerations will throw additional light on the point.*

There are three kinds of things that move us to choose, and three that move us to avoid them: on the one hand, the beautiful or noble, the advantageous, the pleasant; on the other hand, the ugly or base, the

* Reading ἔτι. See Stewart.

hurtful, the painful. Now, the good man is apt to go right, and the bad man to go wrong, about them all, but especially about pleasure: for pleasure is not only common to man with animals, but also accompanies all pursuit or choice; since the noble, and the advantageous also, are pleasant in idea.

Again, the feeling of pleasure has been fostered in 8
us all from our infancy by our training, and has thus
become so engrained in our life that it can scarce be
washed out.* And, indeed, we all more or less make
pleasure our test in judging of actions. For this 9
reason too, then, our whole inquiry must be concerned
with these matters; since to be pleased and pained in
the right or the wrong way has great influence on our
actions.

Again, to fight with pleasure is harder than to 10
fight with wrath (which Heraclitus says is hard), and
virtue, like art, is always more concerned with what
is harder; for the harder the task the better is success.
For this reason also, then, both [moral] virtue or
excellence and the science of the state must always
be concerned with pleasures and pains; for he that
behaves rightly with regard to them will be good,
and he that behaves badly will be bad.

We will take it as established, then, that [moral] 11
excellence or virtue has to do with pleasures and pains;
and that the acts which produce it develop it, and
also, when differently done, destroy it; and that it
manifests itself in the same acts which produced it.

* Actions and the accompanying feelings of pleasure and pain have so grown together, that it is impossible to separate the former and judge them apart: *cf.* X. 4, 11.

The conditions of virtuous action as distinct from artistic production.

4. But here we may be asked what we mean by saying that men can become just and temperate only by doing what is just and temperate: surely, it may be said, if their acts are just and temperate, they themselves are already just and temperate, as they are grammarians and musicians if they do what is grammatical and musical.

We may answer, I think, firstly, that this is not quite the case even with the arts. A man may do something grammatical [or write something correctly] by chance, or at the prompting of another person: he will not be grammatical till he not only does something grammatical, but also does it grammatically [or like a grammatical person], *i.e.* in virtue of his own knowledge of grammar.

But, secondly, the virtues are not in this point analogous to the arts. The products of art have their excellence in themselves, and so it is enough if when produced they are of a certain quality; but in the case of the virtues, a man is not said to act justly or temperately [or like a just or temperate man] if what he does merely be of a certain sort—he must also be in a certain state of mind when he does it; *i.e.*, first of all, he must know what he is doing; secondly, he must choose it, and choose it for itself; and, thirdly, his act must be the expression of a formed and stable character. Now, of these conditions, only one, the knowledge, is necessary for the possession of any art; but for the possession of the virtues knowledge is of little or no avail, while the other conditions that result from repeatedly doing what is just and temperate are not a little important, but all-important.

The thing that is done, therefore, is called just or 4
temperate when it is such as the just or temperate man would do; but the man who does it is not just or temperate, unless he also does it in the spirit of the just or the temperate man.

It is right, then, to say that by doing what is just 5
a man becomes just, and temperate by doing what is temperate, while without doing thus he has no chance of ever becoming good.

But most men, instead of doing thus, fly to 6
theories, and fancy that they are philosophizing and that this will make them good, like a sick man who listens attentively to what the doctor says and then disobeys all his orders. This sort of philosophizing will no more produce a healthy habit of mind than this sort of treatment will produce a healthy habit of body.

Virtue not an emotion, nor a faculty, but a trained faculty or habit;

5. We have next to inquire what excellence or 1
virtue is.

A quality of the soul is either (1) a passion or emotion, or (2) a power or faculty, or (3) a habit or trained faculty; and so virtue must be one of these three. By (1) a passion or emotion we mean appetite, 2
anger, fear, confidence, envy, joy, love, hate, longing, emulation, pity, or generally that which is accompanied by pleasure or pain; (2) a power or faculty is that in respect of which we are said to be capable of being affected in any of these ways, as, for instance, that in respect of which we are able to be angered or pained or to pity; and (3) a habit or trained faculty is that in respect of which we are well or ill regulated or disposed in the matter of our affections; as, for instance, in the matter of being angered, we are ill

regulated if we are too violent or too slack, but if we are moderate in our anger we are well regulated. And so with the rest.

Now, the virtues are not emotions, nor are the vices—(1) because we are not called good or bad in respect of our emotions, but are called so in respect of our virtues or vices; (2) because we are neither praised nor blamed in respect of our emotions (a man is not praised for being afraid or angry, nor blamed for being angry simply, but for being angry in a particular way), but we are praised or blamed in respect of our virtues or vices; (3) because we may be angered or frightened without deliberate choice, but the virtues are a kind of deliberate choice, or at least are impossible without it; and (4) because in respect of our emotions we are said to be moved, but in respect of our virtues and vices we are not said to be moved, but to be regulated or disposed in this way or in that.

For these same reasons also they are not powers or faculties; for we are not called either good or bad for being merely capable of emotion, nor are we either praised or blamed for this. And further, while nature gives us our powers or faculties, she does not make us either good or bad. (This point, however, we have already treated.)

If, then, the virtues be neither emotions nor faculties, it only remains for them to be habits or trained faculties.

6. We have thus found the genus to which virtue belongs; but we want to know, not only that it is a trained faculty, but also what species of trained faculty it is. *viz., the habit of choosing the mean.*

We may safely assert that the virtue or excellence of a thing causes that thing both to be itself in good condition and to perform its function well. The excellence of the eye, for instance, makes both the eye and its work good; for it is by the excellence of the eye that we see well. So the proper excellence of the horse makes a horse what he should be, and makes him good at running, and carrying his rider, and standing a charge. 2

If, then, this holds good in all cases, the proper excellence or virtue of man will be the habit or trained faculty that makes a man good and makes him perform his function well. 3

How this is to be done we have already said, but we may exhibit the same conclusion in another way, by inquiring what the nature of this virtue is. 4

Now, if we have any quantity, whether continuous or discrete,* it is possible to take either a larger [or too large], or a smaller [or too small], or an equal [or fair] amount, and that either absolutely or relatively to our own needs.

By an equal or fair amount I understand a mean amount, or one that lies between excess and deficiency.

By the absolute mean, or mean relatively to the thing itself, I understand that which is equidistant from both extremes, and this is one and the same for all.

By the mean relatively to us I understand that

* A line (or a generous emotion) is a "continuous quantity;" you can part it where you please: a rouleau of sovereigns is a "discrete quantity," made up of definite parts, and primarily separable into them.

which is neither too much nor too little for us; and this is not one and the same for all.

For instance, if ten be larger [or too large] and two be smaller [or too small], if we take six we take the mean relatively to the thing itself [or the arithmetical mean]; for it exceeds one extreme by the same amount by which it is exceeded by the other extreme: and this is the mean in arithmetical proportion.

But the mean relatively to us cannot be found in this way. If ten pounds of food is too much for a given man to eat, and two pounds too little, it does not follow that the trainer will order him six pounds: for that also may perhaps be too much for the man in question, or too little; too little for Milo, too much for the beginner. The same holds true in running and wrestling.

And so we may say generally that a master in any art avoids what is too much and what is too little, and seeks for the mean and chooses it—not the absolute but the relative mean.

If, then, every art or science perfects its work in this way, looking to the mean and bringing its work up to this standard (so that people are wont to say of a good work that nothing could be taken from it or added to it, implying that excellence is destroyed by excess or deficiency, but secured by observing the mean; and good artists, as we say, do in fact keep their eyes fixed on this in all that they do), and if virtue, like nature, is more exact and better than any art, it follows that virtue also must aim at the mean—virtue of course meaning moral virtue or excellence;

for it has to do with passions and actions, and it is these that admit of excess and deficiency and the mean. For instance, it is possible to feel fear, confidence, desire, anger, pity, and generally to be affected pleasantly and painfully, either too much or too little,
in either case wrongly; but to be thus affected at the 11
right times, and on the right occasions, and towards the right persons, and with the right object, and in the right fashion, is the mean course and the best
course, and these are characteristics of virtue. And 12
in the same way our outward acts also admit of excess and deficiency, and the mean or due amount.

Virtue, then, has to deal with feelings or passions and with outward acts, in which excess is wrong and deficiency also is blamed, but the mean amount is praised and is right—both of which are characteristics of virtue.

Virtue, then, is a kind of moderation (μεσότης τις),* 13
inasmuch as it aims at the mean or moderate amount (τὸ μέσον).

Again, there are many ways of going wrong (for 14
evil is infinite in nature, to use a Pythagorean figure, while good is finite), but only one way of going right; so that the one is easy and the other hard—easy to miss the mark and hard to hit. On this account also, then, excess and deficiency are characteristic of vice, hitting the mean is characteristic of virtue:

"Goodness is simple, ill takes any shape."

Virtue, then, is a habit or trained faculty of choice, 15

* μεσότης, the abstract name for the quality, is quite untranslatable.

the characteristic of which lies in moderation or observance of the mean relatively to the persons concerned, as determined by reason, *i.e.* by the reason by which the prudent man would determine it. And it is a moderation, firstly, inasmuch as it comes in the middle or mean between two vices, one on the side of excess, the other on the side of defect;
16 and, secondly, inasmuch as, while these vices fall short of or exceed the due measure in feeling and in action, it finds and chooses the mean, middling, or moderate amount.

17 Regarded in its essence, therefore, or according to the definition of its nature, virtue is a moderation or middle state, but viewed in its relation to what is best and right it is the extreme of perfection.

18 But it is not all actions nor all passions that admit of moderation; there are some whose very names imply badness, as malevolence, shamelessness, envy, and, among acts, adultery, theft, murder. These and all other like things are blamed as being bad in themselves, and not merely in their excess or deficiency. It is impossible therefore to go right in them; they are always wrong: rightness and wrongness in such things (*e.g.* in adultery) does not depend upon whether it is the right person and occasion and manner, but the mere doing of any one of them is wrong.

19 It would be equally absurd to look for moderation or excess or deficiency in unjust cowardly or profligate conduct; for then there would be moderation in excess or deficiency, and excess in excess, and deficiency in deficiency.

20 The fact is that just as there can be no excess

or deficiency in temperance or courage because the mean or moderate amount is, in a sense, an extreme, so in these kinds of conduct also there can be no moderation or excess or deficiency, but the acts are wrong however they be done. For, to put it generally, there cannot be moderation in excess or deficiency, nor excess or deficiency in moderation.

This must be applied to the several virtues.

7. But it is not enough to make these general statements [about virtue and vice]: we must go on and apply them to particulars [*i.e.* to the several virtues and vices]. For in reasoning about matters of conduct general statements are too vague,* and do not convey so much truth as particular propositions. It is with particulars that conduct is concerned:† our statements, therefore, when applied to these particulars, should be found to hold good.

These particulars then [*i.e.* the several virtues and vices and the several acts and affections with which they deal], we will take from the following table.‡

Moderation in the feelings of fear and confidence is courage: of those that exceed, he that exceeds in fearlessness has no name (as often happens), but he that exceeds in confidence is foolhardy, while he that exceeds in fear, but is deficient in confidence, is cowardly.

* Or "cover more ground, but convey less truth than particular propositions," if we read κοινότεροι with most manuscripts.

† In a twofold sense: my conduct cannot be virtuous except by exhibiting the particular virtues of justice, temperance, etc.; again, my conduct cannot be just except by being just in particular cases to particular persons.

‡ The Greek seems to imply that this is a generally accepted list, but Aristotle repeatedly has to coin names: *cf. infra*, § 11.

3 Moderation in respect of certain pleasures and also (though to a less extent) certain pains is temperance, while excess is profligacy. But defectiveness in the matter of these pleasures is hardly ever found, and so this sort of people also have as yet received no name: let us put them down as "void of sensibility."

4 In the matter of giving and taking money, moderation is liberality, excess and deficiency are prodigality and illiberality. But both vices exceed and fall short in giving and taking in contrary ways: the prodigal exceeds in spending, but falls short in taking; while the illiberal man exceeds in taking, but falls short in
5 spending. (For the present we are but giving an outline or summary, and aim at nothing more; we shall afterwards treat these points in greater detail.)

6 But, besides these, there are other dispositions in the matter of money: there is a moderation which is called magnificence (for the magnificent is not the same as the liberal man: the former deals with large sums, the latter with small), and an excess which is called bad taste or vulgarity, and a deficiency which is called meanness; and these vices differ from those which are opposed to liberality: how they differ will be explained later.

7 With respect to honour and disgrace, there is a moderation which is high-mindedness, an excess which may be called vanity, and a deficiency which is little-mindedness.

8 But just as we said that liberality is related to magnificence, differing only in that it deals with small sums, so here there is a virtue related to high-minded-

ness, and differing only in that it is concerned with small instead of great honours. A man may have a due desire for honour, and also more or less than a due desire: he that carries this desire to excess is called ambitious, he that has not enough of it is called unambitious, but he that has the due amount has no name. There are also no abstract names for the characters, except "ambition," corresponding to ambitious. And on this account those who occupy the extremes lay claim to the middle place. And in common parlance, too, the moderate man is sometimes called ambitious and sometimes unambitious, and sometimes the ambitious man is praised and sometimes
the unambitious. Why this is we will explain 9
afterwards; for the present we will follow out our plan and enumerate the other types of character.

In the matter of anger also we find excess and 10
deficiency and moderation. The characters themselves hardly have recognized names, but as the moderate man is here called gentle, we will call his character gentleness; of those who go into extremes, we may take the term wrathful for him who exceeds, with wrathfulness for the vice, and wrathless for him who is deficient, with wrathlessness for his character.

Besides these, there are three kinds of moderation, 11
bearing some resemblance to one another, and yet different. They all have to do with intercourse in speech and action, but they differ in that one has to do with the truthfulness of this intercourse, while the other two have to do with its pleasantness—one of the two with pleasantness in matters of amusement, the other with pleasantness in all the relations of

life. We must therefore speak of these qualities also in order that we may the more plainly see how, in all cases, moderation is praiseworthy, while the extreme courses are neither right nor praiseworthy, but blamable.

In these cases also names are for the most part wanting, but we must try, here as elsewhere, to coin names ourselves, in order to make our argument clear and easy to follow.

12 In the matter of truth, then, let us call him who observes the mean a true [or truthful] person, and observance of the mean truth [or truthfulness]: pretence, when it exaggerates, may be called boasting, and the person a boaster; when it understates, let the names be irony and ironical.

13 With regard to pleasantness in amusement, he who observes the mean may be called witty, and his character wittiness; excess may be called buffoonery, and the man a buffoon; while boorish may stand for the person who is deficient, and boorishness for his character.

With regard to pleasantness in the other affairs of life, he who makes himself properly pleasant may be called friendly, and his moderation friendliness; he that exceeds may be called obsequious if he have no ulterior motive, but a flatterer if he has an eye to his own advantage; he that is deficient in this respect, and always makes himself disagreeable, may be called a quarrelsome or peevish fellow.

14 Moreover, in mere emotions * and in our conduct with regard to them, there are ways of observing the

* i.e. which do not issue in act like those hitherto mentioned.

mean; for instance, shame (αἰδώς), is not a virtue, but yet the modest (αἰδήμων) man is praised. For in these matters also we speak of this man as observing the mean, of that man as going beyond it (as the shame-faced man whom the least thing makes shy), while he who is deficient in the feeling, or lacks it altogether, is called shameless; but the term modest (αἰδήμων) is applied to him who observes the mean.

Righteous indignation, again, hits the mean between envy and malevolence. These have to do with feelings of pleasure and pain at what happens to our neighbours. A man is called righteously indignant when he feels pain at the sight of undeserved prosperity, but your envious man goes beyond him and is pained by the sight of any one in prosperity, while the malevolent man is so far from being pained that he actually exults in the misfortunes of his neighbours.

But we shall have another opportunity of discussing these matters.

As for justice, the term is used in more senses than one; we will, therefore, after disposing of the above questions, distinguish these various senses, and show how each of these kinds of justice is a kind of moderation.

And then we will treat of the intellectual virtues in the same way.

The two vicious extremes are opposed to one another and to the intermediate virtue.

8. There are, as we said, three classes of disposition, viz. two kinds of vice, one marked by excess, the other by deficiency, and one kind of virtue, the observance of the mean. Now, each is in a way opposed to each, for the extreme dispositions are opposed both

to the mean or moderate disposition and to one another, while the moderate disposition is opposed to both the extremes. Just as a quantity which is equal to a given quantity is also greater when compared with a less, and less when compared with a greater quantity, so the mean or moderate dispositions exceed as compared with the defective dispositions, and fall short as compared with the excessive dispositions, both in feeling and in action; *e.g.* the courageous man seems foolhardy as compared with the coward, and cowardly as compared with the foolhardy; and similarly the temperate man appears profligate in comparison with the insensible, and insensible in comparison with the profligate man; and the liberal man appears prodigal by the side of the illiberal man, and illiberal by the side of the prodigal man.

And so the extreme characters try to displace the mean or moderate character, and each represents him as falling into the opposite extreme, the coward calling the courageous man foolhardy, the foolhardy calling him coward, and so on in other cases.

But while the mean and the extremes are thus opposed to one another, the extremes are strictly contrary to each other rather than to the mean; for they are further removed from one another than from the mean, as that which is greater than a given magnitude is further from that which is less, and that which is less is further from that which is greater, than either the greater or the less is from that which is equal to the given magnitude.

Sometimes, again, an extreme, when compared with the mean, has a sort of resemblance to it, as foolhardiness to courage, or prodigality to liberality; but there is the greatest possible dissimilarity between the extremes.

Again, "things that are as far as possible removed from each other" is the accepted definition of contraries, so that the further things are removed from each other the more contrary they are.

In comparison with the mean, however, it is some- 6
times the deficiency that is the more opposed, and sometimes the excess; *e.g.* foolhardiness, which is excess, is not so much opposed to courage as cowardice, which is deficiency; but insensibility, which is lack of feeling, is not so much opposed to temperance as profligacy, which is excess.

The reasons for this are two. One is the reason 7
derived from the nature of the matter itself: since one extreme is, in fact, nearer and more similar to the mean, we naturally do not oppose it to the mean so strongly as the other; *e.g.* as foolhardiness seems more similar to courage and nearer to it, and cowardice more dissimilar, we speak of cowardice as the opposite rather than the other: for that which is further removed from the mean seems to be more opposed to it.

This, then, is one reason, derived from the nature 8
of the thing itself. Another reason lies in ourselves: and it is this—those things to which we happen to be more prone by nature appear to be more opposed to the mean: *e.g.* our natural inclination is rather towards indulgence in pleasure, and so we more easily fall into profligate than into regular habits: those courses, then, in which we are more apt to run to great lengths are spoken of as more opposed to the

mean; and thus profligacy, which is an excess, is more opposed to temperance than the deficiency is.

1 9. We have sufficiently explained, then, that moral virtue is moderation or observance of the mean, and in what sense, viz. (1) as holding a middle position between two vices, one on the side of excess, and the other on the side of deficiency, and (2) as aiming at the mean or moderate amount both in feeling and in action.

The mean hard to hit, and is a matter of perception, not of reasoning.

2 And on this account it is a hard thing to be good; for finding the middle or the mean in each case is a hard thing, just as finding the middle or centre of a circle is a thing that is not within the power of everybody, but only of him who has the requisite knowledge.

Thus any one can be angry—that is quite easy; any one can give money away or spend it: but to do these things to the right person, to the right extent, at the right time, with the right object, and in the right manner, is not what everybody can do, and is by no means easy; and that is the reason why right doing is rare and praiseworthy and noble.

3 He that aims at the mean, then, should first of all strive to avoid that extreme which is more opposed to it, as Calypso * bids Ulysses—

> "Clear of these smoking breakers keep thy ship."

4 For of the extremes one is more dangerous, the other less. Since then it is hard to hit the mean precisely, we must "row when we cannot sail," as the proverb has it, and choose the least of two evils;

* Hom., Od., xii. 101–110, and 219–220: Calypso should be Circe.

and that will be best effected in the way we have
described.

And secondly we must consider, each for himself,
what we are most prone to—for different natures are
inclined to different things—which we may learn by
the pleasure or pain we feel. And then we must bend 5
ourselves in the opposite direction; for by keeping
well away from error we shall fall into the middle
course, as we straighten a bent stick by bending it
the other way.

But in all cases we must be especially on our guard 6
against pleasant things, and against pleasure; for we
can scarce judge her impartially. And so, in our
behaviour towards her, we should imitate the behaviour
of the old counsellors towards Helen,* and
in all cases repeat their saying: if we dismiss her we
shall be less likely to go wrong.

This then, in outline, is the course by which we 7
shall best be able to hit the mean.

But it is a hard task, we must admit, especially in
a particular case. It is not easy to determine, for
instance, how and with whom one ought to be angry,
and upon what grounds, and for how long; for public
opinion sometimes praises those who fall short, and
calls them gentle, and sometimes applies the term
manly to those who show a harsh temper.

In fact, a slight error, whether on the side of excess 8
or deficiency, is not blamed, but only a considerable
error; for then there can be no mistake. But it is
hardly possible to determine by reasoning how far or
to what extent a man must err in order to incur

* Hom., Il., iii. 154-164.

blame; and indeed matters that fall within the scope of perception never can be so determined. Such matters lie within the region of particulars, and can only be determined by perception.

So much then is plain, that the middle character is in all cases to be praised, but that we ought to incline sometimes towards excess, sometimes towards deficiency; for in this way we shall most easily hit the mean and attain to right doing.

BOOK III.

CHAPTERS 1–5. THE WILL.

An act is involuntary when done (a) under compulsion, or (b) through ignorance: (a) means not originated by doer, (b) means through ignorance of the circumstances: voluntary then means originated with knowledge of circumstances.

1. VIRTUE, as we have seen, has to do with feel- 1
ings and actions. Now, praise * or blame is given only to what is voluntary; that which is involuntary receives pardon, and sometimes even pity.

It seems, therefore, that a clear distinction between the voluntary and the involuntary is necessary for
those who are investigating the nature of virtue, and 2
will also help legislators in assigning rewards and punishments.

That is generally held to be involuntary which is 3
done under compulsion or through ignorance.

"Done under compulsion" means that the cause is external, the agent or patient contributing nothing towards it; as, for instance, if he were carried somewhere by a whirlwind or by men whom he could not resist.

But there is some question about acts done in order 4
to avoid a greater evil, or to obtain some noble end; *e.g.* if a tyrant were to order you to do something dis-

* It must be remembered that "virtue" is synonymous with "praiseworthy habit;" I. 13, 20; II. 9, 9.

graceful, having your parents or children in his power, who were to live if you did it, but to die if you did not—it is a matter of dispute whether such acts are involuntary or voluntary.

5 Throwing a cargo overboard in a storm is a somewhat analogous case. No one voluntarily throws away his property if nothing is to come of it,* but any sensible person would do so to save the life of himself and the crew.

6 Acts of this kind, then, are of a mixed nature, but they more nearly resemble voluntary acts. For they are desired or chosen at the time when they are done, and the end or motive of an act is that which is in view at the time. In applying the terms voluntary and involuntary, therefore, we must consider the state of the agent's mind at the time. Now, he wills the act at the time; for the cause which sets the limbs going lies in the agent in such cases and where the cause lies in the agent, it rests with him to do or not to do.

Such acts, then, are voluntary, though in themselves [or apart from these qualifying circumstances] we may allow them to be involuntary; for no one would choose anything of this kind on its own account.

7 And, in fact, for actions of this sort men are sometimes praised,† *e.g.* when they endure something disgraceful or painful in order to secure some great and noble result: but in the contrary case they are

* ἁπλῶς, "without qualification:" no one chooses loss of property simply, but loss of property with saving of life is what all sensible people would choose.

† Which shows that the acts are regarded as voluntary.

blamed; for no worthy person would endure the extremity of disgrace when there was no noble result in view, or but a trifling one.

But in some cases we do not praise, but pardon, *i.e.* when a man is induced to do a wrong act by pressure which is too strong for human nature and
which no one could bear. Though there are some cases 8
of this kind, I think, where the plea of compulsion is inadmissible,* and where, rather than do the act, a man ought to suffer death in its most painful form; for instance, the circumstances which "compelled" Alcmæon in Euripides† to kill his mother seem absurd.

It is sometimes hard to decide whether we ought 9
to do this deed to avoid this evil, or whether we ought to endure this evil rather than do this deed; but it is still harder to abide by our decisions: for generally the evil which we wish to avoid is something painful, the deed we are pressed to do is something disgraceful; and hence we are blamed or praised according as we do or do not suffer ourselves to be compelled.

What kinds of acts, then, are to be called com- 10
pulsory?

I think our answer must be that, in the first place,

* οὐκ ἔστιν ἀναγκασθῆναι, "compulsion is impossible." If the act was compulsory it was not my act, I cannot be blamed: there are some acts, says Aristotle, for which we could not forgive a man, for which, whatever the circumstances, we must blame him; therefore no circumstances *can* compel him, or compulsion is impossible. The argument is, in fact, "I ought not, therefore I can not (am able not to do it),"—like Kant's, "I ought, therefore I can." But, if valid at all, it is valid universally, and the conclusion should be that the body only can be compelled, and not the will—that a compulsory *act* is impossible.

† The same lost play is apparently quoted in V. 9, 1.

when the cause lies outside and the agent has no part in it, the act is called, without qualification, "compulsory" [and therefore involuntary]; but that, in the second place, when an act that would not be voluntarily done for its own sake is chosen now in preference to this given alternative, the cause lying in the agent, such an act must be called "involuntary in itself," or "in the abstract," but "now, and in preference to this alternative, voluntary." But an act of the latter kind is rather of the nature of a voluntary act: for acts fall within the sphere of particulars; and here the particular thing that is done is voluntary.

It is scarcely possible, however, to lay down rules for determining which of two alternatives is to be preferred; for there are many differences in the particular cases.

11 It might, perhaps, be urged that acts whose motive is something pleasant or something noble are compulsory, for here we are constrained by something outside us.

But if this were so,* all our acts would be compulsory; for these are the motives of every act of every man.†

Again, acting under compulsion and against one's will is painful, but action whose motive is something pleasant or noble involves pleasure.‡ It is absurd,

* Reading οὕτω.

† Therefore, strictly speaking, a "compulsory act" is a contradiction in terms; the real question is, "What is an act?"

‡ Therefore, since these are the motives of every act, all voluntary action involves pleasure. If we add "when successful," this quite agrees with Aristotle's theory of pleasure in Books VII. and X.

then, to blame things outside us instead of our own readiness to yield to their allurements, and, while we claim our noble acts as our own, to set down our disgraceful actions to "pleasant things outside us."

Compulsory, then, it appears, is that of which the 12
cause is external, the person compelled contributing nothing thereto.

What is done through ignorance is always "not- 13
voluntary," but is "involuntary" * when the agent is pained afterwards and sorry when he finds what he has done.† For when a man, who has done something through ignorance, is not vexed at what he has done, you cannot indeed say that he did it voluntarily, as he did not know what he was doing, but neither can you say that he did it involuntarily or unwillingly, since he is not sorry.

A man who has acted through ignorance, then, if he is sorry afterwards, is held to have done the deed involuntarily or unwillingly; if he is not sorry afterwards we may say (to mark the distinction) he did the deed "not-voluntarily;" for, as the case is different, it is better to have a distinct name.

Acting through ignorance, however, seems to be 14
different from acting in ignorance. For instance, when a man is drunk or in a rage he is not thought

* *i.e.* not merely "not-willed," but done "unwillingly," or "against the agent's will." Unfortunately our usage recognizes no such distinction between "not-voluntary" and "involuntary."

† ἐν μεταμελείᾳ, lit. "when the act involves change of mind." This, under the circumstances, can only mean that the agent who willed the act, not seeing the true nature of it at the time, is sorry afterwards, when he comes to see what he has done

to act *through* ignorance, but through intoxication or rage, and yet not knowingly, but *in* ignorance.

Every vicious man, indeed, is ignorant of* what
ought to be done and what ought not to be done, and
it is this kind of error that makes men unjust and
15 bad generally. But the term "involuntary" is not
properly applied to cases in which a man is ignorant
of what is fitting.† The ignorance that makes an
act involuntary is not this ignorance of the principles
which should determine preference (this constitutes
vice),—not, I say, this ignorance of the universal (for
we blame a man for this), but ignorance of the
particulars, of the persons and things affected by the
act. These are the grounds of pity and pardon; for
he who is ignorant of any of these particulars acts
involuntarily.

16 It may be as well, then, to specify what these particulars are, and how many. They are—first, the doer; secondly, the deed; and, thirdly, the object or person affected by it; sometimes also that wherewith (*e.g.* the instrument with which) it is done, and that for the sake of which it is done (*e.g.* for protection), and the way in which it is done (*e.g.* gently or violently.)

17 Now, a man cannot (unless he be mad) be igno-

* *i.e.* forms a wrong judgment; *cf.* ἡ μοχθηρία διαψεύδεσθαι ποιεῖ περὶ τὰς πρακτικὰς ἀρχάς, VI. 12, 10: not that the vicious man does not know that such a course is condemned by society, but he does not assent to society's rules—adopts other maxims contrary to them.

† τὸ συμφέρον, what conduces to a given end, expedient. The meaning of the term varies with the end in view: here the end in view is the supreme end, happiness: τὸ συμφέρον, then, means here the rule of conduct to which, in a given case, the agent must conform in order to realize this end; *cf.* II. 2, 3.

rant of all these particulars; for instance, he evidently cannot be ignorant of the doer: for how can he not know himself?

But a man may be ignorant of what he is doing; *e.g.* a man who has said something will sometimes plead that the words escaped him unawares, or that he did not know that the subject was forbidden (as Æschylus pleaded in the case of the Mysteries); or a man might plead that when he discharged the weapon he only intended to show the working of it, as the prisoner did in the catapult case. Again, a man might mistake his son for an enemy, as Merope does,* or a sharp spear for one with a button, or a heavy stone for a pumice-stone. Again, one might kill a man with a drug intended to save him, or hit him hard when one wished merely to touch him (as boxers do when they spar with open hands).

Ignorance, then, being possible with regard to all 18
these circumstances, he who is ignorant of any of them is held to have acted involuntarily, and especially when he is ignorant of the most important particulars; and the most important seem to be the persons affected and the result.†

Besides this, however, the agent must be grieved 19
and sorry for what he has done, if the act thus ignorantly committed is to be called involuntary [not merely not-voluntary].

* In a lost play of Euripides, believing her son to have been murdered, she is about to kill her son himself as the murderer. See Stewart.

† τὸ οὗ ἕνεκα usually is the intended result (and so ἕνεκα τίνος in § 16), but of course it is only the actual result that the agent can be ignorant of.

20 But now, having found that an act is involuntary when done under compulsion or through ignorance, we may conclude that a voluntary act is one which is originated by the doer with knowledge of the particular circumstances of the act.

21 For I venture to think that it is incorrect to say that acts done through anger or desire are involuntary.

22 In the first place, if this be so we can no longer allow that any of the other animals act voluntarily, nor even children.

23 Again, does the saying mean that none of the acts which we do through desire or anger are voluntary, or that the noble ones are voluntary and the disgraceful ones involuntary? Interpreted in the latter sense, it is surely ridiculous, as the cause of both is the same.
24 If we take the former interpretation, it is absurd, I think, to say that we ought to desire a thing, and also to say that its pursuit is involuntary; but, in fact, there are things at which we ought to be angry, and things which we ought to desire, *e.g.* health and learning.

25 Again, it seems that what is done unwillingly is painful, while what is done through desire is pleasant.

26 Again, what difference is there, in respect of involuntariness, between wrong deeds done upon calculation and wrong deeds done in anger? Both alike
27 are to be avoided, but the unreasoning passions or feelings seem to belong to the man just as much as does the reason, so that the acts that are done under the impulse of anger or desire are also the man's acts.* To make such actions involuntary, therefore, would be too absurd.

* Reason can modify action only by modifying feeling. Every

Purpose, a mode of will, means choice after deliberation.

2. Now that we have distinguished voluntary from 1
involuntary acts, our next task is to discuss choice or purpose. For it seems to be most intimately connected with virtue, and to be a surer test of character than action itself.

It seems that choosing is willing, but that the two 2
terms are not identical, willing being the wider. For children and other animals have will, but not choice or purpose; and acts done upon the spur of the moment are said to be voluntary, but not to be done with deliberate purpose.

Those who say that choice is appetite, or anger, or 3
wish, or an opinion of some sort, do not seem to give a correct account of it.

In the first place, choice is not shared by irrational creatures, but appetite and anger are.

Again, the incontinent man acts from appetite 4
and not from choice or purpose, the continent man from purpose and not from appetite.

Again, appetite may be contrary to purpose, but 5
one appetite can not be contrary to another appetite.*

Again, the object of appetite [or aversion] is the pleasant or the painful, but the object of purpose [as such] is neither painful nor pleasant.

action issues from a feeling or passion (πάθος), which feeling (and therefore the resultant action) is mine (the outcome of my character, and therefore imputable to me), whether it be modified by reason (deliberation, calculation) or no.

* Two appetites may pull two *different*, but not *contrary* ways (ἐναντιοῦται): that which not merely diverts but restrains me from satisfying an appetite must be desire of a different kind, *e.g.* desire to do what is right. Ἐπιθυμία is used loosely in cap. 1 for desire (ὄρεξις), here more strictly for appetite, a species of desire, purpose (προαίρεσις) being another species: *cf.* infra, **3**, 19.

6 Still less can purpose be anger (θυμός); for acts done in anger seem to be least of all done of purpose or deliberate choice.

7 Nor yet is it wish, though it seem very like; for we cannot purpose or deliberately choose the impossible, and a man who should say that he did would be thought a fool; but we may wish for the impossible, *e.g.* to escape death.

8 Again, while we may wish what never could be effected by our own agency (*e.g.* the success of a particular actor or athlete), we never purpose or deliberately choose such things, but only those that we think may be effected by our own agency.

9 Again, we are more properly said to wish the end, to choose the means; *e.g.* we wish to be healthy, but we choose what will make us healthy: we wish to be happy, and confess the wish, but it would not be correct to say we purpose or deliberately choose to be happy; for we may say roundly that purpose or choice deals with what is in our power.

10 Nor can it be opinion; for, in the first place, anything may be matter of opinion—what is unalterable and impossible no less than what is in our power; and, in the second place, we distinguish opinion according as it is true or false, not according as it is good or bad, as we do with purpose or choice.

11 We may say, then, that purpose is not the same as opinion in general; nor, indeed, does any one maintain this.

But, further, it is not identical with a particular kind of opinion. For our choice of good or evil makes us morally good or bad, holding certain opinions does not.

Again, we choose to take or to avoid a good or evil 12
thing; we opine what its nature is, or what it is good for, or in what way; but we cannot opine to take or to avoid.

Again, we commend a purpose for its rightness 13
or correctness, an opinion for its truth.

Again, we choose a thing when we know well that it is good; we may have an opinion about a thing of which we know nothing.

Again, it seems that those who are best at choosing 14
are not always the best at forming opinions, but that some who have an excellent judgment fail, through depravity, to choose what they ought.

It may be said that choice or purpose must be 15
preceded or accompanied by an opinion or judgment; but this makes no difference: our question is not that, but whether they are identical.

What, then, is choice or purpose, since it is none 16
of these?

It seems, as we said, that what is chosen or purposed is willed, but that what is willed is not always chosen or purposed.

The required differentia, I think, is "after previous 17
deliberation." For choice or purpose implies calculation and reasoning. The name itself, too, seems to indicate this, implying that something is chosen before or in preference to other things.*

3. Now, as to deliberation, do we deliberate about 1

* προαίρεσις, lit. "choosing before." Our "preference" exactly corresponds here, but unfortunately cannot always be employed.

everything, and may anything whatever be matter for deliberation, or are there some things about which deliberation is impossible? *on what we can do—not on ends, but means.*

2 By "matter for deliberation" we should understand, I think, not what a fool or a maniac, but what a rational being would deliberate about.

3 Now, no one deliberates about eternal or unalterable things, *e.g.* the system of the heavenly bodies, or the incommensurability of the side and the diagonal of a square.

4 Again, no one deliberates about things which
change, but always change in the same way (whether
the cause of change be necessity, or nature, or any
5 other agency), *e.g.* the solstices and the sunrise;* nor
about things that are quite irregular, like drought and
wet; nor about matters of chance, like the finding
of a treasure.

6 Again, even human affairs are not always matter of deliberation; *e.g.* what would be the best constitution for Scythia is a question that no Spartan would deliberate about.

The reason why we do not deliberate about these things is that none of them are things that we can ourselves effect.

7 But the things that we do deliberate about are matters of conduct that are within our control. And these are the only things that remain; for besides nature and necessity and chance, the only remaining cause of change is reason and human agency in general. Though we must add that men severally deliberate about what they can themselves do.

* These are instances of "necessity;" a tree grows by "nature," i.e. by its own natural powers.

A further limitation is that where there is exact 8
and absolute knowledge, there is no room for deliberation; *e.g.* writing: for there is no doubt how the letters should be formed.

We deliberate, then, about things that are brought about by our own agency, but not always in the same way; *e.g.* about medicine and money-making, and about navigation more than about gymnastic, inasmuch as it is not yet reduced to so perfect a system,
and so on; but more about matters of art than matters 9
of science, as there is more doubt about them.

Matters of deliberation, then, are matters in 10
which there are rules that generally hold good, but in which the result cannot be predicted, *i.e.* in which there is an element of uncertainty. In important matters we call in advisers, distrusting our own powers of judgment.

It is not about ends, but about means that we 11
deliberate. A physician does not deliberate whether he shall heal, nor an orator whether he shall persuade, nor a statesman whether he shall make a good system of laws, nor a man in any other profession about his end; but, having the proposed end in view, we consider how and by what means this end can be attained; and if it appear that it can be attained by various means, we further consider which is the easiest and best; but if it can only be attained by one means, we consider how it is to be attained by this means, and how this means itself is to be secured, and so on, until we come to the first link in the chain of causes, which is last in the order of discovery.

For in deliberation we seem to inquire and to
analyze in the way described, just as we analyze a
geometrical figure in order to learn how to construct
12 it* (and though inquiry is not always deliberation—
mathematical inquiry, for instance, is not—deliberation is always inquiry); that which is last in the
analysis coming first in the order of construction.

13 If we come upon something impossible, we give up the plan; *e.g.* if it needs money, and money cannot be got: but if it appear possible, we set to work. By possible I mean something that can be done by *us;* and what can be done by our friends can in a manner be done by us; for it is we who set our friends to work.

14 Sometimes we have to find out instruments, sometimes how to use them; and so on with the rest: sometimes we have to find out what agency will produce the desired effect, sometimes how or through whom this agency is to be set at work.

15 It appears, then, that a man, as we have already
said, originates his acts; but that he deliberates about
that which he can do himself, and that what he
16 does is done for the sake of something else.† For

* If we have to construct a geometrical figure, we first "suppose it done," then analyze the imagined figure in order to see the conditions which it implies and which imply it, and continue the chain till we come to some thing (drawing of some lines) which we already know how to do.

† *Cf.* III. 2, 9, and 5, 1, and X. 7, 5. There is no real inconsistency between this and the doctrine that the end of life is life, that the good act is to be chosen for its own sake (II. 4, 3), because it is noble (III. 7, 13): for the end is not outside the means; happiness or the perfect life is the complete system of those acts, and the real nature of each act is determined by its rela-

he cannot deliberate about the end, but about the means to the end; nor, again, can he deliberate about particular facts, *e.g.* whether this be a loaf, or whether it be properly baked: these are matters of immediate perception. And if he goes on deliberating for ever he will never come to a conclusion.

But the object of deliberation and the object of choice or purpose are the same, except that the latter is already fixed and determined; when we say, "this is chosen" or "purposed," we mean that it has been selected after deliberation. For we always stop in our inquiry how to do a thing when we have traced back the chain of causes to ourselves, and to the commanding part of ourselves; for this is the part that chooses. 17

This may be illustrated by the ancient constitutions which Homer describes; for there the kings announce to the people what they have chosen. 18

Since, then, a thing is said to be chosen or purposed when, being in our power, it is desired after deliberation, choice or purpose may be defined as deliberate desire for something in our power; for we first deliberate, and then, having made our decision thereupon, we desire in accordance with deliberation. 19

Let this stand, then, for an account in outline of choice or purpose, and of what it deals with, viz. means to ends. 20

We wish for the end,

4. Wish, we have already said, is for the end; but 1

tion to this system; to choose it as a means to this end is to choose it for itself.

whereas some hold that the object of wish is the good others hold that it is what seems good. *the real or apparent good.*

2 Those who maintain that the object of wish* is the good have to admit that what those wish for who choose wrongly is not object of wish (for if so it would be good; but it may so happen that it was
3 bad); on the other hand, those who maintain that the object of wish is what seems good have to admit that there is nothing which is naturally object of wish, but that each wishes for what seems good to him—different and even contrary things seeming good to different people.

4 As neither of these alternatives quite satisfies us, perhaps we had better say that the good is the real object of wish (without any qualifying epithet), but that what seems good is object of wish to each man. The good man, then, wishes for the real object of wish; but what the bad man wishes for may be anything whatever; just as, with regard to the body, those who are in good condition find those things healthy that are really healthy, while those who are diseased find other things healthy (and it is just the same with things bitter, sweet, hot, heavy, etc.): for the good or ideal man judges each case correctly, and in each case what is true seems true to him.

For, corresponding to each of our trained faculties, there is a special form of the noble and the pleasant,

* *βουλητόν.* This word hovers between two senses, (1) wished for, (2) to be wished for, just as *αἱρετόν* hovers between (1) desired, (2) desirable. The difficulty, as here put, turns entirely upon the equivocation; but at bottom lies the fundamental question, whether there be a common human nature, such that we can say, "This kind of life is man's real life."

and perhaps there is nothing so distinctive of the good or ideal man as the power he has of discerning these special forms in each case, being himself, as it were, their standard and measure.

What misleads people seems to be in most cases pleasure; it seems to be a good thing, even when it is not. So they choose what is pleasant as good, and shun pain as evil.

Virtue and vice are alike voluntary: our acts are our own; for we are punished for them: if this be our character, we have made it by repeated acts: even bodily vices are blamable when thus formed. We cannot plead that our notion of good depends on our nature; for (1) vice would still be as voluntary as virtue, (2) we help to make ourselves what we are.

5. We have seen that, while we wish for the end, we deliberate upon and choose the means thereto.

Actions that are concerned with means, then, will be guided by choice, and so will be voluntary.

But the acts in which the virtues are manifested are concerned with means.*

Therefore virtue depends upon ourselves: and vice likewise. For where it lies with us to do, it lies with us not to do. Where we can say no, we can say yes. If then the doing a deed, which is noble, lies with us, the not doing it, which is disgraceful, lies with us; and if the not doing, which is noble, lies with us, the doing, which is disgraceful, also lies with us. But if the doing and likewise the not doing of noble or base deeds lies with us, and if this is, as we found, identical with being good or bad, then it follows that it lies with us to be worthy or worthless men.

And so the saying—

> "None would be wicked, none would not be blessed,"

---

* Each virtuous act is desired and chosen as a means to realizing a particular virtue, and this again is desired as a part or constituent of, and so as a means to, that perfect self-realization which is happiness: *cf.* 3, 15.

seems partly false and partly true: no one indeed is blessed against his will; but vice is voluntary.

5 If we deny this, we must dispute the statements made just now, and must contend that man is not the originator and the parent of his actions, as of his children.

6 But if those statements commend themselves to us, and if we are unable to trace our acts to any other sources than those that depend upon ourselves, then that whose source is within us must itself depend upon us and be voluntary.

7 This seems to be attested, moreover, by each one of us in private life, and also by the legislators; for they correct and punish those that do evil (except when it is done under compulsion, or through ignorance for which the agent is not responsible), and honour those that do noble deeds, evidently intending to encourage the one sort and discourage the other. But no one encourages us to do that which does not depend on ourselves, and which is not voluntary: it would be useless to be persuaded not to feel heat or pain or hunger and so on, as we should feel them all the same.

8 I say "ignorance for which the agent is not responsible," for the ignorance itself is punished by the law, if the agent appear to be responsible for his ignorance, *e.g.* for an offence committed in a fit of drunkenness the penalty is doubled: for the origin of the offence lies in the man himself; he might have avoided the intoxication, which was the cause of his ignorance. Again, ignorance of any of the ordinances of the law, which a man ought to know and easily
9 can know, does not avert punishment. And so in

other cases, where ignorance seems to be the result of negligence, the offender is punished, since it lay with him to remove this ignorance; for he might have taken the requisite trouble.

It may be objected that it was the man's character 10
not to take the trouble.

We reply that men are themselves responsible for acquiring such a character by a dissolute life, and for being unjust or profligate in consequence of repeated acts of wrong, or of spending their time in drinking and so on. For it is repeated acts of a particular kind that give a man a particular character.

This is shown by the way in which men train 11
themselves for any kind of contest or performance: they practise continually.

Not to know, then, that repeated acts of this or 12
that kind produce a corresponding character or habit, shows an utter want of sense.

Moreover, it is absurd to say that he who acts 13
unjustly does not wish to be unjust, or that he who behaves profligately does not wish to be profligate.

But if a man knowingly does acts which must make
him unjust, he will be voluntarily unjust; though it 14
does not follow that, if he wishes it, he can cease to
be unjust and be just, any more than he who is sick
can, if he wishes it, be whole. And it may be that
he is voluntarily sick, through living incontinently
and disobeying the doctor. At one time, then, he had
the option not to be sick, but he no longer has it now
that he has thrown away his health. When you
have discharged a stone it is no longer in your power
to call it back; but nevertheless the throwing and

casting away of that stone rests with you; for the beginning of its flight depended upon you.*

Just so the unjust or the profligate man at the beginning was free not to acquire this character, and therefore he is voluntarily unjust or profligate; but now that he has acquired it, he is no longer free to put it off.

15 But it is not only our mental or moral vices that are voluntary; bodily vices also are sometimes voluntary, and then are censured. We do not censure natural ugliness, but we do censure that which is due to negligence and want of exercise. And so with weakness and infirmity: we should never reproach a man who was born blind, or had lost his sight in an illness or by a blow—we should rather pity him; but we should all censure a man who had blinded himself by excessive drinking or any other kind of profligacy.

16 We see, then, that of the vices of the body it is those that depend on ourselves that are censured, while those that do not depend on ourselves are not censured. And if this be so, then in other fields also those vices that are blamed must depend upon ourselves.

17 Some people may perhaps object to this.

"All men," they may say, "desire that which appears good to them, but cannot control this appearance; a man's character, whatever it be, decides what shall appear to him to be the end."

* My act is mine, and does not cease to be mine because I would undo it if I could; and so, further, since we made the habits whose bonds we cannot now unloose, we are responsible, not merely for the acts which made them, but also for the acts which they now produce "in spite of us:" what constrains us is ourselves.

If, I answer, each man be in some way responsible for his habits or character, then in some way he must be responsible for this appearance also.

But if this be not the case, then a man is not responsible for, or is not the cause of, his own evil doing, but it is through ignorance of the end that he does evil, fancying that thereby he will secure the greatest good: and the striving towards the true end does not depend on our own choice, but a man must be born with a gift of sight, so to speak, if he is to discriminate rightly and to choose what is really good: and he is truly well-born who is by nature richly endowed with this gift; for, as it is the greatest and the fairest gift, which we cannot acquire or learn from another, but must keep all our lives just as nature gave it to us, to be well and nobly born in this respect is to be well-born in the truest and completest sense.

Now, granting this to be true, how will virtue be any more voluntary than vice?

For whether it be nature or anything else that 18
determines what shall appear to be the end, it is determined in the same way for both alike, for the good man as for the bad, and both alike refer all their acts of whatever kind to it.

And so whether we hold that it is not merely 19
nature that decides what appears to each to be the end (whatever that be), but that the man himself contributes something; or whether we hold that the end is fixed by nature, but that virtue is voluntary, inasmuch as the good man voluntarily takes the steps to that end—in either case vice will be just as volun-

tary as virtue; for self is active in the bad man just as much as in the good man, in choosing the particular acts at least, if not in determining the end.

If then, as is generally allowed, the virtues are voluntary (for we do, in fact, in some way help to make our character, and, by being of a certain character, give a certain complexion to our idea of the end), the vices also must be voluntary; for all this applies equally to them.

We have thus described in outline the nature of the virtues in general, and have said that they are forms of moderation or modes of observing the mean, and that they are habits or trained faculties, and that they show themselves in the performance of the same acts which produce them, and that they depend on ourselves and are voluntary, and that they follow the guidance of right reason. But our particular acts are not voluntary in the same sense as our habits: for we are masters of our acts from beginning to end when we know the particular circumstances; but we are masters of the beginnings only of our habits or characters, while their growth by gradual steps is imperceptible, like the growth of disease. Inasmuch, however, as it lay with us to employ or not to employ our faculties in this way, the resulting characters are on that account voluntary.

Now let us take up each of the virtues again in turn, and say what it is, and what its subject is, and how it deals with it; and in doing this, we shall at the same time see how many they are. And, first of all, let us take courage.

BOOK III. CHAPTER 6.—END OF BOOK V. THE SEVERAL MORAL VIRTUES AND VICES.

Of courage and the opposite vices.

6. We have already said that courage is modera- 1
tion or observance of the mean with respect to feelings of fear and confidence.

Now, fear evidently is excited by fearful things, 2
and these are, roughly speaking, evil things; and so fear is sometimes defined as "expectation of evil."

Fear, then, is excited by evil of any kind, *e.g.* by 3
disgrace, poverty, disease, friendlessness, death; but it does not appear that every kind gives scope for courage. There are things which we actually ought to fear, which it is noble to fear and base not to fear, *e.g.* disgrace. He who fears disgrace is an honourable man, with a due sense of shame, while he who fears it not is shameless (though some people stretch the word courageous so far as to apply it to him; for he has a certain resemblance to the courageous man, courage also being a kind of fearlessness). Poverty, per- 4
haps, we ought not to fear, nor disease, nor generally those things that are not the result of vice, and do not depend upon ourselves. But still to be fearless in regard to these things is not strictly courage; though here also the term is sometimes applied in virtue of a certain resemblance. There are people,

for instance, who, though cowardly in the presence of the dangers of war, are yet liberal and bold in the spending of money.

5 On the other hand, a man is not to be called cowardly for fearing outrage to his children or his wife, or for dreading envy and things of that kind, nor courageous for being unmoved by the prospect of a whipping.

6 In what kind of terrors, then, does the courageous man display his quality? Surely in the greatest; for no one is more able to endure what is terrible. But of all things the most terrible is death; for death is our limit, and when a man is once dead it seems that there is no longer either good or evil for him.

7 It would seem, however, that even death does not on all occasions give scope for courage, *e.g.* death by water or by disease.

8 On what occasions then? Surely on the noblest occasions: and those are the occasions which occur in war; for they involve the greatest and the noblest danger.

9 This is confirmed by the honours which courage receives in free states and at the hands of princes.

10 The term courageous, then, in the strict sense, will be applied to him who fearlessly faces an honourable death and all sudden emergencies which involve death; and such emergencies mostly occur in war.

11 Of course the courageous man is fearless in the presence of illness also, and at sea, but in a different way from the sailors; for the sailors, because of their

experience, are full of hope when the landsmen are already despairing of their lives and filled with aversion at the thought of such a death.

Moreover, the circumstances which especially call 12
out courage are those in which prowess may be displayed, or in which death is noble; but in these forms of death there is neither nobility nor room for prowess.

7. Fear is not excited in all men by the same 1
things, but yet we commonly speak of fearful things that surpass man's power to face. Such things, then, inspire fear in every rational man. But the fearful things that a man may face differ in importance and in being more or less fearful (and so with the things that inspire confidence). Now, the courageous man 2
always keeps his presence of mind (so far as a man can). So though he will fear these fearful things, he will endure them as he ought and as reason bids him, for the sake of that which is noble;* for this is the end or aim of virtue.

But it is possible to fear these things too much or 3
too little, and again to take as fearful what is not really so. And thus men err sometimes by fearing 4
the wrong things, sometimes by fearing in the wrong manner or at the wrong time, and so on.

And all this applies equally to things that inspire confidence.

He, then, that endures and fears what he ought 5
from the right motive, and in the right manner, and

* τοῦ καλοῦ ἕνεκα, the highest expression that Aristotle has for the moral motive, = καλοῦ ἕνεκα (§ 6) and ὅτι καλόν (§ 13), "as a means to or as a constituent part of the noble life."

at the right time, and similarly feels confidence, is courageous.

For the courageous man regulates both his feeling and his action according to the merits of each case and as reason bids him.

6 But the end or motive of every manifestation of a habit or exercise of a trained faculty is the end or motive of the habit or trained faculty itself.

Now, to the courageous man courage is essentially a fair or noble thing.

Therefore the end or motive of his courage is also noble; for everything takes its character from its end.

It is from a noble motive, therefore, that the courageous man endures and acts courageously in each particular case.*

7 Of the characters that run to excess, he that exceeds in fearlessness has no name (and this is often the case, as we have said before); but a man would be either a maniac or quite insensible to pain who should fear nothing, not even earthquakes and breakers, as they say is the case with the Celts.

He that is over-confident in the presence of
8 fearful things is called foolhardy. But the foolhardy man is generally thought to be really a braggart, and to pretend a courage which he has not: at least he wishes to seem what the courageous man really is in the presence of danger; so he imitates him
9 where he can. And so your foolhardy man is generally a coward at bottom: he blusters so long as he

* The courageous man desires the courageous act for the same reason for which he desires the virtue itself, viz. simply because it is noble: see note on § 2.

can do so safely,* but turns tail when real danger comes.

He who is over-fearful is a coward; for he fears what he ought not, and as he ought not, etc. 10

He is also deficient in confidence; but his character rather displays itself in excess of fear in the presence of pain.

The coward is also despondent, for he is frightened at everything. But it is the contrary with the courageous man; for confidence implies hopefulness. 11

Thus the coward and the foolhardy and the courageous man display their characters in the same circumstances, behaving differently under them: for while the former exceed or fall short, the latter behaves moderately and as he ought; and while the foolhardy are precipitate and eager before danger comes, but fall away in its presence, the courageous are keen in action, but quiet enough beforehand. 12

Courage then, as we have said, is observance of the mean with regard to things that excite confidence or fear, under the circumstances which we have specified, and chooses its course and sticks to its post because it is noble to do so, or because it is disgraceful not to do so. 13

But to seek death as a refuge from poverty, or love, or any painful thing, is not the act of a brave man, but of a coward. For it is effeminacy thus to fly from vexation; and in such a case death is accepted not because it is noble, but simply as an escape from evil.

* ἐν τούτοις, i.e. ἐν οἷς δύναται, so long as he can imitate the courageous man without being courageous.

8. Courage proper, then, is something of this sort. But besides this there are five other kinds of courage so called.

Of courage improperly so called

First, "political courage," which most resembles true courage.

Citizens seem often to face dangers because of legal pains and penalties on the one hand, and honours on the other. And on this account the people seem to be most courageous in those states where cowards are disgraced and brave men honoured.

This, too, is the kind of courage which inspires Homer's characters, *e.g.* Diomede and Hector.

> "Polydamas will then reproach me first," *

says Hector; and so Diomede:

> "Hector one day will speak among his folk
> And say, 'The son of Tydeus at my hand——'" †

This courage is most like that which we described above, because its impulse is a virtuous one, viz. a sense of honour (αἰδώς), and desire for a noble thing (glory), and aversion to reproach, which is disgraceful.

We might, perhaps, put in the same class men who are forced to fight by their officers; but they are inferior, inasmuch as what impels them is not a sense of honour, but fear, and what they shun is not disgrace, but pain. For those in authority compel them in Hector's fashion—

> "Whoso is seen to skulk and shirk the fight
> Shall nowise save his carcase from the dogs." ‡

* Il., xxii. 200. † Ibid., viii. 148, 149.
‡ Ibid., xv. 348, ii. 391.

And the same thing is done by commanders who 5
order their men to stand, and flog them if they run,
or draw them up with a ditch in their rear, and so
on: all alike, I mean, employ compulsion.

But a man ought to be courageous, not under compulsion, but because it is noble to be so.

Secondly, experience in this or that matter is 6
sometimes thought to be a sort of courage; and this
indeed is the ground of the Socratic notion that
courage is knowledge.

This sort of courage is exhibited by various persons in various matters, but notably by regular troops in military affairs; for it seems that in war there are many occasions of groundless alarm, and with these the regulars are better acquainted; so they appear to be courageous, simply because the other troops do not understand the real state of the case.

Again, the regular troops by reason of their
experience are more efficient both in attack and
defence; for they are skilled in the use of their
weapons, and are also furnished with the best kind
of arms for both purposes. So they fight with the 8
advantage of armed over unarmed men, or of trained
over untrained men; for in athletic contests also it
is not the bravest men that can fight best, but those
who are strongest and have their bodies in the best
order.

But these regular troops turn cowards whenever 9
the danger rises to a certain height and they find
themselves inferior in numbers and equipment; then
they are the first to fly, while the citizen-troops stand

and are cut to pieces, as happened at the temple of Hermes.* For the citizens deem it base to fly, and hold death preferable to saving their lives on these terms; but the regulars originally met the danger only because they fancied they were stronger, and run away when they learn the truth, fearing death more than disgrace. But that is not what we mean by courageous.

10 *Thirdly*, people sometimes include rage within the meaning of the term courage.

Those who in sheer rage turn like wild beasts on those who have wounded them are taken for courageous, because the courageous man also is full of rage; for rage is above all things eager to rush on danger; so we find in Homer, "Put might into his rage," and "roused his wrath and rage," and "fierce wrath breathed through his nostrils," and "his blood boiled." For all these expressions seem to signify the awakening and the bursting out of rage.

11 The truly courageous man, then, is moved to act by what is noble, rage helping him: but beasts are moved by pain, *i.e.* by blows or by fear; for in a wood or a marsh they do not attack man. And so beasts are not courageous, since it is pain and rage that drives them to rush on danger, without foreseeing any of the terrible consequences. If this be courage, then asses must be called courageous when they are hungry; for though you beat them they will not leave off eating. Adulterers also are moved to do many bold deeds by their lust.

* Outside Coronea, when the town was betrayed, in the Sacred War.

Being driven to face danger by pain or rage, then, 12
is not courage proper. However, this kind of courage, whose impulse is rage, seems to be the most natural, and, when deliberate purpose and the right motive are added to it, to become real courage.

Again, anger is a painful state, the act of revenge is pleasant; but those who fight from these motives [*i.e.* to avoid the pain or gain the pleasure] may fight well, but are not courageous: for they do not act because it is noble to act so, or as reason bids, but are driven by their passions; though they bear some resemblance to the courageous man.

Fourthly, the sanguine man is not properly called 13
courageous: he is confident in danger because he has often won and has defeated many adversaries. The two resemble one another, since both are confident; but whereas the courageous man is confident for the reasons specified above, the sanguine man is confident because he thinks he is superior and will win without
receiving a scratch. (People behave in the same sort 14
of way when they get drunk; for then they become sanguine.) But when he finds that this is not the case, he runs away; while it is the character of the courageous man, as we saw, to face that which is terrible to a man even when he sees the danger, because it is noble to do so and base not to do so.

And so (it is thought) it needs greater courage to 15
be fearless and cool in sudden danger than in danger that has been foreseen; for behaviour in the former case must be more directly the outcome of formed character, since it is less dependent on preparation. When we see what is coming we may choose to meet

it, as the result of calculation and reasoning, but when it comes upon us suddenly we must choose according to our character.

16 *Fifthly,* those who are unaware of their danger sometimes appear to be courageous, and in fact are not very far removed from the sanguine persons we last spoke of, only they are inferior in that they have not necessarily any opinion of themselves, which the sanguine must have. And so while the latter hold their ground for some time, the former, whose courage was due to a false belief, run away the moment they perceive or suspect that the case is different; as the Argives did when they engaged the Spartans under the idea that they were Sicyonians.*

17 Thus we have described the character of the courageous man, and of those who are taken for courageous.

But there is another point to notice.

How courage involves both pain and pleasure.

1 9. Courage is concerned, as we said, with feelings both of confidence and of fear, yet it is not equally concerned with both, but more with occasions of fear: it is the man who is cool and behaves as he ought on such occasions that is called courageous, rather than he who behaves thus on occasions that inspire confidence.

2 And so, as we said, men are called courageous for enduring painful things.

Courage, therefore, brings pain, and is justly praised; for it is harder to endure what is painful than to abstain from what is pleasant.

3 I do not, of course, mean to say that the end of

* The incident is narrated by Xenophon, Hell., iv. 10.

courage is not pleasant, but that it seems to be hidden from view by the attendant circumstances, as is the case in gymnastic contests also. Boxers, for instance, have a pleasant end in view, that for which they strive, the crown and the honours; but the blows they receive are grievous to flesh and blood, and painful, and so are all the labours they undergo; and as the latter are many, while the end is small, the pleasantness of the end is hardly apparent.

If, then, the case of courage is analogous, death 4
and wounds will be painful to the courageous man and against his will, but he endures them because it is noble to do so or base not to do so.

And the more he is endowed with every virtue, and the happier he is, the more grievous will death be to him; for life is more worth living to a man of his sort than to any one else, and he deprives himself knowingly of the very best things; and it is painful to do that. But he is no less courageous because he feels this pain; nay, we may say he is even more courageous, because in spite of it he chooses noble conduct in battle in preference to those good things.

Thus we see that the rule that the exercise of a 5
virtue is pleasant* does not apply to all the virtues, except in so far as the end is attained.

Still there is, perhaps, no reason why men of this 6
character should not be less efficient as soldiers than those who are not so courageous, but have nothing good to lose; for such men are reckless of risk, and will sell their lives for a small price.

Here let us close our account of courage; it will 7

* *Cf.* I. 8, 10, f.

not be hard to gather an outline of its nature from what we have said.

1 10. After courage, let us speak of temperance, for these two seem to be the virtues of the irrational parts of our nature. *Of temperance.*

We have already said that temperance is moderation or observance of the mean with regard to pleasures (for it is not concerned with pains so much, nor in the same manner); profligacy also manifests itself in the same field.

Let us now determine what kind of pleasures these are.

2 First, let us accept as established the distinction between the pleasures of the body and the pleasures of the soul, such as the pleasures of gratified ambition or love of learning.

When he who loves honour or learning is delighted by that which he loves, it is not his body that is affected, but his mind. But men are not called either temperate or profligate for their behaviour with regard to these pleasures; nor for their behaviour with regard to any other pleasures that are not of the body. For instance, those who are fond of gossip and of telling stories, and spend their days in trifles, are called babblers, but not profligate; nor do we apply this term to those who are pained beyond measure at the loss of money or friends.

3 Temperance, then, will be concerned with the pleasures of the body, but not with all of these even: for those who delight in the use of their eyesight, in colours and forms and painting, are not called either temperate or profligate; and yet it would seem that

it is possible to take delight in these things too as one ought, and also more or less than one ought.

And so with the sense of hearing: a man is never 4
called profligate for taking an excessive delight in music or in acting, nor temperate for taking a proper delight in them.

Nor are these terms applied to those who delight 5
(unless it be accidentally) in smells. We do not say that those who delight in the smell of fruit or roses or incense are profligate, but rather those who delight in the smell of unguents and savoury dishes; for the profligate delights in these smells because they remind him of the things that he lusts after.

You may, indeed, see other people taking delight 6
in the smell of food when they are hungry; but only a profligate takes delight in such smells [constantly], as he alone is [constantly] lusting after such things.

The lower animals, moreover, do not get pleasure 7
through these senses, except accidentally. It is not the scent of a hare that delights a dog, but the eating of it; only the announcement comes through his sense of smell. The lion rejoices not in the lowing of the ox, but in the devouring of him; but as the lowing announces that the ox is near, the lion appears to delight in the sound itself. So also, it is not seeing a stag or a wild goat that pleases him, but the anticipation of a meal.

Temperance and profligacy, then, have to do with 8
those kinds of pleasure which are common to the lower animals, for which reason they seem to be slavish and brutal; I mean the pleasures of touch and taste.

9 Taste, however, seems to play but a small part here, or perhaps no part at all. For it is the function of taste to distinguish flavours, as is done by wine-tasters and by those who season dishes; but it is by no means this discrimination of objects that gives delight (to profligates, at any rate), but the actual enjoyment of them, the medium of which is always the sense of touch, alike in the pleasures of eating, of drinking, and of sexual intercourse.

10 And hence a certain gourmand wished that his throat were longer than a crane's, thereby implying that his pleasure was derived from the sense of touch.

That sense, then, with which profligacy is concerned is of all senses the commonest or most widespread; and so profligacy would seem to be deservedly of all vices the most censured, inasmuch as it attaches not to our human, but to our animal nature.

11 To set one's delight in things of this kind, then, and to love them more than all things, is brutish.

And further, the more manly sort even of the pleasures of touch are excluded from the sphere of profligacy, such as the pleasures which the gymnast finds in rubbing and the warm bath; for the profligate does not cultivate the sense of touch over his whole body, but in certain parts only.

1 11. Now, of our desires or appetites some appear to be common to the race, others to be individual and acquired.

Thus the desire of food is natural [or common to the race]; every man when he is in want desires meat or drink, or sometimes both, and sexual intercourse, as Homer says, when he is young and vigorous.

But not all men desire to satisfy their wants in 2
this or that particular way, nor do all desire the same things; and therefore such desire appears to be peculiar to ourselves, or individual.

Of course it is also partly natural: different people are pleased by different things, and yet there are some things which all men like better than others.

Firstly, then, in the matter of our natural or 3
common desires but few err, and that only on one side, viz. on the side of excess; *e.g.* to eat or drink of whatever is set before you till you can hold no more is to exceed what is natural in point of quantity, for natural desire or appetite is for the filling of our want simply. And so such people are called "belly-mad," implying that they fill their bellies too full.

It is only utterly slavish natures that acquire this vice.

Secondly, with regard to those pleasures that are 4
individual [*i.e.* which attend the gratification of our individual desires] many people err in various ways.

Whereas people are called fond of this or that because they delight either in wrong things, or to an unusual degree, or in a wrong fashion, profligates exceed in all these ways. For they delight in some things in which they ought not to delight (since they are hateful things), and if it be right to delight in any of these things they delight in them more than is right and more than is usual.

It is plain, then, that excess in these pleasures is 5
profligacy, and is a thing to be blamed.

But in respect of the corresponding pains the case

is not the same here as it was with regard to courage: a man is not called temperate for bearing them, and profligate for not bearing them; but the profligate man is called profligate for being more pained than he ought at not getting certain pleasant things (his pain being caused by his pleasure *), and the temperate man is called temperate because the absence of these pleasant things or the abstinence from them is not painful to him.

The profligate, then, desires all pleasant things or those that are most intensely pleasant, and is led by his desire so as to choose these in preference to all other things. And so he is constantly pained by failing to get them and by lusting after them: for all appetite involves pain; but it seems a strange thing to be pained for the sake of pleasure.

People who fall short in the matter of pleasure, and take less delight than they ought in these things, are hardly found at all; for this sort of insensibility is scarcely in human nature. And indeed even the lower animals discriminate kinds of food, and delight in some and not in others; and a being to whom nothing was pleasant, and who found no difference between one thing and another, would be very far removed from being a man. We have no name for such a being, because he does not exist.

But the temperate man observes the mean in these things. He takes no pleasure in those things that the profligate most delights in (but rather disdains

* *Cf.* VII. **14**, 2: "the opposite of this excessive pleasure [*i.e.* going without a wrong pleasure] is not pain, except to the man who sets his heart on this excessive pleasure."

them), nor generally in the wrong things, nor very much in any of these things,* and when they are absent he is not pained, nor does he desire them, or desires them but moderately, not more than he ought, nor at the wrong time, etc.; but those things which, being pleasant, at the same time conduce to health and good condition, he will desire moderately and in the right manner, and other pleasant things also, provided they are not injurious, or incompatible with what is noble, or beyond his means; for he who cares for them then, cares for them more than is fitting, and the temperate man is not apt to do that, but rather to be guided by right reason.

How profligacy is more voluntary than cowardice.

12. Profligacy seems to be more voluntary than 1
cowardice.

For a man is impelled to the former by pleasure, to the latter by pain; but pleasure is a thing we choose, while pain is a thing we avoid. Pain puts us beside 2
ourselves and upsets the nature of the sufferer, while pleasure has no such effect. Profligacy, therefore, is more voluntary.

Profligacy is for these reasons more to be blamed than cowardice, and for another reason too, viz. that it is easier to train one's self to behave rightly on these occasions [*i.e.* those in which profligacy is displayed]; for such occasions are constantly occurring in our lives, and the training involves no risk; but with occasions of fear the contrary is the case.

Again, it would seem that the habit of mind or 3
character called cowardice is more voluntary than the particular acts in which it is exhibited. It is not

* *i.e.* the pleasures of taste and touch.

painful to be a coward, but the occasions which exhibit cowardice put men beside themselves through fear of pain, so that they throw away their arms and altogether disgrace themselves; and hence these particular acts are even thought to be compulsory.

In the case of the profligate, on the contrary, the particular acts are voluntary (for they are done with appetite and desire), but the character itself less so; for no one desires to be a profligate.

The term "profligacy" we apply also to childish faults,* for they have some sort of resemblance. It makes no difference for our present purpose which of the two is named after the other, but it is plain that the later is named after the earlier.

And the metaphor, I think, is not a bad one: what needs "chastening" or "correction"† is that which inclines to base things and which has great powers of expansion. Now, these characteristics are nowhere so strongly marked as in appetite and in childhood; children too [as well as the profligate] live according to their appetites, and the desire for pleasant things is most pronounced in them. If then this element be not submissive and obedient to the governing principle, it will make great head: for in an irrational being the desire for pleasant things is insatiable and ready to gratify itself in any way, and the gratification of the appetite increases the natural tendency, and if the gratifications are great and intense they even thrust out reason altogether. The gratifications of appetite,

* Of course the English term is not so used.

† κόλασις, chastening; ἀκόλαστος, unchastened, incorrigible, profligate.

therefore, should be moderate and few, and appetite
should be in no respect opposed to reason (this is
what we mean by submissive and "chastened"), but 8
subject to reason as a child should be subject to his
tutor.

And so the appetites of the temperate man should 9
be in harmony with his reason; for the aim of both
is that which is noble: the temperate man desires
what he ought, and as he ought, and when he ought;
and this again is what reason prescribes.

This, then, may be taken as an account of tem- 10
perance.

BOOK IV.

THE SAME—*Continued.*

1 **1.** LIBERALITY, of which we will next speak, seems to be moderation in the matter of wealth. What we commend in a liberal man is his behaviour, not in war, nor in those circumstances in which temperance is commended, nor yet in passing judgment, but in the giving and taking of wealth, and especially *Of liberality*
2 in the giving—wealth meaning all those things whose value can be measured in money.

3 But both prodigality and illiberality are at once excess and defect in the matter of wealth.

Illiberality always means caring for wealth more than is right; but prodigality sometimes stands for a combination of vices. Thus incontinent people, who squander their money in riotous living, are called
4 prodigals. And so prodigals are held to be very worthless individuals, as they combine a number of vices.

But we must remember that this is not the proper
5 use of the term; for the term "prodigal" (ἄσωτος) is intended to denote a man who has one vice, viz. that of wasting his substance: for he is ἄσωτος,* or "prodigal," who is destroyed through his own fault, and

* ἄσωτος, ἀ priv. and σῶς, σώζειν.

the wasting of one's substance is held to be a kind of destruction of one's self, as one's life is dependent upon it. This, then, we regard as the proper sense of the term "prodigality."

Anything that has a use may be used well or ill. 6

Now, riches is abundance of useful things (τὰ χρήσιμα).

But each thing is best used by him who has the virtue that is concerned with that thing.

Therefore he will use riches best who has the virtue that is concerned with wealth * (τὰ χρήματα), i.e. the liberal man.

Now, the ways of using wealth are spending and 7
giving, while taking and keeping are rather the ways of acquiring wealth. And so it is more distinctive of the liberal man to give to the right people than to take from the right source and not to take from the wrong source. For it is more distinctive of virtue to do good to others than to have good done to you, and to act nobly than not to act basely: but it is
plain that doing good and acting nobly go with the 8
giving, while having good done to you and not acting basely go with the taking.

Again, we are thankful to him who gives, not to him who does not take; and so also we praise the former rather than the latter.

Again, it is easier not to take than to give; for we 9
are more inclined to be too stingy with our own goods than to take another's.

* The connection is plainer in the original, because τὰ χρήματα, "wealth," is at once seen to be identical with τὰ χρήσιμα, "useful things," and connected with χρεία, "use."

10 Again, it is those who give that are commonly
called liberal; while those who abstain from taking
are not praised for their liberality especially, but
11 rather for their justice; and those who take are not
praised at all.

Again, of all virtuous characters the liberal man is perhaps the most beloved, because he is useful; but his usefulness lies in his giving.

12 But virtuous acts, we said, are noble, and are done for the sake of that which is noble. The liberal man, therefore, like the others, will give with a view to, or for the sake of, that which is noble, and give rightly; *i.e.* he will give the right things to the right persons at the right times—in short, his giving will have all the characteristics of right giving.

13 Moreover, his giving will be pleasant to him, or at least painless; for virtuous acts are always pleasant or painless—certainly very far from being painful.

14 He who gives to the wrong persons, or gives from some other motive than desire for that which is noble, is not liberal, but must be called by some other name.

Nor is he liberal who gives with pain; for that shows that he would prefer * the money to the noble action, which is not the feeling of the liberal man.

15 The liberal man, again, will not take from wrong sources; for such taking is inconsistent with the character of a man who sets no store by wealth.

16 Nor will he be ready to beg a favour; for he who confers benefits on others is not usually in a hurry to receive them.

* Were it not for some extraneous consideration, *e.g.* desire to stand well with his neighbours.

But from right sources he will take (*e.g.* from his 17
own property), not as if there were anything noble in taking, but simply as a necessary condition of giving. And so he will not neglect his property, since he wishes by means of it to help others. But he will refuse to give to any casual person, in order that he may have wherewithal to give to the right persons, at the right times, and where it is noble to give.

It is very characteristic of the liberal man * to 18
go even to excess in giving, so as to leave too little for himself; for disregard of self is part of his character.

In applying the term liberality we must take 19
account of a man's fortune; for it is not the amount of what is given that makes a gift liberal, but the liberal habit or character of the doer; and this character proportions the gift to the fortune of the giver. And so it is quite possible that the giver of the smaller sum may be the more liberal man, if his means be smaller.

Those who have inherited a fortune seem to be 20
more liberal than those who have made one; for they have never known want; and all men are particularly fond of what themselves have made, as we see in parents and poets.

It is not easy for a liberal man to be rich, as he is not apt to take or to keep, but is apt to spend, and cares for money not on its own account, but only for the sake of giving it away.

* This is strictly a departure from the virtue; but Aristotle seems often to pass insensibly from the abstract ideal of a virtue to its imperfect embodiment in a complex character. *Cf. infra.* cap. 3.

21 Hence the charge often brought against fortune, that those who most deserve wealth are least blessed with it. But this is natural enough; for it is just as impossible to have wealth without taking trouble about it, as it is to have anything else.

22 Nevertheless the liberal man will not give to the wrong people, nor at the wrong times; for if he did, he would no longer be displaying true liberality, and, after spending thus, would not have enough to
23 spend on the right occasions. For, as we have already said, he is liberal who spends in proportion to his fortune, on proper objects, while he who exceeds this is prodigal. And so princes * are not called prodigal, because it does not seem easy for them to exceed the measure of their possessions in gifts and expenses.

24 Liberality, then, being moderation in the giving and taking of wealth, the liberal man will give and spend the proper amount on the proper objects, alike in small things and in great, and that with pleasure; and will also take the proper amount from the proper sources. For since the virtue is moderation in both giving and taking, the man who has the virtue will do both rightly. Right taking is consistent with right giving, but any other taking is contrary to it. Those givings and takings, then, that are consistent with one another are found in the same person, while those that are contrary to one another manifestly are not.

25 But if a liberal man happen to spend anything in

* No single English word can convey the associations of the Greek *τύραννος*, a monarch who has seized absolute power, not necessarily one who abuses it.

a manner contrary to what is right and noble, he will be pained, but moderately and in due measure; for it is a characteristic of virtue to be pleased and pained on the right occasions and in due measure.

The liberal man, again, is easy to deal with in 26
money matters; it is not hard to cheat him, as he
does not value wealth, and is more apt to be vexed 27
at having failed to spend where he ought, than to be pained at having spent where he ought not—the sort of man that Simonides would not commend.*

The prodigal, on the other hand, errs in these 28
points also; he is not pleased on the right occasions nor in the right way, nor pained: but this will be clearer as we go on.

We have already said that both prodigality and 29
illiberality are at once excess and deficiency, in two things, viz. giving and taking (expenditure being included in giving). Prodigality exceeds in giving and in not taking, but falls short in taking; illiberality falls short in giving, but exceeds in taking—in small things, we must add.

Now, the two elements of prodigality are not 30
commonly united in the same person: † it is not easy for a man who never takes to be always giving; for private persons soon exhaust their means of giving, and it is to private persons that the name is generally applied.‡

A prodigal of this kind [*i.e.* in whom both the 31

* See Stewart.

† *i.e.* in men of some age and fixed character; they often coexist in very young men, he says, but cannot possibly coexist for long.

‡ As he has already said in effect, *supra*, § 23

elements are combined], we must observe, would seem to be not a little better than an illiberal man. For he is easily cured by advancing years and by lack of means, and may come to the middle course. For he has the essential points of the liberal character; he gives and abstains from taking, though he does neither well nor as he ought. If then he can be trained to this, or if in any other way this change in his nature can be effected, he will be liberal; for then he will give to whom he ought, and will not take whence he ought not. And so he is generally thought to be not a bad character; for to go too far in giving and in not taking does not show a vicious or ignoble nature so much as a foolish one.

A prodigal of this sort, then, seems to be much better than an illiberal man, both for the reasons already given, and also because the former does good to many, but the latter to no one, not even to himself.

But most prodigals, as has been said, not only give wrongly, but take from wrong sources, and are in this respect illiberal. They become grasping because they wish to spend, but cannot readily do so, as their supplies soon fail. So they are compelled to draw from other sources. At the same time, since they care nothing for what is noble, they will take quite recklessly from any source whatever; for they long to give, but care not a whit how the money goes or whence it comes.

And so their gifts are not liberal; for they are not noble, nor are they given with a view to that which is noble, nor in the right manner. Sometimes they enrich those who ought to be poor, and will give nothing to men of well-regulated character, while they give a great deal to those who flatter them, or furnish them with any other pleasure. And thus the greater part of them are profligates; for, being ready to part with their money, they are apt to lavish it on riotous living, and as they do not shape their lives with a view to that which is noble, they easily fall away into the pursuit of pleasure.

The prodigal, then, if he fail to find guidance, 36
comes to this, but if he get training he may be brought to the moderate and right course.

But illiberality is incurable; for old age and all 37
loss of power seems to make men illiberal.

It also runs in the blood more than prodigality; the generality of men are more apt to be fond of money than of giving.

Again, it is far-reaching, and has many forms; for 38
there seem to be many ways in which one can be illiberal.

It consists of two parts—deficiency in giving, and excess of taking; but it is not always found in its entirety; sometimes the parts are separated, and one man exceeds in taking, while another falls short
in giving. Those, for instance, who are called by such 39
names as niggardly, stingy, miserly, all fall short in giving, but do not covet other people's goods, or wish to take them.

Some are impelled to this conduct by a kind of honesty, or desire to avoid what is disgraceful—I mean that some of them seem, or at any rate profess, to be saving, in order that they may never be compelled to do anything disgraceful; *e.g.* the cheeseparer * (and those like him), who is so named because of the extreme lengths to which he carries his unwillingness to give.

But others are moved to keep their hands from their neighbours' goods only by fear, believing it to be no easy thing to take the goods of others, without having one's own goods taken in turn; so they are content with neither taking nor giving.

Others, again, exceed in the matter of taking so far as to make any gain they can in any way whatever, *e.g.* those who ply debasing trades, brothel-keepers and such like, and usurers who lend out small sums at a high rate. For all these make money from improper sources to an improper extent.

The common characteristic of these last seems to be the pursuit of base gain; for all of them endure reproach for the sake of gain, and that a small gain. For those who make improper gains in improper ways on a large scale are not called illiberal, *e.g.* tyrants who sack cities and pillage temples; they are rather called wicked, impious, unjust. The dice-sharper, however, and the man who steals clothes at the bath, or the common thief, are reckoned among the illiberal; for they all make base gains; *i.e.* both the thief and the sharper ply their trade and endure reproach for gain, and the thief for the sake of his booty endures the greatest dangers, while the sharper makes gain out of his friends, to whom he ought to give. Both then, wishing to make gain in improper ways, are seekers of base gain; and all such ways of making money are illiberal.

* Lit. "cummin-splitter."

But illiberality is rightly called the opposite of 44
liberality; for it is a worse evil than prodigality, and men are more apt to err in this way than in that which we have described as prodigality.

Let this, then, be taken as our account of liberality, 45
and of the vices that are opposed to it.

2. Our next task would seem to be an examina- 1
tion of magnificence. For this also seems to be a virtue that is concerned with wealth.

But it does not, like liberality, extend over the whole field of money transactions, but only over those that involve large expenditure; and in these it goes beyond liberality in largeness. For, as its very name (μεγαλοπρέπεια) suggests, it is suitable expenditure on
a large scale. But the largeness is relative: the 2
expenditure that is suitable for a man who is fitting out a war-ship is not the same as that which is suitable for the chief of a sacred embassy.

What is suitable, then, is relative to the person,
and the occasion, and the business on hand. Yet he 3
who spends what is fitting on trifling or moderately important occasions is not called magnificent; *e.g.* the man who can say, in the words of the poet—

"To many a wandering beggar did I give;"

but he who spends what is fitting on great occasions. For the magnificent man is liberal, but a man may be liberal without being magnificent.

The deficiency of this quality is called meanness; 4
the excess of it is called vulgarity, bad taste, etc.; the characteristic of which is not spending too much on proper objects, but spending ostentatiously on im-

proper objects and in improper fashion. But we will speak of them presently.

5 But the magnificent man is like a skilled artist;
he can see what a case requires, and can spend great
6 sums tastefully. For, as we said at the outset, a
habit or type of character takes its complexion
from the acts in which it issues and the things it
produces. The magnificent man's expenses, therefore,
must be great and suitable.

What he produces then will also be of the same nature; for only thus will the expense be at once great and suitable to the result.

The result, then, must be proportionate to the expenditure, and the expenditure proportionate to th result, or even greater.

7 Moreover, the magnificent man's motive in thus spending his money will be desire for that which is noble; for this is the common characteristic of all the virtues.

8 Further, he will spend gladly and lavishly; for a
9 minute calculation of cost is mean. He will inquire
how the work can be made most beautiful and most
elegant, rather than what its cost will be, and how
it can be done most cheaply.

10 So the magnificent man must be liberal also; for the liberal man, too, will spend the right amount in the right manner; only, both the amount and the manner being right, magnificence is distinguished from liberality (which has the same * sphere of action) by greatness—I mean by actual magnitude of amount spent: and secondly, where the amount spent is the

* Reading ταὐτά.

same, the result of the magnificent man's expenditure will be more magnificent.*

For the excellence of a possession is not the same as the excellence of a product or work of art: as a possession, that is most precious or estimable which is worth most, *e.g.* gold; as a work of art, that is most estimable which is great and beautiful: for the sight of such a work excites admiration, and a magnificent thing is always admirable; indeed, excellence of work on a great scale is magnificence.

Now, there is a kind of expenditure which is 11
called in a special sense estimable or honourable, such as expenditure on the worship of the gods (*e.g.* offerings, temples, and sacrifices), and likewise all expenditure on the worship of heroes, and again all public service which is prompted by a noble ambition; *e.g.* a man may think proper to furnish a chorus or a war-ship, or to give a public feast, in a handsome style.

But in all cases, as we have said, we must have 12
regard to the person who spends, and ask who he is, and what his means are; for expenditure should be proportionate to circumstances, and suitable not only to the result but to its author.

And so a poor man cannot be magnificent: he 13
has not the means to spend large sums suitably: if he tries, he is a fool; for he spends disproportionately and in a wrong way; but an act must be done in the

* A worthy expenditure of £100,000 would be magnificent from its mere amount; but even £100 may be spent in a magnificent manner (by a man who can afford it), *e.g.* in buying a rare engraving for a public collection: *cf.* § 17 and 18.

14 right way to be virtuous. But such expenditure is becoming in those who have got the requisite means, either by their own efforts or through their ancestors or their connections, and who have birth and reputation, etc.; for all these things give a man a certain greatness and importance.

15 The magnificent man, then, is properly a man of this sort, and magnificence exhibits itself most properly in expenditure of this kind, as we have said; for this is the greatest and most honourable kind of expenditure: but it may also be displayed on private occasions, when they are such as occur but once in a man's life, *e.g.* a wedding or anything of that kind; or when they are of special interest to the state or the governing classes, *e.g.* receiving strangers and sending them on their way, or making presents to them and returning their presents; for the magnificent man does not lavish money on himself, but on public objects; and gifts to strangers bear some resemblance to offerings to the gods.

16 But a magnificent man will build his house too in a style suitable to his wealth; for even a fine house is a kind of public ornament. And he will spend money more readily on things that last; for these
17 are the noblest. And on each occasion he will spend what is suitable—which is not the same for gods as for men, for a temple as for a tomb.

And since every expenditure may be great after its kind, great expenditure on a great occasion being most magnificent,* and then in a less degree that which is great for the occasion, whatever it be

* ἁπλῶς seems unnecessary.

(for the greatness of the result is not the same as the greatness of the expense; *e.g.* the most beautiful ball or the most beautiful bottle that can be got is a magnificent present for a child, though its price is something small and mean), it follows that it is characteristic of the magnificent man to do magnificently that which he does, of whatever kind it be (for such work cannot easily be surpassed), and to produce a result proportionate to the expense.

This, then, is the character of the magnificent man.

The man who exceeds (whom we call vulgar) exceeds, as we said, in spending improperly. He spends great sums on little objects, and makes an unseemly display; *e.g.* if he is entertaining the members of his club, he will give them a wedding feast; if he provides the chorus for a comedy, he will bring his company on the stage all dressed in purple, as they did at Megara. And all this he will do from no desire for what is noble or beautiful, but merely to display his wealth, because he hopes thereby to gain admiration, spending little where he should spend much, and much where he should spend little.

But the mean man will fall short on every occasion, and, even when he spends very large sums, will spoil the beauty of his work by niggardliness in a trifle, never doing anything without thinking twice about it, and considering how it can be done at the least possible cost, and bemoaning even that, and thinking he is doing everything on a needlessly large scale.

Both these characters, then, are vicious, but they do not bring reproach, because they are neither injurious to others nor very offensive in themselves.

3. High-mindedness would seem from its very name (μεγαλοψυχία) to have to do with great things; let us first ascertain what these are. *Of high-mindedness*

It will make no difference whether we consider the quality itself, or the man who exhibits the quality.

By a high-minded man we seem to mean one who claims much and deserves much: for he who claims much without deserving it is a fool; but the possessor of a virtue is never foolish or silly. The man we have described, then, is high-minded.

He who deserves little and claims little is temperate [or modest], but not high-minded: for high-mindedness [or greatness of soul] implies greatness, just as beauty implies stature; small men may be neat and well proportioned, but cannot be called beautiful.

He who claims much without deserving it is vain (though not every one who claims more than he deserves is vain).

He who claims less than he deserves is little-minded, whether his deserts be great or moderate, or whether they be small and he claims still less: but the fault would seem to be greatest in him whose deserts are great; for what would he do if his deserts were less than they are?

The high-minded man, then, in respect of the greatness of his deserts occupies an extreme position, but in that he behaves as he ought, observes the mean; for he claims that which he deserves, while all the others claim too much or too little.

If, therefore, he deserves much and claims much, and most of all deserves and claims the greatest

things, there will be one thing with which he will be
especially concerned. For desert has reference to 10
external good things. Now, the greatest of external good things we may assume to be that which we render to the gods as their due, and that which people in high stations most desire, and which is the prize appointed for the noblest deeds. But the thing that answers to this description is honour, which, we may safely say, is the greatest of all external goods. Honours and dishonours, therefore, are the field in which the high-minded man behaves as he ought.

And indeed we may see, without going about to 11
prove it, that honour is what high-minded men are concerned with; for it is honour that they especially claim and deserve.

The little-minded man falls short, whether we 12
compare his claims with his own deserts or with what the high-minded man claims for himself.

The vain or conceited man exceeds what is due to 13
himself, though he does not exceed the high-minded man in his claims.*

But the high-minded man, as he deserves the 14
greatest things, must be a perfectly good or excellent man; for the better man always deserves the greater things, and the best possible man the greatest possible things. The really high-minded man, therefore, must be a good or excellent man. And indeed greatness in every virtue or excellence would seem to be necessarily implied in being a high-minded or great-souled man.

* For that is impossible.

15 It would be equally inconsistent with the high-minded man's character to run away swinging his arms, and to commit an act of injustice; for what thing is there for love of which he would do anything unseemly, seeing that all things are of little account to him?

Survey him point by point and you will find that the notion of a high-minded man that is not a good or excellent man is utterly absurd. Indeed, if he were not good, he could not be worthy of honour; for honour is the prize of virtue, and is rendered to the good as their due.

16 High-mindedness, then, seems to be the crowning grace, as it were, of the virtues; it makes them greater, and cannot exist without them. And on this account it is a hard thing to be truly high-minded; for it is impossible without the union of all the virtues.

17 The high-minded man, then, exhibits his character especially in the matter of honours and dishonours and at great honour from good men he will be moderately pleased, as getting nothing more than his due, or even less; for no honour can be adequate to complete virtue; but nevertheless he will accept it, as they have nothing greater to offer him. But honour from ordinary men and on trivial grounds he will utterly despise; for that is not what he deserves. And dishonour likewise he will make light of; for he will never merit it.

18 But though it is especially in the matter of honours, as we have said, that the high-minded man displays his character, yet he will also observe the mean in his feelings with regard to wealth and power

and all kinds of good and evil fortune, whatever may befall him, and will neither be very much exalted by prosperity, nor very much cast down by adversity; seeing that not even honour affects him as if it were a very important thing. For power and wealth are desirable for honour's sake (at least, those who have them wish to gain honour by them). But he who thinks lightly of honour must think lightly of them also.

And so high-minded men seem to look down upon everything.

But the gifts of fortune also are commonly thought 19
to contribute to high-mindedness. For those who are well born are thought worthy of honour, and those who are powerful or wealthy; for they are in a position of superiority, and that which is superior in any good thing is always held in greater honour. And so these things do make people more high-minded in a
sense; for such people find honour from some. But 20
in strictness it is only the good man that is worthy of honour, though he that has both goodness and good fortune is commonly thought to be more worthy of honour. Those, however, who have these good things without virtue, neither have any just claim to great things, nor are properly to be called high-minded; for neither is possible without complete virtue.

But those who have these good things readily 21
come to be supercilious and insolent. For without virtue it is not easy to bear the gifts of fortune becomingly; and so, being unable to bear them, and thinking themselves superior to everybody else, such people look down upon others, and yet themselves do

whatever happens to please them. They imitate the high-minded man without being really like him, and they imitate him where they can; that is to say, they do not exhibit virtue in their acts, but they look down upon others. For the high-minded man never looks down upon others without justice (for he estimates them correctly), while most men do so for quite irrelevant reasons.

The high-minded man is not quick to run into petty dangers, and indeed does not love danger, since there are few things that he much values; but he is ready to incur a great danger, and whenever he does so is unsparing of his life, as a thing that is not worth keeping at all costs.

It is his nature to confer benefits, but he is ashamed to receive them; for the former is the part of a superior, the latter of an inferior. And when he has received a benefit, he is apt to confer a greater in return; for thus his creditor will become his debtor and be in the position of a recipient of his favour.

It seems, moreover, that such men remember the benefits which they have conferred better than those which they have received (for the recipient of a benefit is inferior to the benefactor, but such a man wishes to be in the position of a superior), and that they like to be reminded of the one, but dislike to be reminded of the other; and this is the reason why we read * that Thetis would not mention to Zeus the services she had done him, and why the Lacedæmonians, in treating with the Athenians, re-

* Homer, Il. i. 394 f., 503 f.

minded them of the benefits received by Sparta rather than of those conferred by her.

It is characteristic of the high-minded man, again, 26
never or reluctantly to ask favours, but to be ready to confer them, and to be lofty in his behaviour to those who are high in station and favoured by fortune, but affable to those of the middle ranks; for it is a difficult thing and a dignified thing to assert superiority over the former, but easy to assert it over the latter. A haughty demeanour in dealing with the great is quite consistent with good breeding, but in dealing with those of low estate is brutal, like showing off one's strength upon a cripple.

Another of his characteristics is not to rush in 27
wherever honour is to be won, nor to go where others take the lead, but to hold aloof and to shun an enterprise, except when great honour is to be gained, or a great work to be done—not to do many things, but great things and notable.

Again, he must be open in his hate and in 28
his love (for it is cowardly to dissemble your feelings and to care less for truth than for what people will think of you), and he must be open in word and in deed (for his consciousness of superiority makes him outspoken, and he is truthful
except in so far as he adopts an ironical tone in 29
his intercourse with the masses), and he must be unable to fashion his life to suit another, except he be a friend; for that is servile: and so all flatterers or hangers on of great men are of a slavish nature, and men of low natures become flatterers.

30 Nor is he easily moved to admiration; for nothing is great to him.

He readily forgets injuries; for it is not consistent with his character to brood on the past, especially on past injuries, but rather to overlook them.

31 He is no gossip; he will neither talk about himself nor about others; for he cares not that men should praise him, nor that others should be blamed (though, on the other hand, he is not very ready to bestow praise); and so he is not apt to speak evil of others, not even of his enemies, except with the express purpose of giving offence.

32 When an event happens that cannot be helped or is of slight importance, he is the last man in the world to cry out or to beg for help; for that is the conduct of a man who thinks these events very important.

33 He loves to possess beautiful things that bring no profit, rather than useful things that pay; for this is characteristic of the man whose resources are in himself.

34 Further, the character of the high-minded man seems to require that his gait should be slow, his voice deep, his speech measured; for a man is not likely to be in a hurry when there are few things in which he is deeply interested, nor excited when he holds nothing to be of very great importance: and these are the causes of a high voice and rapid movements.

This, then, is the character of the high-minded man.

35 But he that is deficient in this quality is called little-minded; he that exceeds, vain or conceited.

Now these two also do not seem to be bad—for they do no harm—though they are in error.

For the little-minded man, though he deserves good things, deprives himself of that which he deserves, and so seems to be the worse for not claiming these good things, and for misjudging himself; for if he judged right he would desire what he deserves, as it is good. I do not mean to say that such people seem to be fools, but rather too retiring. But a misjudgment of this kind does seem actually to make them worse; for men strive for that which they deserve, and shrink from noble deeds and employments of which they think themselves unworthy, as well as from mere external good things.

But vain men are fools as well as ignorant of 36
themselves, and make this plain to all the world: for they undertake honourable offices for which they are unfit, and presently stand convicted of incapacity they dress in fine clothes and put on fine airs and so on; they wish everybody to know of their good fortune; they talk about themselves, as if that were the way to honour.

But little-mindedness is more opposed to high- 37
mindedness than vanity is; for it is both commoner and worse.

High-mindedness, then, as we have said, has to do 38
with honour on a large scale.

4. But it appears (as we said at the outset) that 1
there is also a virtue concerned with honour, which bears the same relation to high-mindedness that liberality bears to magnificence; *i.e.* both the virtue in question and liberality have nothing to do with

great things, but cause us to behave properly in matters of moderate or of trifling importance. Just as in the taking and giving of money it is possible to observe the mean, and also to exceed or fall short of it, so it is possible in desire for honour to go too far or not far enough, or, again, to desire honour from the right source and in the right manner.

A man is called ambitious or fond of honour (φιλότιμος) in reproach, as desiring honour more than he ought, and from wrong sources; and a man is called unambitious, or not fond of honour (ἀφιλότιμος) in reproach, as not desiring to be honoured even for noble deeds.

But sometimes a man is called ambitious or fond of honour in praise, as being manly and fond of noble things; and sometimes a man is called unambitious or not fond of honour in praise, as being moderate and temperate (as we said at the outset).

It is plain, then, that there are various senses in which a man is said to be fond of a thing, and that the term fond of honour has not always the same sense, but that as a term of praise it means fonder than most men, and as a term of reproach it means fonder than is right. But, as there is no recognized term for the observance of the mean, the extremes fight, so to speak, for what seems an empty place. But wherever there is excess and defect there is also a mean: and honour is in fact desired more than is right, and less: therefore * it may also be desired to the right degree: this character then is praised, being observance of the mean in the matter of honour, though it

* Reading ἔστι δή.

has no recognized name. Compared with ambition, it seems to be lack of ambition; compared with lack of ambition, it seems to be ambition; compared with both at once, it seems in a way to be both at once.
This, we may observe, also happens in the case of 6
the other virtues. But in this case the extreme characters seem to be opposed to one another [instead of to the moderate character], because the character that observes the mean has no recognized name.

Of gentleness.

5. Gentleness is moderation with respect to anger. 1
But it must be noted that we have no recognized name for the mean, and scarcely any recognized names for the extremes. And so the term gentleness, which properly denotes an inclination towards deficiency in anger (for which also we have no recognized name), is applied to the mean.*

The excess may be called wrathfulness; for the 2
emotion concerned is wrath or anger, though the things that cause it are many and various.

He then who is angry on the right occasions and 3
with the right persons, and also in the right manner, and at the right season, and for the right length of time, is praised; we will call him gentle, therefore, since gentleness is used as a term of praise. For the

* The reader will please overlook the gap which is caused by the withdrawal of a note which stood here in former editions, but which with Bywater's text is no longer required.

man who is called gentle wishes not to lose his
balance, and not to be carried away by his emotions
or passions, but to be angry only in such manner,
and on such occasions, and for such period as reason
4 shall prescribe. But he seems to err rather on the
side of deficiency; he is loth to take vengeance and
very ready to forgive.

5 But the deficiency—call it wrathlessness or
what you will—is censured. Those who are not
angered by what ought to anger them seem to be
foolish, and so do those who are not angry as and
6 when and with whom they ought to be; for such a
man seems to feel nothing and to be pained by
nothing, and, as he is never angered, to lack spirit to
defend himself. But to suffer one's self to be insulted,
or to look quietly on while one's friends are being
insulted, shows a slavish nature.

7 It is possible to exceed in all points, *i.e.* to be angry with persons with whom one ought not, and at things at which one ought not to be angry, and more than one ought, and more quickly, and for a longer time. All these errors, however, are not found in the same person. That would be impossible; for evil is self-destructive, and, if it appears in its entirety, becomes quite unbearable.

8 So we find that wrathful men get angry very soon, and with people with whom and at things at which they ought not, and more than they ought; but they soon get over their anger, and that is a very good point in their character. And the reason is that they do not keep in their anger, but, through the quickness of their temper, at once retaliate, and so let

what is in them come to light, and then have done with it.

But those who are called choleric are excessively 9
quick-tempered, and apt to be angered at anything and on any occasion; whence the name (ἀκρόχολοι).

Sulky men are hard to appease and their anger 10
lasts long, because they keep it in. For so soon as we retaliate we are relieved: vengeance makes us cease from our anger, substituting a pleasant for a painful state. But the sulky man, as he does not thus relieve himself, bears the burden of his wrath about with him; for no one even tries to reason him out of it, as he does not show it, and it takes a long time to digest one's anger within one's self. Such men are exceedingly troublesome to themselves and their dearest friends.

Lastly, hard (χαλεπός) is the name we give to 11
those who are offended by things that ought not to offend them, and more than they ought, and for a longer time, and who will not be appeased without vengeance or punishment.

Of the two extremes the excess is the more opposed 12
to gentleness; for it is commoner (as men are naturally more inclined to vengeance); and a hard-tempered person is worse to live with [than one who is too easy-tempered].

What we said some time ago * is made abundantly 13
manifest by what we have just been saying; it is not easy to define how, and with whom, and at what, and for how long one ought to be angry—how far it is right to go, and at what point misconduct begins.

* II. 9 7.

He who errs slightly from the right course is not blamed, whether it be on the side of excess or of deficiency; for sometimes we praise those who fall short and call them gentle, and sometimes those who behave hardly are called manly, as being able to rule. But what amount and kind of error makes a man blamable can scarcely be defined; for it depends upon the particular circumstances of each case, and can only be decided by immediate perception.

14 But so much at least is manifest, that on the one hand the habit which observes the mean is to be praised, *i.e.* the habit which causes us to be angry with the right persons, at the right things, in the right manner, etc.; and that, on the other hand, all habits of excess or deficiency deserve censure—slight censure if the error be trifling, graver censure if it be considerable, and severe censure if it be great.

It is evident, therefore, that we must strive for the habit which observes the mean.

15 This then may be taken as our account of the habits which have to do with anger.

1 **6.** In the matter of social intercourse, *i.e.* the living *Of agreeableness.*
with others and joining with them in conversation
and in common occupations, some men show themselves what is called obsequious — those who to
please you praise everything, and never object to
anything, but think they ought always to avoid
2 giving pain to those whom they meet. Those who
take the opposite line, and object to everything and
never think for a moment what pain they may give,
are called cross and contentious.

3 It is sufficiently plain that both these habits

merit censure, and that the habit which takes the
middle course between them is to be commended—
the habit which makes a man acquiesce in what he
ought and in the right manner, and likewise refuse
to acquiesce. This habit or type of character has no 4
recognized name, but seems most nearly to resemble
friendliness (φιλία). For the man who exhibits this
moderation is the same sort of man that we mean
when we speak of an upright friend, except that
then affection also is implied. This differs from 5
friendliness in that it does not imply emotion and
affection for those with whom we associate; for he
who has this quality acquiesces when he ought, not
because he loves or hates, but because that is his
character. He will behave thus alike to those whom
he knows and to those whom he does not know,
to those with whom he is intimate and to those
with whom he is not intimate, only that in each
case he will behave as is fitting; for we are not
bound to show the same consideration to strangers
as to intimates, nor to take the same care not to pain
them.

We have already said in general terms that such 6
a man will behave as he ought in his intercourse
with others, but we must add that, while he tries to
contribute to the pleasure of others and to avoid
giving them pain, he will always be guided by reference to that which is noble and fitting. It seems to 7
be with the pleasures and pains of social intercourse
that he is concerned. Now, whenever he finds that
it is not noble, or is positively hurtful to himself, to
contribute to any of these pleasures, he will refuse to

acquiesce and will prefer to give pain. And if the pleasure is such as to involve discredit, and no slight discredit, or some injury to him who is the source of it, while his opposition will give a little pain, he will not acquiesce, but will set his face against it. But he will behave differently according as he is in the company of great people or ordinary people, of intimate friends or mere acquaintances, and so on, rendering to each his due; preferring, apart from other considerations, to promote pleasure, and loth to give pain, but regulating his conduct by consideration of the consequences, if they be considerable—by consideration, I mean, of what is noble and fitting. And thus for the sake of great pleasure in the future he will inflict a slight pain now.

The man who observes the mean, then, is something of this sort, but has no recognized name.

The man who always makes himself pleasant, if he aims simply at pleasing and has no ulterior object in view, is called obsequious; but if he does so in order to get some profit for himself, either in the way of money or of money's worth, he is a flatterer.

But he who sets his face against everything is, as we have already said, cross and contentious.

But the extremes seem here to be opposed to one another [instead of to the mean], because there is no name for the mean.

7. The moderation which lies between boastfulness and irony (which virtue also lacks a name) seems to display itself in almost the same field. *Of truthfulness.*

It will be as well to examine these qualities also; for we shall know more about human character, when we have gone through each of its forms; and we shall be more fully assured that the virtues are modes of observing the mean, when we have surveyed them all and found that this is the case with every one of them.

We have already spoken of the characters that are displayed in social intercourse in the matter of pleasure and pain; let us now go on to speak in like manner of those who show themselves truthful or untruthful in what they say and do, and in the pretensions they put forward.

First of all, then, the boaster seems to be fond of 2
pretending to things that men esteem, though he has
them not, or not to such extent as he pretends; the 3
ironical man, on the other hand, seems to disclaim
what he has, or to depreciate it; while he who ob- 4
serves the mean, being a man who is "always himself" (αὐθέκαστός τις), is truthful in word and deed, confessing the simple facts about himself, and neither exaggerating nor diminishing them.

Now, each of these lines of conduct may be pur- 5
sued either with an ulterior object or without one.

When he has no ulterior object in view, each man speaks and acts and lives according to his character.

But falsehood in itself is vile and blamable; 6
truth is noble and praiseworthy in itself.

And so the truthful man, as observing the mean, is praiseworthy, while the untruthful characters are both blamable, but the boastful more than the ironical.

Let us speak then of each of them, and first of the truthful character.

We must remember that we are not speaking of 7

the man who tells the truth in matters of business, or in matters which come within the sphere of injustice and justice (for these matters would belong to another
8 virtue); the man we are considering is the man who in cases where no such important issues are involved is truthful in his speech and in his life, because that is his character.

Such a man would seem to be a good man (ἐπιεικής). For he who loves truth, and is truthful where nothing depends upon it, will still more surely tell the truth where serious interests are involved; he will shun falsehood as a base thing here, seeing that he shunned it elsewhere, apart from any consequences: but such a man merits praise.

9 He inclines rather towards under-statement than over-statement of the truth; and this seems to be the more suitable course, since all exaggeration is offensive.

10 On the other hand, he who pretends to more than he has with no ulterior object [the boaster proper] seems not to be a good character (for if he were he would not take pleasure in falsehood), but to be silly rather than bad.

11 But of boasters who have an ulterior object, he whose object is reputation or honour is not very severely censured (just as the boaster proper is not), but he whose object is money, or means of making money, is held in greater reproach.

12 But we must observe that what distinguishes the boaster proper from the other kinds of boasters, is not his faculty of boasting, but his preference for boasting: the boaster proper is a boaster by habit, and

because that is his character; just as there is on the one hand the liar proper, who delights in falsehood itself, and on the other hand the liar who lies through desire of honour or gain.

Those who boast with a view to reputation pretend to those things for which a man is commended or is thought happy; those whose motive is gain pretend to those things which are of advantage to others, and whose absence may escape detection, *e.g.* to skill in magic or in medicine. And so it is usually something of this sort that men pretend to and boast of; for the conditions specified are realized in them. 13

Ironical people, on the other hand, with their depreciatory way of speaking of themselves, seem to be of a more refined character; for their motive in speaking thus seems to be not love of gain, but desire to avoid parade: but what they disclaim seems also * to be especially that which men esteem—of which Socrates was an instance. 14

But those who disclaim † petty advantages which they evidently possess are called affected (βαυκοπανοῦργοι), and are more easily held in contempt. And sometimes this self-depreciation is scarcely distinguishable from boasting, as for instance dressing like a Spartan; for there is something boastful in extreme depreciation as well as in exaggeration. 15

But those who employ irony in moderation, and speak ironically in matters that are not too obvious and palpable, appear to be men of refinement. 16

* The things that the boaster pretends to are *also* the things that the ironical man disclaims.

† Omitting προσποιούμενοι. See Bywater.

17 Finally, the boaster seems to be especially the opposite of the truthful man; for he is worse than the ironical man.

1 8. Again, since relaxation is an element in our life, and one mode of relaxation is amusing conversation, it seems that in this respect also there is a proper way of mixing with others; *i.e.* that there are things that it is right to say, and a right way of saying them: and the same with hearing; though here also it will make a difference what kind of people they are in whose presence you are speaking, or to whom you are listening.

2 And it is plain that it is possible in these matters also to go beyond, or to fall short of, the mean.

3 Now, those who go to excess in ridicule seem to be buffoons and vulgar fellows, striving at all costs for a ridiculous effect, and bent rather on raising a laugh than on making their witticisms elegant and inoffensive to the subject of them. While those who will never say anything laughable themselves, and frown on those who do, are considered boorish and morose. But those who jest gracefully are called witty, or men of ready wit (εὐτράπελοι), as it were ready or versatile men.

For* a man's character seems to reveal itself in these sallies or playful movements, and so we judge of his moral constitution by them, as we judge of his body by its movements.

4 But through the prominence given to ridiculous things, and the excessive delight which most people

* What follows explains why all these terms have a specific moral meaning.

take in amusement and jesting, the buffoon is often
called witty because he gives delight. But that there
is a difference, and a considerable difference, between
the two is plain from what we have said.

An element in the character that observes the 5
mean in these matters is tact. A man of tact will
only say and listen to such things as it befits an
honest man and a gentleman to say and listen to;
for there are things that it is quite becoming for such
a man to say and to listen to in the way of jest, and
the jesting of a gentleman differs from that of a man
of slavish nature, and the jesting of an educated from
that of an uneducated man.

This one may see by the difference between the old 6
comedy and the new: the fun of the earlier writers
is obscenity, of the later innuendo; and there is no
slight difference between the two as regards decency.

Can good jesting, then, be defined as making 7
jests that befit a gentleman, or that do not pain the
hearer, or that even give him pleasure? Nay, surely
a jest that gives pleasure to the hearer is something
quite indefinite, for different things are hateful and
pleasant to different people.

But the things that he will listen to will be of the 8
same sort [as those that he will say, whatever that
be]: jests that a man can listen to he can, we think,
make himself.

So then there are jests that he will not make 9
[though we cannot exactly define them]; for to
make a jest of a man is to vilify him in a way, and
the law forbids certain kinds of vilification, and ought
perhaps also to forbid certain kinds of jesting.

10 The refined and gentlemanly man, therefore, will thus regulate his wit, being as it were a law to himself.

This then is the character of him who observes the mean, whether we call him a man of tact or a man of ready wit.

The buffoon, on the other hand, cannot resist an opportunity for a joke, and, if he can but raise a laugh, will spare neither himself nor others, and will say things which no man of refinement would say, and some of which he would not even listen to.

The boor, lastly, is wholly useless for this kind of
intercourse; he contributes nothing, and takes every-
11 thing in ill part. And yet recreation and amusement
seem to be necessary ingredients in our life.

12 In conclusion, then, the modes just described of observing the mean in social life are three in number,* and all have to do with conversation or joint action of some kind: but they differ in that one has to do with truth, while the other two are concerned with what is pleasant; and of the two that are concerned with pleasure, one finds its field in our amusements, the other in all other kinds of social intercourse.

Of the feeling of shame.

1 9. Shame (αἰδώς) cannot properly be spoken of
as a virtue; for it is more like a feeling or emotion
than a habit or trained faculty. At least, it is
2 defined as a kind of fear of disgrace, and its effects
are analogous to those of the fear that is excited by
danger; for men blush when they are ashamed, while
the fear of death makes them pale. Both then seem
to be in a way physical, which is held to be a mark

* Friendliness, truthfulness, wit.

of a feeling or emotion, rather than of a habit or trained faculty.

Again, it is a feeling which is not becoming at all 3
times of life, but only in youth; it is thought proper
for young people to be ready to feel shame, because,
as their conduct is guided by their emotions, they
often are misled, but are restrained from wrong
actions by shame.

And so we praise young men when they are ready to feel shame, but no one would praise a man of more advanced years for being apt to be ashamed; for we consider that he ought not to do anything which could make him ashamed of himself.

Indeed, shame is not the part of a good man, since 4
it is occasioned by vile acts (for such acts should not
be done: nor does it matter that some acts are really 5
shameful, others shameful in public estimation only;
for neither ought to be done, and so a man ought not
to be ashamed); it is the part of a worthless man 6
and the result* of being such as to do something
shameful.

But supposing a man's character to be such that, if he were to do one of these shameful acts, he would be ashamed, it is absurd for him to fancy that he is a good man on that account; for shame is only felt at voluntary acts, and a good man will never voluntarily do vile acts.

At the utmost, shame would be hypothetically 7
good; that is to say, supposing he were to do the act,
a good man would be ashamed: but there is nothing
hypothetical about the virtues.

* Reading καὶ τῷ εἶναι. Bywater.

Again, granting that it is bad to be shameless, or not to be ashamed to do shameful things, it does not therefore follow that it is good to do them and be ashamed of it.

8 Continence,* in the same way, is not a virtue, but something between virtue and vice.

But we will explain this point about continence later; † let us now treat of justice.

* The continent man desires the evil which he ought not to desire, and so is not good; but he does not do it, and so is not bad: thus continence also might be called "hypothetically good"; granting the evil desire (which excludes goodness proper), the best thing is to master it.

† Book VII.

BOOK V.

THE SAME—*concluded.* JUSTICE.

Preliminary. Two senses of justice distinguished. Of justice (1) = obedience to law, = complete virtue.

1. We now have to inquire about justice and in- 1
justice, and to ask what sort of acts they are concerned with, and in what sense justice observes the mean, and what are the extremes whose mean is that which
is just. And in this inquiry we will follow the same 2
method as before.

We see that all men intend by justice to signify 3
the sort of habit or character that makes men apt to do what is just, and which further makes them act justly * and wish what is just; while by injustice they intend in like manner to signify the sort of character that makes men act unjustly and wish what is unjust. Let us lay this down, then, as an outline to work upon.

We thus oppose justice and injustice, because a 4
habit or trained faculty differs in this respect both from a science and a faculty or power. I mean that whereas both of a pair of opposites come under the same science or power, a habit which produces a

* A man may "do that which is just" without "acting justly:" *cf. supra*, II. 4, 3, and *infra*, cap. 8.

certain result does not also produce the opposite result; *e.g.* health produces healthy manifestations only, and not unhealthy; for we say a man has a healthy gait when he walks like a man in health.

5 [Not that the two opposites are unconnected.] In the first place, a habit is often known by the opposite habit, and often by its causes and results: if we know what good condition is, we can learn from that what bad condition is; and, again, from that which conduces to good condition we can infer what good condition itself is, and conversely from the latter can infer the former. For instance, if good condition be firmness of flesh, it follows that bad condition is flabbiness of flesh, and that what tends to produce firmness of flesh conduces to good condition.

6 And, in the second place, if one of a pair of opposite terms have more senses than one, the other term will also, as a general rule, have more than one; so that here, if the term "just" have several senses, the term "unjust" also will have several.

7 And in fact it seems that both "justice" and "injustice" have several senses, but, as the different things covered by the common name are very closely related, the fact that they are different escapes notice and does not strike us, as it does when there is a great disparity—a great difference, say, in outward appearance—as it strikes every one, for instance, that the κλείς (*clavis*, collar-bone) which lies under the neck of an animal is different from the κλείς (*clavis*, key) with which we fasten the door.

8 Let us then ascertain in how many different senses we call a man unjust.

Firstly, he who breaks the laws is considered unjust, and, secondly, he who takes more than his share, or the unfair man.

Plainly, then, a just man will mean (1) a law-abiding and (2) a fair man.

A just thing then will be (1) that which is in accordance with the law, (2) that which is fair; and the unjust thing will be (1) that which is contrary to law, (2) that which is unfair.

But since the unjust man, in one of the two senses 9
of the word, takes more than his share, the sphere of his action will be good things—not all good things, but those with which good and ill fortune are concerned, which are always good in themselves, but not always good for us—the things that we men pray for and pursue, whereas we ought rather to pray that what is good in itself may be good for us, while we choose that which is good for us.

But the unjust man does not always take more 10
than his share; he sometimes take less, viz. of those things which are bad in the abstract; but as the lesser evil is considered to be in some sort good, and taking more means taking more good, he is said to
take more than his share. But in any case he is 11
unfair; for this is a wider term which includes the other.

We found that the law-breaker is unjust, and 12
the law-abiding man is just. Hence it follows that whatever is according to law is just in one sense of the word. [And this, we see, is in fact the case;] for what the legislator prescribes is according to law, and is always said to be just.

13 Now, the laws prescribe about all manner of
things, aiming at the common interest of all, or of the
best men, or of those who are supreme in the state
(position in the state being determined by reference to
personal excellence, or to some other such standard);
and so in one sense we apply the term just to whatever tends to produce and preserve the happiness
of the community, and the several elements of that
14 happiness. The law bids us display courage (as not
to leave our ranks, or run, or throw away our arms),
and temperance (as not to commit adultery or outrage), and gentleness (as not to strike or revile our
neighbours), and so on with all the other virtues and
vices, enjoining acts and forbidding them, rightly
when it is a good law, not so rightly when it is a
hastily improvised one.

15 Justice, then, in this sense of the word, is complete virtue, with the addition that it is displayed towards others. On this account it is often spoken of as the chief of the virtues, and such that "neither evening nor morning star is so lovely;" and the saying has become proverbial, "Justice sums up all virtues in itself."

It is complete virtue, first of all, because it is the exhibition of complete virtue: it is also complete because he that has it is able to exhibit virtue in dealing with his neighbours, and not merely in his private affairs; for there are many who can be virtuous enough at home, but fail in dealing with their neighbours.

16 This is the reason why people commend the saying of Bias, "Office will show the man;" for he that

is in office *ipso facto* stands in relation to others,*
and has dealings with them.

This, too, is the reason why justice alone of all 17
the virtues is thought to be another's good, as implying this relation to others; for it is another's interest that justice aims at—the interest, namely, of the ruler or of our fellow-citizens.

While then the worst man is he who displays 18
vice both in his own affairs and in his dealings with his friends, the best man is not he who displays virtue in his own affairs merely, but he who displays virtue towards others; for this is the hard thing to do.

Justice, then, in this sense of the word, is not a part 19
of virtue, but the whole of it; and the injustice which is opposed to it is not a part of vice, but the whole of it.

How virtue differs from justice in this sense is 20
plain from what we have said; it is one and the same character differently viewed: † viewed in relation to others, this character is justice; viewed simply as a certain character,‡ it is virtue.

Of justice (2) = fairness, how related to justice (1). What is just in distribution distinguished from what is just in correction.

2. We have now to examine justice in that sense 1
in which it is a part of virtue—for we maintain that there is such a justice—and also the corresponding kind of injustice.

That the word is so used is easily shown. In the 2
case of the other kinds of badness, the man who displays them, though he acts unjustly [in one sense of the word], yet does not take more than his share:

* While his children are regarded as parts of him, and even his wife is not regarded as an independent person: *cf. infra*, 6, 8.

† Or "differently manifested:" the phrase is used in both senses.

‡ Putting comma after ἁπλῶς instead of after ἕξις (Trendelenburg).

for instance, when a man throws away his shield through cowardice, or reviles another through ill temper, or through illiberality refuses to help another with money. But when he takes more than his share, he displays perhaps no one of these vices, nor does he display them all, yet he displays a kind of badness (for we blame him), namely, injustice [in the second sense of the word].

We see, then, that there is another sense of the word injustice, in which it stands for a part of that injustice which is coextensive with badness, and another sense of the word unjust, in which it is applied to a part only of those things to which it is applied in the former sense of "contrary to law."

Again, if one man commits adultery with a view to gain, and makes money by it, and another man does it from lust, with expenditure and loss of money, the latter would not be called grasping, but profligate, while the former would not be called profligate, but unjust [in the narrower sense]. Evidently, then, he would be called unjust because of his gain.

* Once more, acts of injustice, in the former sense, are always referred to some particular vice, as if a man commits adultery, to profligacy; if he deserts his comrade in arms, to cowardice; if he strikes another, to anger: but in a case of unjust gain, the act is referred to no other vice than injustice.

It is plain then that, besides the injustice which

* This is not merely a repetition of what has been said in § 2: acts of injustice (2) are there distinguished from acts of injustice (1) by the motive (gain), here by the fact that they are referred to no other vice than injustice.

is coextensive with vice, there is a second kind of injustice, which is a particular kind of vice, bearing the same name * as the first, because the same generic conception forms the basis of its definition; *i.e.* both display themselves in dealings with others, but the sphere of the second is limited to such things as honour, wealth, security (perhaps some one name might be found to include all this class †), and its motive is the pleasure of gain, while the sphere of the first is coextensive with the sphere of the good man's action.

We have ascertained, then, that there are more 7
kinds of justice than one, and that there is another kind besides that which is identical with complete virtue; we now have to find what it is, and what are its characteristics.

We have already distinguished two senses in 8
which we speak of things as unjust, viz. (1) contrary to law, (2) unfair; and two senses in which we speak of things as just, viz. (1) according to law, (2) fair.

The injustice which we have already considered corresponds to unlawful.

But since unfair is not the same as unlawful, but 9
differs from it as the part from the whole (for unfair is always unlawful, but unlawful is not always unfair), unjust and injustice in the sense corresponding to

* Before (1, 7) the two kinds of injustice were called *ὁμώνυμα*, *i.e.* strictly, "things that have nothing in common but the name;" here they are called *συνώνυμα*, "different things bearing a common name because they belong to the same genus," as a man and an ox are both called animals: *cf.* Categ. I. 1.

† *τὰ ἐκτὸς ἀγαθά* is the name which Aristotle most frequently uses, sometimes *τὰ ἁπλῶς ἀγαθά*, as *supra*, 1, 9.

unfair will not be the same as unjust and injustice in the sense corresponding to unlawful, but different as the part from the whole; for this injustice is a part of complete injustice, and the corresponding justice is a part of complete justice. We must therefore speak of justice and injustice, and of that which is just and that which is unjust, in this limited sense.

10 We may dismiss, then, the justice which coincides with complete virtue and the corresponding injustice, the former being the exercise of complete virtue towards others, the latter of complete vice.

It is easy also to see how we are to define that which is just and that which is unjust in their corresponding senses [according to law and contrary to law]. For the great bulk, we may say, of the acts which are according to law are the acts which the law commands with a view to complete virtue; for the law orders us to display all the virtues and none of the vices in our lives.

11 But the acts which tend to produce complete virtue are those of the acts according to law which are prescribed with reference to the education of a man as a citizen. As for the education of the individual as such, which tends to make him simply a good man, we may reserve the question whether it belongs to the science of the state or not; for it is possible that to be a good man is not the same as to be a good citizen of any state whatever.*

12 But of justice as a part of virtue, and of that

* The two characters coincide perfectly only in the perfect state: *cf.* Pol. III. 4, 1276 b16 f.

which is just in the corresponding sense, one kind is that which has to do with the distribution of honour, wealth, and the other things that are divided among the members of the body politic (for in these circumstances it is possible for one man's share to be unfair or fair as compared with another's); and another kind is that which has to give redress in private transactions.

The latter kind is again subdivided; for private 13
transactions are (1) voluntary, (2) involuntary.

"Voluntary transactions or contracts" are such as selling, buying, lending at interest, pledging, lending without interest, depositing, hiring: these are called "voluntary contracts," because the parties enter into them of their own will.

"Involuntary transactions," again, are of two kinds: one involving secrecy, such as theft, adultery, poisoning, procuring, corruption of slaves, assassination, false witness; the other involving open violence, such as assault, seizure of the person, murder, rape, maiming, slander, contumely.

Of what is just in distribution, and its rule of geometrical proportion.

3. The unjust man [in this limited sense of the 1
word], we say, is unfair, and that which is unjust is unfair.

Now, it is plain that there must be a mean which lies between what is unfair on this side and on that.
And this is that which is fair or equal; for any 2
act that admits of a too much and a too little admits also of that which is fair.

If then that which is unjust be unfair, that which 3
is just will be fair, which indeed is admitted by all without further proof.

But since that which is fair or equal is a mean between two extremes, it follows that what is just will be a mean.

4 But equality or fairness implies two terms at least.*

It follows, then, that that which is just is both a mean quantity and also a fair amount relatively to something else and to certain persons—in other words, that, on the one hand, as a mean quantity it implies certain other quantities, *i.e.* a more and a less; and, on the other hand, as an equal or fair amount it involves two quantities,† and as a just amount it involves certain persons.

5 That which is just, then, implies four terms at least: two persons to whom justice is done, and two things.

6 And there must be the same "equality" [*i.e.* the same ratio] between the persons and the things: as the things are to one another, so must the persons be. For if the persons be not equal, their shares will not be equal; and this is the source of disputes and accusations, when persons who are equal do not receive equal shares, or when persons who are not equal receive equal shares.

7 This is also plainly indicated by the common phrase "according to merit." For in distribution all men allow that what is just must be according to merit or worth of some kind, but they do not all adopt the same standard of worth; in democratic states

* If this amount be equal, it must be equal to something else; if my share is fair, I must be sharing with one other person at least.

† A's share and B's.

they take free birth as the standard,* in oligarchic states they take wealth, in others noble birth, and in the true aristocratic state virtue or personal merit.

We see, then, that that which is just is in some sort 8
proportionate. For not abstract numbers only, but all things that can be numbered, admit of proportion; proportion meaning equality of ratios, and requiring four terms at least.

That discrete proportion † requires four terms is 9
evident at once. Continuous proportion also requires four terms: for in it one term is employed as two and is repeated; for instance, $\frac{a}{b} = \frac{b}{c}$. The term b then is repeated; and so, counting b twice over, we find that the terms of the proportion are four in number.

That which is just, then, requires that there be 10
four terms at least, and that the ratio between the two pairs be the same, *i.e.* that the persons stand to one another in the same ratio as the things.

Let us say, then, $\frac{a}{b} = \frac{c}{d}$, or *alternando* $\frac{a}{c} = \frac{b}{d}$. 11

The sums of these new pairs then will stand to one another in the original ratio $\left[\ i.e.\ \frac{a+c}{b+d} = \frac{a}{b} \text{ or } \frac{c}{d}\right]$.

But these are the pairs which the distribution joins together; ‡ and if the things be assigned in this manner, the distribution is just.

* Counting all free men as equals entitled to equal shares.

† *e.g.* $\frac{a}{b} = \frac{c}{d}$.

‡ Assigning or joining certain quantities of goods (c and d) to certain persons (a and b).

12 This joining, then, of *a* to *c* and of *b* to *d* is that which is just in distribution; and that which is just in this sense is a mean quantity, while that which is unjust is that which is disproportionate; for that which is proportionate is a mean quantity, but that which is just is, as we said, proportionate.

13 This proportion is called by the mathematicians a geometrical proportion; for it is when four terms are in geometrical proportion that the sum [of the first and third] is to the sum [of the second and fourth] in the original ratio [of the first to the second or the third to the fourth].

14 But this proportion [as applied in justice] cannot be a continuous proportion; for one term cannot represent both a person and a thing.

That which is just, then, in this sense is that
which is proportionate; but that which is unjust
is that which is disproportionate. In the latter
case one quantity becomes more or too much, the
other less or too little. And this we see in practice;
for he who wrongs another gets too much, and
he who is wronged gets too little of the good in
15 question: but of the evil conversely; for the lesser
evil stands in the place of good when compared
16 with the greater evil: for the lesser evil is more
desirable than the greater, but that which is desirable
is good, and that which is more desirable is a greater
good.

17 This then is one form of that which is just.

1 4. It remains to treat of the other form, viz. that which is just in the way of redress, the sphere of

Of that which is just in correction and its rule of arith-

metical proportion. which is private transactions, whether voluntary or involuntary.

This differs in kind from the former. 2

For that which is just in the distribution of a common stock of good things is always in accordance with the proportion above specified (even when it is a common fund that has to be divided, the sums which the several participants take must bear the same ratio to one another as the sums they have put in), and that which is unjust in the corresponding sense is that which violates this proportion.

But that which is just in private transactions * is 3
indeed fair or equal in some sort, and that which is unjust is unfair or unequal; but the proportion to be observed here is not a geometrical proportion as above, but an arithmetical one.

For it makes no difference whether a good man defrauds a bad one, or a bad man a good one, nor whether a man who commits an adultery be a good or a bad man; the law looks only to the difference created by the injury, treating the parties themselves as equal, and only asking whether the one has done, and the other suffered, injury or damage.

That which is unjust, then, is here something 4
unequal [or unfair] which the judge tries to make equal [or fair]. For even when one party is struck and the other strikes, or one kills and the other is killed, that which is suffered and that which is done

* In the way of redress, as given by the law-courts: later on (cap. 5) he gives as an after-thought the kind of justice which ought to regulate buying and selling, etc. See note on p. 152.

may be said to be unequally or unfairly divided; the judge then tries to restore equality by the penalty or loss which he inflicts upon the offender, subtracting it from his gain.

5 For in such cases, though the terms are not always quite appropriate, we generally talk of the doer's "gain" (*e.g.* the striker's) and the sufferer's
6 "loss;" but when the suffering has been assessed by the court, what the doer gets is called "loss" or penalty, and what the sufferer gets is called "gain."

What is fair or equal, then, is a mean between more or too much and less or too little; but gain and loss are both more or too much and less or too little in opposite ways, *i.e.* gain is more or too much good and less or too little evil, and loss the opposite of this.

And in the mean between them, as we found, lies that which is equal or fair, which we say is just.

That which is just in the way of redress, then, is the mean between loss and gain.

7 When disputes arise, therefore, men appeal to the judge:* and an appeal to the judge is an appeal to that which is just; for the judge is intended to be as it were a living embodiment of that which is just; and men require of a judge that he shall be moderate [or observe the mean], and sometimes even call judges "mediators" (μεσιδίους), signifying that

* The δικασταί at Athens combined the functions of judge and jury.

if they get the mean they will get that which is just.

That which is just, then, must be a sort of mean, if the judge be a "mediator." 8

But the judge restores equality; it is as if he found a line divided into two unequal parts, and were to cut off from the greater that by which it exceeds the half, and to add this to the less.

But when the whole is equally divided, the parties are said to have their own, each now receiving an equal or fair amount.

But the equal or fair amount is here the *arithmetic* mean between the more or too much and the less or too little. And so it is called δίκαιον (just) because there is equal division (δίχα); δίκαιον being in fact equivalent to δίχαιον, and δικαστής (judge) to διχαστής. 9

If you cut off a part from one of two equal lines and add it to the other, the second is now greater than the first by two such parts (for if you had only cut off the part from the first without adding it to the second, the second would have been greater by only one such part); the second exceeds the mean by one such part, and the mean also exceeds the first by one. 10

Thus we can tell how much to take away from him who has more or too much, and how much to add to him who has less or too little: to the latter's portion must be added that by which it falls short of the mean, and from the former's portion must be taken away that by which it exceeds the mean. 11

12 To illustrate this, let A A′, B B′, C C′ be three equal lines:—

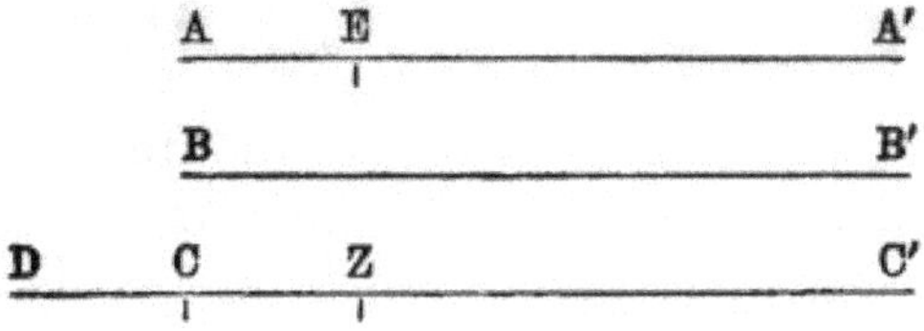

A E A′

B B′

D C Z C′

From A A′ let A E be cut off; and let C D [equal to A E] be added to C C′; then the whole D C C′ exceeds E A′ by C D and C Z [equal to A E or C D], and exceeds B B′ by C D.

And this * holds good not only in geometry, but in the arts also; they could not exist unless that which is worked upon received an impression corresponding in kind and quantity and quality to the exertions of the artist.

13 But these terms, "loss" and "gain," are borrowed from voluntary exchange. For in voluntary exchange having more than your own is called gaining, and having less than you started with is called losing (in buying and selling, I mean, and in the other trans-

* The point to be illustrated is, that in these private transactions what one man gains is equal to what the other loses, so that the penalty that will restore the balance can be exactly measured. Of this principle (on which the possibility of justice does in fact depend) Aristotle first gives a simple geometrical illustration, and then says that the same law holds in all that man does: what is suffered by the patient (whether person, as in medicine, or thing, as in sculpture or agriculture) is the same as what is done by the agent. This paragraph occurs again in the next chapter (5, 9): but it can hardly have come into this place by accident; we rather see the author's thought growing as he writes. I follow Trendelenburg (who omits the passage here) in inserting ὃ before ἐποίει, but not in omitting τὸ before πάσχον.

actions in which the law allows free play); but when 14
the result to each is neither more nor less but the
very same amount with which he started, then they
say that they have their own, and are neither losers
nor gainers. That which is just, then, is a mean
between a gain and a loss, which are both contrary
to the intention,* and consists in having after the
transaction the equivalent of that which you had
before it.

Simple requital is not identical with what is just, but proportionate requital is what is just in exchange; and this is effected by means of money. We can now give a general definition of justice (2).

5. Some people, indeed, go so far as to think that 1
simple requital is just. And so the Pythagoreans
used to teach; for their definition of what is just was
simply that what a man has done to another should
be done to him.

But this simple requital does not correspond either 2
with that which is just in distribution or with that
which is just in the way of redress (though they try 3
to make out that this is the meaning of the Rhada-
manthine rule—

"To suffer that which thou hast done is just");

for in many cases it is quite different. For instance, 4
if an officer strike a man, he ought not to be struck
in return; and if a man strike an officer, he ought
not merely to be struck, but to be punished.

* For the aim of trade is neither profit nor loss, but fair exchange, *i.e.* exchange (on the principle laid down in ch. 5) which leaves the position of the parties as the state fixed it (by distributive justice, ch. 3). But when in the private transactions of man with man this position is disturbed, *i.e.* whenever either unintentionally, by accident or negligence, or intentionally, by force or fraud, one has bettered his position at the expense of another, corrective justice steps in to redress the balance. I read *αὐτὰ δι' αὐτῶν* and accept Stewart's interpretation of these words, and in part Jackson's interpretation of *τῶν παρὰ τὸ ἑκούσιον*, but cannot entirely agree with either as to the sense of the whole passage.

5 Further, it makes a great difference whether what was done to the other was done with his consent or against it.

6 But it is true that, in the interchange of services, this is the rule of justice that holds society together, viz. requital—but proportionate requital, and not simple repayment of equals for equals. For the very existence of a state depends upon proportionate return. If men have suffered evil, they seek to return it; if not, if they cannot requite an injury, we count their condition slavish. And again, if men have received good, they seek to repay it: for otherwise there is no exchange of services; but it is by this exchange that we are bound together in society.

7 This is the reason why we set up a temple of the graces [charities, χάριτες] in sight of all men, to remind them to repay that which they receive; for this is the special characteristic of charity or grace. We ought to return the good offices of those who have been gracious to us, and then again to take the lead in good offices towards them.

8 But proportionate interchange is brought about by "cross conjunction."

For instance, let A stand for a builder, B for a shoemaker, C for a house, D for shoes.*

* We had before (3, 11, 12) as the rule of distributive justice $\frac{A}{B} = \frac{C}{D}$, and the distribution was expressed by the "joining" (σύζευξις) of the opposite or corresponding symbols, A and C, B and D. Here we have the same two pairs of symbols, ranged opposite to each other as before; but the *exchange* will be expressed by joining A to D and B to C, *i.e.* by "cross conjunction" or by drawing diagonal lines (ἡ κατὰ διάμετρον σύζευξις) from A to D and B to C.

The builder then must take some of the shoemaker's work, and give him his own work in exchange.

Now, the desired result will be brought about if requital take place after proportionate equality has first been established.*

If this be not done, there is no equality, and intercourse becomes impossible; for there is no reason why the work of the one should not be worth more than the work of the other. Their work, then, must be brought to an equality [or appraised by a common standard of value].

This is no less true of the other arts and professions [than of building and shoemaking]; for they could not exist if that which the patient [client or consumer] receives did not correspond in quantity and quality with that which the agent [artist or producer] does or produces.†

* *i.e.* (as will presently appear), it must first be determined how much builder's work is equal to a given quantity of shoemaker's work: *i.e.* the price of the two wares must first be settled; that done, they simply exchange shilling's worth for shilling's worth (ἀντιπεπονθός); *e.g.* if a four-roomed cottage be valued at £100, and a pair of boots at £1, the builder must supply such a cottage in return for 100 such pairs of boots (or their equivalent).

Fixing the price of the articles is called securing equality, because, evidently, it means fixing how much of one article shall be considered equal to a given quantity of the other. It is called securing *proportionate* equality, because, as we shall see, the question that has to be determined is, "in what ratio must work be exchanged in order to preserve the due ratio between the workers?"

† Benefit to consumer = cost to producer; *e.g.* if £100 be a fair price for a picture, it must fairly represent both the benefit to the purchaser and the effort expended on it by the artist. I follow Trendelenburg in inserting ὃ before ἐποίει, but not in omitting τὸ before πάσχον. *Cf.* note on 4, 12.

For it is not between two physicians that exchange of services takes place, but between a physician and a husbandman, and generally between persons of different professions and of unequal worth; these unequal persons, then, have to be reduced to equality [or measured by a common standard].*

10 All things or services, then, which are to be exchanged must be in some way reducible to a common measure.

For this purpose money was invented, and serves as a medium of exchange; for by it we can measure everything, and so can measure the superiority and inferiority of different kinds of work—the number of shoes, for instance, that is equivalent to a house or to a certain quantity of food.

What is needed then is that so many shoes shall bear to a house (or a measure of corn) the same ratio that a builder [or a husbandman] bears to a shoemaker.† For unless this adjustment be effected, no dealing or exchange of services can take place; and it cannot be effected unless the things to be exchanged can be in some way made equal.

11 We want, therefore, some one common measure of value, as we said before.

This measure is, in fact, the need for each other's services which holds the members of a society together; for if men had no needs, or no common

* The persons have to be appraised as well as their work; but, as we soon see, these are two sides of the same thing: the relative value at which persons are estimated by society is indicated by the relative value which society puts upon their services, and this is indicated by the price put upon a certain quantity of their work.

† See note on § 12.

needs, there would either be no exchange, or a different sort of exchange from that which we know.

But money has been introduced by convention as a kind of substitute for need or demand; and this is why we call it *νόμισμα*, because its value is derived, not from nature, but from law (*νόμος*), and can be altered or abolished at will.

Requital then will take place after the wares 12
have been so equated [by the adjustment of prices] that the quantity of shoemaker's work bears to the quantity of husbandman's work [which exchanges for it] the same ratio that husbandman bears to shoemaker.* But this adjustment must be made,† not at the time of exchange (for then one of the two parties would get both the advantages‡), but while they are still in possession of their own wares; if this be

* *e.g.* suppose the husbandman is twice as good a man as the shoemaker, then, if the transaction is to follow the universal rule of justice and leave their relative position unaltered, in exchange for a certain quantity of husbandman's work the shoemaker must give twice as much of his own. The price, that is, of corn and shoes must be so adjusted that, if a quarter of corn sell for 50*s.* and three pair of shoes sell for the same sum, the three pair of shoes must represent twice as much labour as the quarter of corn. Aristotle speaks loosely of the ratio between the shoes and the corn, etc., but as their value is *ex hypothesi* the same, and as the relative size, weight, and number of articles is quite accidental (*e.g.* we might as well measure the corn by bushels or by pounds), the ratio intended can only be the ratio between the quantities of labour. He omits to tell us that these quantities must be measured by time, but the omission is easily supplied. He omits also to tell us how the relative worth of the persons is to be measured, but he has already said all that is necessary in **3**, 7.

† Lit. "they must be reduced to proportion," *i.e.*, in strictness, the four terms (two persons and two things).

‡ *i.e.* have his superiority counted twice over. His (*e.g.* the husbandman's) superiority over the other party (the shoemaker) has

done, they are put on an equal footing and can make an exchange, because this kind of equality can be established between them.

If A stand for a husbandman and C for a certain quantity of his work (or corn), B will stand for a shoemaker, and D for that quantity of shoemaker's work that is valued as equal to C.

If they could not requite each other in this way, interchange of services would be impossible.

13 That it is our need which forms, as it were, a common bond to hold society together, is seen from the fact that people do not exchange unless they are in need of one another's services (each party of the services of the other, or at least one party of the service of the other), as when that which one has, *e.g.* wine, is needed by other people who offer to export corn in return. This article, then [the corn to be exported], must be made equal [to the wine that is imported].*

14 But even if we happen to want nothing at the moment, money is a sort of guarantee that we shall be able to make an exchange at any future time when we happen to be in need; for the man who brings money must always be able to take goods in exchange.

been already taken into account in fixing the price of a quarter of corn as equal to three pairs of shoes: this is one advantage which is fairly his; but it would be plainly unfair if, at the time of exchange, the husbandman were to demand 50*s.* worth of shoes for 25*s.* worth of corn, on the ground that he was twice as good a man: *cf.* Munro, *Journal of Classical and Sacred Philology*, vol. ii. p. 58 f. In the text I have followed Trendelenburg's stopping, throwing the words εἰ δὲ μὴ . . . ἄκρον into a parenthesis.

* *i.e.* each must be valued in money, so that so many quarters of corn shall exchange for so many hogsheads of wine.

Money is, indeed, subject to the same conditions as other things: its value is not always the same; but still it tends to be more constant than the value of anything else.

Everything, then, must be assessed in money; for this enables men always to exchange their services, and so makes society possible.

Money, then, as a standard, serves to reduce things to a common measure, so that equal amounts of each may be taken; for there would be no society if there were no exchange, and no exchange if there were no equality, and no equality if it were not possible to reduce things to a common measure.

In strictness, indeed, it is impossible to find any common measure for things so extremely diverse; but our needs give a standard which is sufficiently accurate for practical purposes.

There must, then, be some one common symbol for 15
this, and that a conventional symbol; so we call it money (νόμισμα, νόμος). Money makes all things commensurable, for all things are valued in money. For instance, let A stand for a house, B for ten minæ, C for a bed; and let $A = \frac{B}{2}$, taking a house to be worth or equal to five minæ, and let C (the bed) $= \frac{B}{10}$. We see at once, then, how many beds are equal to one house, viz. five.

It is evident that, before money came into use, 16
all exchange must have been of this kind: it makes no difference whether you give five beds for a house, or the value of five beds.

Thus we have described that which is unjust and 17

that which is just. And now that these are determined, we can see that doing justice is a mean between doing and suffering injustice; for the one is having too much, or more, and the other too little, or less than one's due.

We see also that the virtue justice is a kind of moderation or observance of the mean, but not quite in the same way as the virtues hitherto spoken of. It does indeed choose a mean, but both the extremes fall under the single vice injustice.*

We see also that justice is that habit in respect of which the just man is said to be apt to do deliberately that which is just; that is to say, in dealings between himself and another (or between two other parties), to apportion things, not so that he shall get more or too much, and his neighbour less or too little, of what is desirable, and conversely with what is disadvantageous, but so that each shall get his fair, that is, his proportionate share, and similarly in dealings between two other parties.

18 Injustice, on the contrary, is the character which chooses what is unjust, which is a disproportionate amount, that is, too much and too little of what is advantageous and disadvantageous respectively.

* The mean which justice aims at (the just thing, the due share of goods) lies between two extremes, too much and too little; so far justice is analogous to the other virtues: but whereas in other fields these two extremes are chosen by different and opposite characters (*e.g.* the cowardly and the foolhardy), the character that chooses too much is here the same as that which chooses too little,—too much for himself or his friend, too little for his enemy. (The habitual choice of too little for oneself is neglected as impossible). *Cf.* II. 6, especially § 15–16.

Thus injustice, as we say, is both an excess and a deficiency, in that it chooses both an excess and a deficiency—in one's own affairs choosing excess of what is, as a general rule, advantageous, and deficiency of what is disadvantageous; in the affairs of others making a similarly disproportionate assignment, though in which way the proportion is violated will depend upon circumstances.

But of the two sides of the act of injustice, suffering is a lesser wrong than doing the injustice.

Let this, then, be accepted as our account, in general terms, of the nature of justice and injustice respectively, and of that which is just and that which is unjust.

(One can act unjustly without being unjust.) That which is just in the strict sense is between citizens only, for it implies law.

6. But since it is possible for a man to do an act of injustice without yet being unjust, what acts of injustice are there, such that the doing of them stamps a man at once as unjust in this or that particular way, *e.g.* as a thief, or an adulterer, or a robber?

Perhaps we ought to reply that there is no such difference in the acts.* A man might commit adultery, knowing what he was about, and yet be acting not from a deliberate purpose at all, but from a momentary passion. In such a case, then, a man acts unjustly, but is not unjust; *e.g.* is not a thief though he commits a theft, and is not an adulterer though he commits adultery, and so on.†

* It is in the state of mind of the doer that the difference lies, not in the particular things done: *cf. infra*, cap. 8.

† This passage, cap. 6, §§ 1, 2, seems to have quite a natural connection with what goes before, though the discussion is not carried on here, but in cap. 8. Again, the discussion which begins with

3 We have already explained the relation which
4 requital bears to that which is just. But we must
not fail to notice that what we are seeking is at
once that which is just simply [or without any
qualifying epithet], and that which is just in a state
or between citizens.* Now, this implies men who
associate together in order to supply their deficiencies,
being free men, and upon a footing of equality, either
absolute or proportionate.

Between those who are not upon this footing, then, we cannot speak of that which is just as between citizens (though there is something that can be called just metaphorically). For the term just cannot be properly applied, except where men have a law to appeal to,† and the existence of law implies the existence of injustice; for the administration of the law is the discrimination of what is just from what is unjust.

But injustice implies an act of injustice (though an act of injustice does not always imply injustice) which is taking too much of the goods and too little

the words πῶς μὲν οὖν, cap. 6, § 3, though it has no connection with § 2, comes naturally enough after the end of cap. 5, τὸ ἁπλῶς δίκαιον corresponding to τοῦ δικαίου καὶ ἀδίκου καθόλου. We have, then, two discussions, both growing out of and attached to the discussion which closes with the end of cap. 5, but not connected with each other. If the author had revised the work, he would, no doubt, have fitted these links together; but as he omitted to do so, it is useless for us to attempt, by any rearrangement of the links, to secure the close connection which could only be effected by forging them anew.

* These are not two distinct kinds of justice; justice proper, he means to say, implies a state.

† Only the citizen in an ancient state could appeal to the law in his own person; the non-citizen could only sue through a citizen.

of the evils of life. And so we do not allow an individual to rule over us, but reason or law; for an individual is apt thus to take more for himself, and to become a tyrant.

The magistrate's function, then, is to secure that which is just, and if that which is just, then that which is equal or fair. But it seems that he gets no advantage from his office, if he is just (for he does not take a larger share of the good things of life, except when that larger share is proportionate to his worth; he works, therefore, in the interests of others, which is the reason why justice is sometimes called "another's good," as we remarked before).* Some salary, therefore, must be given him, and this he receives in the shape of honours and privileges; and it is when magistrates are not content with these that they make themselves tyrants.

That which is just as between master and slave, or between father and child, is not the same as this, though like. We cannot speak (without qualification) of injustice towards what is part of one's self—and a man's chattels and his children (until they are of a certain age and are separated from their parent) are as it were a part of him—for no one deliberately chooses to injure himself; so that a man cannot be unjust towards himself.

We cannot speak in this case, then, of that which is unjust, or of that which is just as between citizens; for that, we found, is according to law, and subsists between those whose situation implies law, *i.e.*, as we found, those who participate equally or fairly in governing and being governed.

* *Supra*, 1, 17.

The term just, therefore, is more appropriate to a man's relations to his wife than to his relations to his children and his chattels, and we do speak in this sense of that which is just in a family; but even this is not the same as that which is just between citizens.*

It is in part natural, in part conventional.

7. Now, of that which is just as between citizens, part is natural, part is conventional. That is natural which has the same validity everywhere, and does not depend on our accepting or rejecting it; that is conventional which at the outset may be determined in this way or in that indifferently, but which when once determined is no longer indifferent; *e.g.* that a man's ransom be a mina, or that a sacrifice consist of a goat and not of two sheep; and, again, those ordinances which are made for special occasions, such as the sacrifice to Brasidas [at Amphipolis], and all ordinances that are of the nature of a decree.

Now, there are people who think that what is just is always conventional, because that which is natural is invariable, and has the same validity everywhere, as fire burns here and in Persia, while that which is just is seen to be not invariable.

But this is not altogether true, though it is true in a way. Among the gods, indeed, we may venture to say it is not true at all; but of that which is just among us part is natural, though all is subject to change. Though all is subject to change, nevertheless, I repeat, part is natural and part not.

Nor is it hard to distinguish, among things that may be other than they are, that which is natural

* Which alone is properly just.

from that which is not natural but dependent on law or convention, though both are alike variable. In other fields we can draw the same distinction; we say, for instance, that the right hand is naturally the stronger, though in any man the left may become equally strong.

And so, of that which is just, that part which is conventional and prescribed with a view to a particular end * varies as measures vary; for the measures of wine and of corn are not everywhere the same, but larger where the dealers buy, and smaller where they sell.† So I say that which is just not by nature but merely by human ordinance is not the same everywhere, any more than constitutions are everywhere the same, though there is but one constitution that is naturally the best everywhere.

The terms "just" and "lawful" in each of their several senses stand for universal notions which embrace a number of particulars; *i.e.* the acts are many, but the notion is one, for it is applied to all alike.

"That which is unjust," we must notice, is different from "an act of injustice," and "that which is just" from "an act of justice:" for a thing is unjust either by nature or by ordinance; but this same thing when done is called "an act of injustice," though before it was done it could only be called unjust. And so with "an act of justice" (*δικαίωμα*); though in the latter

* *τὸ ξυμφέρον*, which is usually rendered "expedient," means simply that which conduces to *any* desired end; as the end varies, then, so will the expedient vary: *cf.* III. 1, 15, note.

† *e.g.* the wine-merchant may buy in the cask what he sells in bottle (Stewart).

case we rather employ δικαιοπράγημα as the generic term, and restrict δικαίωμα to the correction of an act of injustice. But as to the several species of acts of justice and injustice, we must postpone for the present the inquiry into their nature and number and the ground which they cover.

The internal conditions of a just or unjust action, and of a just or unjust agent

8. Now that we have ascertained what is just and what is unjust, we may say that a man acts unjustly or justly when he does these things voluntarily; but when he does them involuntarily, he does not, strictly speaking, act either unjustly or justly, but only "accidentally," *i.e.* he does a thing which happens to be just or unjust.* For whether an act is or is not to be called an act of injustice (or of justice) depends upon whether it is voluntary or involuntary; for if it be voluntary the agent is blamed, and at the same time the act becomes an act of injustice: so something unjust may be done, and yet it may not be an act of injustice, *i.e.* if this condition of voluntariness be absent.

By a voluntary act I mean, as I explained before, anything which, being within the doer's control, is done knowingly (*i.e.* with knowledge of the person, the instrument, and the result; *e.g.* the person whom and the instrument with which he is striking, and the effect of the blow), without the intervention at any point of accident or constraint; *e.g.* if another take your hand and with it strike a third person, that is not a voluntary act of yours, for it was not within your control; again, the man you strike may be your father, and you may know that it is a man, or perhaps that it is one of the company, that you are striking

* *Cf.* § 4.

but not know that it is your father; and it must be understood that the same distinction is to be made with regard to the result, and, in a word, to the whole act. That then which either is done in ignorance, or, though not done in ignorance, is not under our control, or is done under compulsion, is involuntary; besides which, there are many natural processes in which we knowingly take an active or a passive part, which cannot be called either voluntary or involuntary, such as growing old and dying.

An accidentally unjust act and an accidentally just 4
act are equally possible; *e.g.* a man might restore a deposit against his will for fear of consequences, and then you could not say that he did what was just or acted justly except accidentally:* and, similarly, a man who against his will was forcibly prevented from restoring a deposit would be said only accidentally to act unjustly or to do that which is unjust.

Voluntary acts, again, are divided into (1) those 5
that are done of set purpose, and (2) those that are done without set purpose; *i.e.* (1) those that are done after previous deliberation, and (2) those that are done without previous deliberation.

Now, there are three ways in which we may hurt 6
our neighbour. Firstly, a hurt done in ignorance is generally called a mistake when there is a misconception as to the person affected, or the thing done, or the instrument, or the result; *e.g.* I may not think to hit,

* *i.e.* he willed the act not as just, but as a means of avoiding the painful consequences; the justice of it, therefore, was not part of the essence of the act to him, was not among the qualities of the act which moved him to choose it, or, in Aristotle's language, was "accidental."

or not to hit with this instrument, or not to hit this person, or not to produce this effect, but an effect follows other than that which was present to my mind; I may mean to inflict a prick, not a wound, or not to wound the person whom I wound, or not to deal a wound of this kind.

7 But [if we draw the distinction more accurately] when the hurt comes about contrary to what might reasonably be expected, it may be called a mishap: but when, though it is not contrary to what might reasonably be expected, there is still no vicious intention, it is a mistake; for a man makes a mistake when he sets the train of events in motion,* but he is unfortunate when an external agency interferes.†

8 Secondly, when the agent acts with knowledge but without previous deliberation, it is an act of injustice; *e.g.* when he is impelled by anger or any of the other passions to which man is necessarily or naturally subject. In doing such hurt and committing such errors, the doer acts unjustly and the acts are acts of injustice, though they are not such as to stamp him as unjust or wicked; for the hurt is not done out of wickedness.

9 But, thirdly, when it is done of set purpose, the doer is unjust and wicked.

On this account acts done in anger are rightly held not to be done of malice aforethought; for he who gave the provocation began it, not he who did the deed in a passion.

* which leads by a natural, though by him unforeseen, sequence to his neighbour's hurt: negligence, or error of judgment.

† and gives a fatal termination to an act that would ordinarily be harmless: accident.

Again, in such cases as this last, what men dispute 10
about is usually not whether the deed was done or not, but what the justice of the case is; for it is an apparent injustice that stirs the assailant's wrath. There is a difference between cases of this kind and disputes about contracts: in the latter the question is a question of fact, and one or other of the parties must be a vicious character, unless his memory be at fault; but in these cases they agree about the facts, but differ as to which side is in the right (whereas the deliberate aggressor knows very well the rights of the case), so that the one thinks that he is wronged, while the other thinks differently.*

But if a man hurt another of set purpose, he acts 11
unjustly, and acts of injustice (*i.e.* violations of what is proportionate and fair), when so done, stamp the doer as an unjust character.

In like manner a man is a just character when he of set purpose acts justly; but he is said to act justly if he merely do voluntarily that which is just.

Of involuntary injuries, on the other hand, some 12
are pardonable, some unpardonable. Errors that are committed not merely in ignorance but by reason of ignorance are pardonable; but those that are committed not through ignorance but rather in ignorance, through some unnatural or inhuman passion, are not pardonable.†

* Throwing the words ὁ δ' ἐπιβουλεύσας οὐκ ἀγνοεῖ into a parenthesis. The passage is easier to construe without the parenthesis, but with a stop after ἀμφισβητοῦσιν.

† In strictness, of course, such acts cannot be called involuntary (ἀκούσια) at all: *cf. supra*, III. 1, where the conditions of an involuntary act are stated more precisely.

Sundry questions about doing and suffering injustice

9. But it may be doubted whether we have sufficiently explained what it is to suffer and to do injustice. First of all, are these terms applicable to such a case as that which is described in those strange verses of Euripides ?—

> "*A.* I slew my mother: that is all my tale.
> *P.* But say, did both or neither will the deed?"

Is it really possible, I mean, to suffer injustice [or be wronged] voluntarily ? or is suffering injustice always involuntary, as doing injustice is always voluntary ?

Again, is suffering injustice always one way or the other (as doing injustice is always voluntary), or is it sometimes voluntary and sometimes involuntary?

Similarly with regard to having justice done to you: doing justice is always voluntary [as doing injustice is], so that one might expect that there is the same relation in both cases between the active and the passive, and that suffering injustice and having justice done to you are either both voluntary or both involuntary. But it would surely be absurd to maintain, even with regard to having justice done to you, that it is always voluntary; for some that have justice done to them certainly do not will it.

Again we may raise the question in this [more general] form: Can a man who has that which is unjust done to him always be said to suffer injustice [or be wronged]? or are there further conditions necessary for suffering as there are for doing injustice?

Both what I do and what I suffer may be (as we saw) "accidentally" just; and so also it may be "accidentally" unjust: for doing that which is unjust is not identical with doing injustice, nor is suffering that which is unjust the same as suffering injustice; and similarly with doing justice and having justice done to you. For to have injustice done to you implies some one that does injustice, and to have justice done to you implies some one that does justice.

But if to do injustice means simply to hurt a man 4
voluntarily, and voluntarily means with knowledge of the person, the instrument, and the manner, then the incontinent man, who voluntarily hurts himself, will voluntarily suffer injustice, and it will be possible for a man to do injustice to himself—the possibility of which last is also one of the questions in dispute.

Again, a man might, through incontinence, volun- 5
tarily suffer himself to be hurt by another also acting voluntarily; so that in this case also a man might voluntarily suffer injustice.

I think rather that the above definition is incorrect, and that to "hurting with knowledge of the person, the instrument, and the manner," we must
add "against his wish."* If we define it so, then a 6
man may voluntarily be hurt and suffer that which is unjust, but cannot voluntarily have injustice done to him. (For no one *wishes* to be hurt,—even the incontinent man does not wish it, but acts contrary to his wish. No one wishes for anything that he does not think good; what the incontinent man does

* βούλησιν is used perhaps for will, as there is no abstract term corresponding to ἑκών. I bracket the last two sentences of § 6, as (in spite of the ingenuity of Jackson and Stewart) the statement seems to me hopelessly confused.

7 is not that which he thinks he ought to do.) But he that gives, as Glaucus gives to Diomede in Homer—

"Gold for his bronze, fivescore kine's worth for nine,"

does not suffer injustice; for the giving rests with him, but suffering injustice does not rest with one's self; there must be some one to do injustice.

8 It is plain, then, that suffering injustice cannot be voluntary.

There are still two questions that we purposed to discuss: (1) Is it the man who assigns or the man who receives a disproportionately large share that does injustice? (2) Is it possible to do injustice to yourself?

9 In the former case, *i.e.* if he who assigns and not he who receives the undue share does injustice, then if a man knowingly and voluntarily gives too much to another and too little to himself, he does injustice to himself. And this is what moderate persons are often thought to do; for the equitable man is apt to take less than his due. But the case is hardly so simple: it may be that he took a larger share of some other good, *e.g.* of good fame or of that which is intrinsically noble.

Again, the difficulty may be got over by reference to our definition of doing injustice; for in this case nothing is done to the man against his wish, so that no injustice is done him, but at most only harm.

10 It is plain, moreover, that the man who makes the unjust award does injustice, but not always he who gets more than his share; for a man does not always do injustice when we can say of what he

does that it is unjust, but only when we can say that he voluntarily does that which is unjust; and that we can only say of the prime mover in the action, which in this case is the distributor and not the receiver.

Again, there are many senses of the word "do," 11
and in a certain sense an inanimate instrument, or my hand, or again my slave under my orders, may be said to slay; but though these may be said to do what is unjust, they cannot be said to act unjustly or to do an act of injustice.

Again, if a man unwittingly gives unjust judg- 12
ment, he does not commit injustice in the sense of contravening that which is just according to law, nor is his judgment unjust in this sense, but in a certain sense it is unjust; for there is a difference between that which is just according to law and that which is just in the primary sense of the word: but if he knowingly gives unjust judgment, he is himself grasping at more than his share, in the shape either of favour with one party or vengeance on the
other. The judge, then, who gives unjust judgment 13
on these grounds, takes more than his due, quite as much as if he received a share of the unjust award; for even in the latter case a judge who awards a piece of land would receive, not land, but money.

Men fancy that as it is in their power to act 14
unjustly, so it is an easy matter to be just. But it is not so. To lie with your neighbour's wife, or to strike your neighbour, or to pass certain coins from your hand to his is easy enough, and always within your power, but to do these acts as the outcome of a certain

character is not an easy matter, nor one which is always within your power.*

15 Similarly men think that to know what is just and what is unjust needs no great wisdom, since any one can inform himself about those things which the law prescribes (though these things are only accidentally, not essentially, just): but to know how these acts must be done and how these distributions must be made in order to be just,—that indeed is a harder matter than to know what conduces to health; though that is no easy matter. It is easy enough to know the meaning of honey, and wine, and hellebore, and cautery, and the knife, but to know how, and to whom, and when they must be applied in order to produce health, is so far from being easy, that to have this knowledge is to be a physician.

16 For the same reason, some people think that the just man is as able to act unjustly as justly, for he is not less but rather more capable than another of performing the several acts, *e.g.* of lying with a woman or of striking a blow, as the courageous man is rather more capable than another of throwing away his shield and turning his back and running away anywhere. But to play the coward or to act unjustly means not merely to do such an act (though the

* You can always do the *acts* if you want to do them, *i.e.* if you will them; but you cannot at will do them in the spirit of a just or an unjust man; for character is the *result* of a series of acts of will: *cf. supra*, III. 5, 22. The contradiction between this and III. 5, 2, is only apparent: we are responsible for our character, though we cannot change it at a moment's notice.

doer might be said "accidentally" to act unjustly),* but to do it in a certain frame of mind; just as to act the part of a doctor and to heal does not mean simply to apply the knife or not to apply it, to give or to withhold a drug, but to do this in a particular fashion.

Justice, lastly, implies persons who participate in 17
those things that, generally speaking, are good, but who can have too much or too little of them. For some—for the gods perhaps—no amount of them is too much; and for others—for the incurably vicious—no amount is beneficial, they are always hurtful; but for the rest of mankind they are useful within certain limits: justice, therefore, is essentially human.

10. We have next to speak of equity and of that 1
which is equitable, and to inquire how equity is related to justice, and that which is equitable to that which is just. For, on consideration, they do not seem to be absolutely identical, nor yet generically different. At one time we praise that which is equitable and the equitable man, and even use the word metaphorically as a term of praise synonymous with good, showing that we consider that the more equitable a thing is the better it is. At another time we reflect and find it strange that what is equitable should be praiseworthy, if it be different from what is just; for, we argue, if it be something else, either what is just is not good, or what is equitable is not good; † if both be good, they are the same.

* *Cf. supra*, 8, 1-4.

† Οὐ δίκαιον I have omitted (after Trendelenburg) as obviously wrong. We may suppose either that the original οὐ σπουδαῖον was altered into οὐ δίκαιον, or (more probably) that οὐ δίκαιον or δίκαιον was inserted by a bungling copyist.

2 These are the reflections which give rise to the difficulty about what is equitable. Now, in a way, they are all correct and not incompatible with one another; for that which is equitable, though it is better than that which is just (in one sense of the word), is yet itself just, and is not better than what is just in the sense of being something generically distinct from it. What is just, then, and what is equitable are generically the same, and both are good, though what is equitable is better.

3 But what obscures the matter is that though what is equitable is just, it is not identical with, but a correction of, that which is just according to law.

4 The reason of this is that every law is laid down in general terms, while there are matters about which it is impossible to speak correctly in general terms. Where, then, it is necessary to speak in general terms, but impossible to do so correctly, the legislator lays down that which holds good for the majority of cases, being quite aware that it does not hold good for all.

The law, indeed, is none the less correctly laid down because of this defect; for the defect lies not in the law, nor in the lawgiver, but in the nature of the subject-matter, being necessarily involved in the very conditions of human action.

5 When, therefore, the law lays down a general rule, but a particular case occurs which is an exception to this rule, it is right, where the legislator fails and is in error through speaking without qualification, to make good this deficiency, just as the lawgiver himself would do if he were present, and as he would

have provided in the law itself if the case had occurred to him.

What is equitable, then, is just, and better than 6
what is just in one sense of the word—not better than what is absolutely just, but better than that which fails through its lack of qualification. And the essence of what is equitable is that it is an amendment of the law, in those points where it fails through the generality of its language.

The reason why the law does not cover all cases is that there are matters about which it is impossible to lay down a law, so that they require a special
decree. For that which is variable needs a variable 7
rule, like the leaden rule employed in the Lesbian style of masonry; as the leaden rule has no fixed shape, but adapts itself to the outline of each stone, so is the decree adapted to the occasion.

We have ascertained, then, what the equitable 8
course is, and have found that it is just, and also better than what is just in a certain sense of the word. And after this it is easy to see what the equitable man is: he who is apt to choose such a course and to follow it, who does not insist on his rights to the damage of others, but is ready to take less than his due, even when he has the law to back him, is called an equitable man; and this type of character is called equitableness, being a sort of justice, and not a different kind of character.

11. The foregoing discussion enables us to answer 1
the question whether it be possible or not for a man to act unjustly to himself.

That which is just in one sense of the word we

found to be those manifestations of the several virtues which the law prescribes: *e.g.* the law does not order a man to kill himself; and what the law does not order it forbids: and, further, when a man, contrary to the law, voluntarily inflicts hurt without provocation, he acts unjustly (voluntarily meaning with knowledge of the person and the instrument). Now, the man who kills himself in a rage voluntarily acts thus against right reason and does what the law forbids: he acts unjustly therefore.

But unjustly to whom? To the state surely, not to himself; for he suffers voluntarily, but no one can have an injustice done him voluntarily. And upon this ground the state actually punishes him, *i.e.* it pronounces a particular kind of disfranchisement upon the man who destroys himself, as one who acts unjustly towards the state.

Again, if we take the word unjust in the other sense, in which it is used to designate not general badness, but a particular species of vice, we find that in this sense also it is impossible to act unjustly to one's self. (This, we found, is different from the former sense of the word: the unjust man in this second sense is bad in the same way as the coward is bad, *i.e.* as having a particular form of vice, not as having a completely vicious character, nor do we mean to say that he displays a completely vicious character when we say that he acts unjustly). For if it were possible, it would be possible for the same thing at the same time to be taken from and added to the same person. But this is impossible; and, in fact, a just deed or an unjust deed always implies more persons than one.

Further, an act of injustice, besides being voluntary, if not deliberate, must be prior to hurt received (for he who, having received some hurt, repays the same that he received is not held to act unjustly); but he who hurts himself suffers that very hurt at the same time that he inflicts it. 5

Again, if it were possible for a man to act unjustly to himself, it would be possible to suffer injustice voluntarily.

Further, a man cannot act unjustly without doing an act of injustice of some particular kind; but no one commits adultery with his own wife, or burglariously breaks through his own walls, or steals his own property. 6

But the whole question about acting unjustly to one's self is settled (without going into detail) by the answer we gave * to the question whether a man could voluntarily suffer injustice.

(It is plain that to suffer and to do injustice are both bad, for the one is to get less and the other more than the mean amount, which corresponds to what is healthy in medicine, or to what promotes good condition in gymnastics: but, though both are bad, to do injustice is the worse; for to do injustice is blamable and implies vice (either completely formed vice, what we call vice simply, or else that which is on the way to become vice; for a voluntary act of injustice does not always imply injustice), but to have injustice done to you is no token of a vicious and unjust character. 7

In itself, then, to be unjustly treated is less bad, but there is nothing to prevent its being accidentally 8

* *Supra*, cap. 9.

the greater evil. Science, however, does not concern itself with these accidents, but calls a pleurisy a greater malady than a stumble; and yet the latter might, on occasion, accidentally become the greater, as, for instance, if a stumble were to cause you to fall and be caught or slain by the enemy.)

9 Though we cannot apply the term just to a man's behaviour towards himself, yet we can apply it metaphorically and in virtue of a certain resemblance to the relations between certain parts of a man's self—not, however, in all senses of the word just, but in that sense in which it is applied to the relations of master and slave, or husband and wife; for this is the sort of relation that exists between the rational and the irrational parts of the soul.

And it is this distinction of parts that leads people to fancy that there is such a thing as injustice to one's self: one part of a man can have something done to it by another part contrary to its desires; and so they think that the term just can be applied to the relations of these parts to one another, just as to the relations of ruler and ruled.*

10 We may now consider that we have concluded our examination of justice and the other moral virtues.

* Whereas, says Aristotle, we cannot speak at all of justice or injustice to one's self, and it is only by way of metaphor that we can apply the terms even to the relations of parts of the self—not strictly, since the parts are not persons.

BOOK VI.

THE INTELLECTUAL VIRTUES.

Must be studied because (a) reason prescribes the mean, (b) they are a part of human excellence. The intellect is (1) scientific, (2) calculative: we want the virtue of each.

1. We said above that what we should choose is neither too much nor too little, but "the mean," and that "the mean" is what "right reason" prescribes. This we now have to explain.

Each of the virtues we have discussed implies (as every mental habit implies) some aim which the rational man keeps in view when he is regulating his efforts; in other words, there must be some standard for determining the several modes of moderation, which we say lie between excess and deficiency, and are in accordance with "right reason." But though this is quite true, it is not sufficiently precise. In any kind of occupation which can be reduced to rational principles, it is quite true to say that we must brace ourselves up and relax ourselves neither too much nor too little, but "in moderation," "as right reason orders;" but this alone would not tell one much; *e.g.* a man would hardly learn how to treat a case by being told to treat it as the art of medicine prescribes, and as one versed in that art would treat it.

So in the case of mental habits or types of character also it is not enough that the rule we have laid down is correct; we need further to know precisely what this right reason is, and what is the standard which it affords.

4 * The virtues or excellences of the mind or soul, it will be remembered, we divided † into two classes, and called the one moral and the other intellectual. The moral excellences or virtues we have already discussed in detail; let us now examine the other class, the intellectual excellences, after some preliminary remarks about the soul.

5 We said before that the soul consists of two parts, the rational and the irrational part. We will now make a similar division of the former, and will assume that there are two rational faculties: (1) that by which we know those things that depend on invariable principles, (2) that by which we know those things that are variable. For to generically different objects must correspond generically different faculties, if, as we hold, it is in virtue of some kind of likeness or kinship with their objects that our faculties are able to know them.

6 Let us call the former the scientific or demonstra-

* This really forms quite a fresh opening, independent of §§ 1–3; and it is one among many signs of the incomplete state in which this part of the treatise was left, that these two openings of Book VI. were never fused together. The scheme of the treatise, as unfolded in Book I. (*cf.* especially I. 7, 13; 13, 20), gives the intellectual virtues an independent place alongside of, or rather above, the moral virtues; now that the latter have been disposed of it naturally remains to consider the former: this is the natural transition which we have in § 4. But besides this the dependence of the moral virtues upon the intellectual virtues makes an examination of the latter absolutely necessary to the completion of the theory of the former; thus we get the transition of §§ 1–3.

† *Supra*, I. 13, 20.

tive, the latter the calculative or deliberative faculty. For to deliberate is the same as to calculate, and no one deliberates about things that are invariable. One division then of the rational faculty may be fairly called the calculative faculty.

Our problem, then, is to find what each of these 7
faculties becomes in its full development, or in its best state; for that will be its excellence or virtue.

But its excellence will bear direct reference to its proper function.

The function of the intellect, both in practice and speculation, is to attain truth.

2. Now, the faculties which guide us in action and 1
in the apprehension of truth are three: sense, reason,* and desire.

The first of these cannot originate action, as we 2
see from the fact that brutes have sense but are incapable of action.

If we take the other two we find two modes of reasoning, viz. affirmation and negation [or assent and denial], and two corresponding modes of desire, viz. pursuit and avoidance [or attraction and repulsion].

Now, moral virtue is a habit or formed faculty of choice or purpose, and purpose is desire following upon deliberation.

It follows, then, that if the purpose is to be all it should be, both the calculation or reasoning must be true and the desire right, and that the very same things must be assented to by the former and pursued by the latter.

This kind of reasoning, then, and this sort of truth has to do with action.

* νοῦς: the word is used here in its widest sense.

3 But speculative reasoning that has to do neither with action nor production is good or bad according as it is true or false simply: for the function of the intellect is always the apprehension of truth; but the function of the practical intellect is the apprehension of truth in agreement with right desire.

4 Purpose, then, is the cause—not the final but the efficient cause or origin—of action, and the origin of purpose is desire and calculation of means; so that purpose necessarily implies on the one hand the faculty of reason and its exercise, and on the other hand a certain moral character or state of the desires; for right action and the contrary kind of action are alike impossible without both reasoning and moral character.

5 Mere reasoning, however, can never set anything going, but only reasoning about means to an end—what may be called practical reasoning (which practical reasoning also regulates production; for in making anything you always have an ulterior object in view—what you make is desired not as an end in itself, but only as a means to, or a condition of, something else; but what you do is an end in itself, for well-doing or right action is the end, and this is the object of desire).

Purpose, then, may be called either a reason that desires, or a desire that reasons; and this faculty of originating action constitutes a man.

6 No past event can be purposed; *e.g.* no one purposes to have sacked Troy; for no one deliberates about that which is past, but about that which is to come, and which is variable: but the past

cannot be undone; so that Agathon is right when he says—

> "This thing alone not God himself can do—
> To make undone that which hath once been done."

We have thus found that both divisions of the reason, or both the intellectual faculties, have the attainment of truth for their function; that developed state of each, then, in which it best attains truth will be its excellence or virtue.

Of the five modes of attaining truth: (1) of demonstrative science of things invariable.

3. Let us describe these virtues then, starting 1
afresh from the beginning.

Let us assume that the modes in which the mind arrives at truth, either in the way of affirmation or negation, are five in number, viz. art, science, prudence, wisdom, reason;* for conception and opinion may be erroneous.

What science is we may learn from the following 2
considerations (for we want a precise account, and must not content ourselves with metaphors). We all suppose that what we know with scientific knowledge is invariable; but of that which is variable we cannot say, so soon as it is out of sight, whether it is in existence or not. The object of science, then, is necessary. Therefore it is eternal: for whatever is of its own nature necessary is eternal: and what is eternal neither begins nor ceases to be.

Further, it is held that all science can be taught, 3
and that what can be known in the way of science can be learnt. But all teaching starts from some-

* νοῦς—used now in a narrower special sense which will presently be explained.

thing already known, as we have explained in the Analytics; for it proceeds either by induction or by syllogism. Now, it is induction that leads the learner up to universal principles, while syllogism starts from these. There are principles, then, from which syllogism starts, which are not arrived at by syllogism, and which, therefore, must be arrived at by induction.*

4 Science, then, may be defined as a habit or formed faculty of demonstration, with all the further qualifications which are enumerated in the Analytics. It is necessary to add this, because it is only when the principles of our knowledge are accepted and known to us in a particular way, that we can properly be said to have scientific knowledge; for unless these principles are better known to us than the conclusions based upon them, our knowledge will be merely accidental.†

This, then, may be taken as our account of science.

1 4. That which is variable includes that which *Of knowledge of things variable,*
man makes and that which man does; but making
2 or production is different from doing or action (here *viz. (2) of art in what we make;*
we adopt the popular distinctions). The habit or formed faculty of acting with reason or calculation, then, is different from the formed faculty of producing with reason or calculation. And so the one cannot include the other; for action is not production, nor is production action.

3 Now, the builder's faculty is one of the arts, and

* Though, as we see later, induction can elicit them from experience only because they are already latent in that experience.

† We may know truths of science, but unless we know these in their necessary connection, we have not scientific knowledge.

may be described as a certain formed faculty of producing with calculation; and there is no art which is not a faculty of this kind, nor is there any faculty of this kind which is not an art: an art, then, is the same thing as a formed faculty of producing with correct calculation.

And every art is concerned with bringing some- 4
thing into being, *i.e.* with contriving or calculating how to bring into being some one of those things that can either be or not be, and the cause of whose production lies in the producer, not in the thing itself which is produced. For art has not to do with that which is or comes into being of necessity, nor with the products of nature; for these have the cause of their production in themselves.

Production and action being different, art of course 5
has to do with production, and not with action. And, in a certain sense, its domain is the same as that of chance or fortune, as Agathon says—

"Art waits on fortune, fortune waits on art."

Art, then, as we said, is a certain formed faculty 6
or habit of production with correct reasoning or calculation, and the contrary of this (ἀτεχνία) is a habit of production with incorrect calculation, the field of both being that which is variable.

and (3) of prudence in what we do, the virtue of the calculative intellect.

5. In order to ascertain what prudence is, we will 1
first ask who they are whom we call prudent.

It seems to be characteristic of a prudent man that he is able to deliberate well about what is good or expedient for himself, not with a view to some particular end, such as health or strength, but with a view to well-being or living well.

2 This is confirmed by the fact that we apply the name sometimes to those who deliberate well in some particular field, when they calculate well the means to some particular good end, in matters that do not fall within the sphere of art. So we may say, generally, that a man who can deliberate well is prudent.

3 But no one deliberates about that which cannot be altered, nor about that which it is not in his power to do.

Now science, we saw, implies demonstration; but things whose principles or causes are variable do not admit of demonstration; for everything that depends upon these principles or causes is also variable; and, on the other hand, things that are necessarily determined do not admit of deliberation. It follows, therefore, that prudence cannot be either a science or an art: it cannot be a science, because the sphere of action is that which is alterable; it cannot be an art, because production is generically different from action.

4 It follows from all this that prudence is a formed faculty that apprehends truth by reasoning or calculation, and issues in action, in the domain of human good and ill; for while production has another end than itself, this is not so with action, since good action or well doing is itself the end.

5 For this reason Pericles and men who resemble him are considered prudent, because they are able to see what is good for themselves and for men; and this we take to be the character of those who are able to manage a household or a state.

This, too, is the reason why we call temperance

σωφροσύνη, signifying thereby that it is the virtue which preserves prudence. But what temperance 6 preserves is this particular kind of judgment. For it is not *any* kind of judgment that is destroyed or perverted by the presentation of pleasant or painful objects (not such a judgment, for instance, as that the angles of a triangle are equal to two right angles), but only judgments about matters of practice. For the principles of practice [or the causes which originate action] * are the ends for the sake of which acts are done; but when a man is corrupted by pleasure or pain, he straightway loses sight of the principle, and no longer sees that this is the end for the sake of which, and as a means to which, each particular act should be chosen and done; for vice is apt to obliterate the principle.

Our conclusion then is that prudence is a formed faculty which apprehends truth by reasoning or calculation, and issues in action, in the field of human good.

Moreover, art [or the artistic faculty] has its excel- 7 lence [or perfect development] in something other than itself, but this is not so with prudence. Again, in the domain of art voluntary error is not so bad as involuntary, but it is worse in the case of prudence, as it is in the case of all the virtues or excellences. It is plain, then, that prudence is a virtue or excellence, and not an art.

And the rational parts of the soul or the intellectual 8 faculties being two in number, prudence will be the

* The conception of the end is at once a cause or source of action and a principle of knowledge; ἀρχή covers both.

virtue of the second, [the calculative part or] the faculty of opinion; for opinion deals with that which is variable, and so does prudence.

But it is something more than "a formed faculty of apprehending truth by reasoning or calculation;" as we see from the fact that such a faculty may be lost, but prudence, once acquired, can never be lost.*

(4) Of intuitive reason as the basis of demonstrative science.

1 6. Science is a mode of judging that deals with universal and necessary truths; but truths that can be demonstrated depend upon principles, and (since science proceeds by demonstrative reasoning) every science has its principles. The principles, then, on which the truths of science depend cannot fall within the province of science, nor yet of art or prudence; for a scientific truth is one that can be demonstrated, but art and prudence have to do with that which is variable.

Nor can they fall within the province of wisdom; for it is characteristic of the wise man to have a demonstrative knowledge of certain things.

2 But the habits of mind or formed faculties by which we apprehend truth without any mixture of error, whether in the domain of things invariable or in the domain of things variable, are science, prudence, wisdom, and reason.† If then no one of the first three (prudence, science, wisdom) can be the faculty

* For it implies a determination of the will which is more permanent in its nature than a merely intellectual habit. And further, when once acquired it must be constantly strengthened by exercise, as occasions for action can never be wanting.

† Art, which is one of the five enumerated above, is here omitted, either in sheer carelessness, or perhaps because it is subordinate to prudence: *cf. supra* 5, 7.

which apprehends these principles, the only possible conclusion is that they are apprehended by reason.

(5) Of wisdom as the union of science and intuitive reason. Comparison of the two intellectual virtues, wisdom and prudence.

7. The term σοφία (wisdom*) is sometimes applied 1 in the domain of the arts to those who are consummate masters of their art; *e.g.* it is applied to Phidias as a master of sculpture, and to Polyclitus for his skill in portrait-statues; and in this application it means nothing else than excellence of art or perfect development of the artistic faculty.

But there are also men who are considered wise, 2 not in part nor in any particular thing (as Homer says in the Margites—

> "Him the gods gave no skill with spade or plough,
> Nor made him wise in aught"),

but generally wise. In this general sense, then, wisdom plainly will be the most perfect of the sciences.

The wise man, then, must not only know what 3 follows from the principles of knowledge, but also know the truth about those principles. Wisdom, therefore, will be the union of [intuitive] reason with [demonstrative] scientific knowledge, or scientific knowledge of the noblest objects with its crowning perfection, so to speak, added to it. For it would be absurd to suppose that the political faculty or prudence is the highest of our faculties, unless indeed man is the best of all things in the universe.

Now, as the terms wholesome and good mean one 4 thing in the case of men and another in the case of fishes, while white and straight always have the same meaning, we must all allow that wise means

* Of course we do not use "wisdom" in this sense

one thing always, while prudent means different things; for we should all say that those who are clear-sighted in their own affairs are prudent, and deem them fit to be entrusted with those affairs. (And for this reason we sometimes apply the term prudent even to animals, when they show a faculty of foresight in what concerns their own life.)

Moreover, it is plain that wisdom cannot be the same as statesmanship. If we apply the term wisdom to knowledge of what is advantageous to ourselves, there will be many kinds of wisdom; for the knowledge of what is good will not be one and the same for all animals, but different for each species. It can no more be one than the art of healing can be one and the same for all kinds of living things.

Man may be superior to all other animals, but that will not make any difference here; for there are other things of a far diviner nature than man, as—to take the most conspicuous instance—the heavenly bodies.

It is plain, then, after what we have said, that wisdom is the union of scientific [or demonstrative] knowledge and [intuitive] reason about objects of the noblest nature.

And on this account people call Anaxagoras and Thales and men of that sort wise, but not prudent, seeing them to be ignorant of their own advantage; and say that their knowledge is something out of the common, wonderful, hard of attainment, nay superhuman, but useless, since it is no human good that they seek.

Prudence, on the other hand, deals with human

affairs, and with matters that admit of deliberation: for the prudent man's special function, as we conceive it, is to deliberate well; but no one deliberates about what is invariable, or about matters in which there is not some end, in the sense of some realizable good. But a man is said to deliberate well (without any qualifying epithet) when he is able, by a process of reasoning or calculation, to arrive at what is best for man in matters of practice.

Prudence, moreover, does not deal in general pro- 7
positions only, but implies knowledge of particular facts also; for it issues in action, and the field of action is the field of particulars.

This is the reason why some men that lack [scientific] knowledge are more efficient in practice than others that have it, especially men of wide experience; for if you know that light meat is digestible and wholesome, but do not know what meats are light, you will not be able to cure people so well as a man who only knows that chicken is light and wholesome.

But prudence is concerned with practice; so that it needs knowledge both of general truths and of particular facts, but more especially the latter.

But here also [*i.e.* in the domain of practice] there must be a supreme form of the faculty [which we will now proceed to consider].

Prudence compared with statesmanship and other forms of knowledge.

8. And in fact statesmanship and prudence are the 1
same faculty, though they are differently manifested.

Of this faculty in its application to the state the 2
supreme form is the legislative faculty, but the special form which deals with particular cases is called by

the generic name statesmanship. The field of the latter is action and deliberation; for a decree directly concerns action, as the last link in the chain.* And on this account those engaged in this field are alone said to be statesmen, for they alone act like handicraftsmen.

8 But it is when applied to the individual and to one's own affairs that this faculty is especially regarded as prudence, and this is the form which receives the generic name prudence or practical wisdom (the other forms being (1) the faculty of managing a household, (2) the legislative faculty, (3) statesmanship [in the narrower sense], which is subdivided into (*a*) the deliberative, (*b*) the judicial faculty).

4 Knowing one's own good, then, would seem to be a kind of knowledge (though it admits of great variety),† and, according to the general opinion, he who knows and attends to his own affairs is prudent, while statesmen are busybodies, as Euripides says—

> "What? was I wise, who might without a care
> Have lived a unit in the multitude
> Like any other unit? . . .
> For those who would excel and do great things——"

For men generally seek their own good, and fancy that is what they should do; and from this opinion comes the notion that these men are prudent.

And yet, perhaps, it is not possible for a man to manage his own affairs well without managing a

* πρακτὸν ὡς τὸ ἔσχατον, *i.e.* as the last link in the chain of causes leading to the proposed end—last in the order of deliberation, but first in the order of events: *cf.* III. 3, 12.

† Varying as the good varies; *cf. supra*, 7, 4, and I. 3, 2.

household and taking part in the management of a state.

Moreover, how a man is to manage his own affairs is not plain and requires consideration. And this is attested by the fact that a young man may become proficient in geometry or mathematics and wise* in these matters, but cannot possibly, it is thought, become prudent. The reason of this is that prudence deals with particular facts, with which experience alone can familiarize us; but a young man must be inexperienced, for experience is the fruit of years.

Why again, we may ask, can a lad be a mathema- 6
tician but not wise, nor proficient in the knowledge of nature? And the answer surely is that mathematics is an abstract science, while the principles of wisdom and of natural science are only to be derived from a large experience; † and that thus, though a young man may repeat propositions of the latter kind, he does not really believe them, while he can easily apprehend the meaning of mathematical terms.

Error in deliberation, again, may lie either in 7
the universal or in the particular judgment; for instance, you may be wrong in judging that all water that weighs heavy is unwholesome, or in judging that this water weighs heavy. But prudence [in 8
spite of its universal judgments] plainly is not science;

* Here in the looser sense, below (§ 6) in the stricter sense, which is the technical meaning of the term in Aristotle: *cf. supra*, **7**, 12.

† He does not mean that the principles of mathematics are not derived from experience, but only that they are derived from the primitive experience which every boy has, being in fact (as we should say) the framework on which the simplest knowledge of an external world is built.

for, as we said,* it deals with the ultimate or particular fact [the last link in the chain], for anything that can be done must be of this nature.

9 And thus it is in a manner opposed to the intuitive reason also: the intuitive reason deals with primary principles which cannot be demonstrated, while prudence deals with ultimate [particular] facts which cannot be scientifically proved, but are perceived by sense—not one of the special senses, but a sense analogous to that by which we perceive in mathematics that this ultimate [particular] figure is a triangle; † for here too our reasoning must come to a stand. But this faculty [by which we apprehend particular facts in the domain of practice] should, after all, be called sense rather than prudence; for prudence cannot be defined thus.‡

1 9. Inquiry and deliberation are not the same; for Of deliberation.
deliberation is a particular kind of inquiry. But we must ascertain what good deliberation is—whether it is a kind of science or opinion, or happy guessing, or something quite different.

2 It is not science; for we do not inquire about that

* *Cf. supra*, § 2.

† The perception "that the ultimate fact is a triangle" (which is the more obvious translation of these words), whether this means "that three lines is the least number that will enclose a space," or "that the possibility of a triangle is a fact that cannot be demonstrated," is in either case not the perception of a *particular* fact; but it is the perception of a particular fact that is needed if the illustration is to be relevant.

‡ The intuitive reason (*νοῦς*) is here opposed to prudence (*φρόνησις*), but presently (cap. 11) is found to be included in it; reason (*νοῦς*) was similarly in cap. 6 opposed to wisdom (*σοφία*), but in cap. 7 found to be included in it.

which we know: but good deliberation is a kind of deliberation, and when we deliberate we inquire and calculate.

Nor is it happy guessing; for we make happy guesses without calculating and in a moment, but we take time to deliberate, and it is a common saying that execution should be swift, but deliberation slow.

Good deliberation, again, is different from sagacity, 3
which is a kind of happy guessing.

Nor is it any kind of opinion.

But since in deliberating ill we go wrong, and in deliberating well we go right, it is plain that good deliberation is a kind of rightness, but a rightness or correctness neither of science nor opinion; for science does not admit of correctness (since it does not admit of error), and correctness of opinion is simply truth; and, further, that concerning which we have an opinion is always something already settled.

Good deliberation, however, is impossible without calculation.

We have no choice left, then, but to say that it is correctness of reasoning (*διάνοια*); for reasoning is not yet assertion: and whereas opinion is not an inquiry, but already a definite assertion, when we are deliberating, whether well or ill, we are inquiring and calculating.

But as good deliberation is a kind of correctness 4
in deliberation, we must first inquire what deliberation means, and what its field is.*

Now, there are various kinds of correctness, and it

* This, however, is not done here, perhaps because it has been already done at length in III. 3.

is plain that not every kind of correctness in deliberation is good deliberation; for the incontinent man or the vicious man may duly arrive, by a process of calculation, at the end which he has in view,* so that he will have deliberated correctly, though what he gains is a great evil. But to have deliberated well is thought to be a good thing; for it is only a particular kind of correctness in deliberation that is called good deliberation—that, namely, which arrives at what is good.

5 But, further, what is good may be arrived at by a false syllogism; I mean that a right conclusion as to what is to be done may be arrived at in a wrong way or upon wrong grounds—the middle term being wrong;† so that what leads to a right conclusion as to what should be done is not good deliberation, unless the grounds also be right.

6 A further difference is that one may arrive at the right conclusion slowly, another rapidly. So we must add yet another condition to the above, and say that good deliberation means coming to a right conclusion as to what is expedient or ought to be done, and coming to it in the right manner and at the right time.

7 Again, we speak of deliberating well simply, and of deliberating well with a view to a particular kind of end. So good deliberation simply [or without any qualifying epithet] is that which leads to right conclusions as to the means to the end simply;

* Omitting ἰδεῖν.

† *e.g.* this act should be done simply because it is just; I may decide to do it for reputation, or for pleasure's sake, or thinking it to be an act of generosity.

a particular kind of good deliberation is that which leads to right conclusions as to the means to a particular kind of end. And so, when we say that prudent men must deliberate well, good deliberation in this case will be correctness in judging what is expedient to that end of which prudence has a true conception.

Of intelligence.

10. The faculty of intelligence or sound intelli- 1
gence, in respect of which we say a man is intelligent or of sound intelligence, is not the same as science generally, nor as opinion (for then all men would be intelligent), nor is it identical with any particular science, such as medicine, which deals with matters of health, and geometry, which deals with magnitudes; for intelligence has not to do with what is eternal and unchangeable, nor has it to do with events of every kind, but only with those that one may doubt and deliberate about. And so it has to do with the same matters as prudence; but they are not identical: prudence issues orders, for its scope is that which is to be done or not to be done; while intelligence discerns merely (intelligence being equivalent to sound intelligence, and an intelligent man to a man of sound intelligence).

Intelligence, in fact, is equivalent neither to the possession nor to the acquisition of prudence; but just as the learner in science is said to show intelligence when he makes use of the scientific knowledge which he hears from his teacher, so in the domain of prudence a man is said to show intelligence when he makes use of the opinions which he hears from others in judging, and judging fitly—

for soundly [when we speak of sound intelligence] means fitly.

4 And from this use of the term with regard to learning comes its employment to denote that faculty which we imply when we call a man intelligent; for we often speak of the intelligence of a learner.

Of judgme[nt]. Of reason intuitive perception as the bas[is] of the practical intellect.

1 **11.** Judgment (what we mean when we speak of a man of kindly judgment, or say a man has judgment) is a correct discernment of that which is equitable. For the equitable man is thought to be particularly kindly in his judgments, and to pass kindly judgments on some things is considered equitable. But kindly judgment (συγγνώμη) is judgment (γνώμη) which correctly discerns that which is equitable—correctly meaning truly.

2 Now, all these four formed faculties which we have enumerated not unnaturally tend in the same direction. We apply all these terms—judgment, intelligence, prudence, and reason—to the same persons, and talk of people as having, at a certain age, already acquired judgment and reason, and as being prudent and intelligent. For all these four faculties deal with ultimate and particular* facts, and it is in virtue of a power of discrimination in the matters with which prudence deals that we call a person intelligent, or a man of sound judgment, or kindly judgment; for equitable is a common term that is applicable to all that is good in our dealings with others.

* All particular facts (τὰ καθ' ἕκαστον) are ultimate (ἔσχατα), i.e. undemonstrable; but not all ultimate facts (ἔσχατα) are particular facts—as presently appears.

But that which is to be done is always some 3
particular thing, something ultimate. As we have seen, it is the business of the prudent man to know it, and intelligence and judgment also have to do with that which is to be done, which is something ultimate.

And the intuitive reason [the last of the four 4
faculties above enumerated] also deals with ultimate truths, in both senses of the word;* for both primary principles and ultimate facts [in the narrower sense of the word ultimate = particular] are apprehended by the intuitive reason, and not by demonstration: on the one hand, in connection with deductions [of general truths in morals and politics],† reason apprehends the unalterable first principles; on the other hand, in connection with practical calculations, reason apprehends the ultimate [particular] alterable fact which forms the minor premise [in the practical syllogism]. These particular judgments, we may say, are given by reason, as they are the source of our conception of the final cause or end of man; the universal principle is elicited from
the particular facts: these particular facts, there- 5
fore, must be apprehended by a sense or intuitive perception; and this is reason.‡

And so it is thought that these faculties are natural, and that while nature never makes a man wise, she does endow men with judgment and intelligence and reason. This is shown by the fact that 6

* Lit. in both directions, *i.e.* not the last only, but the first also.

† *Cf. supra*, 8, 1, 2.

‡ This *αἴσθησις* may be called *νοῦς*, which is the faculty of universals, because the universal (the general conception of human good) is elicited from these particular judgments.

these powers are believed to accompany certain periods of life, and that a certain age is said to bring reason and judgment, implying that they come by nature.

(The intuitive reason, then, is both beginning and end; for demonstration both starts from and terminates in these ultimate truths.)

And on this account we ought to pay the same respect to the undemonstrated assertions and opinions of men of age and experience and prudence as to their demonstrations. For experience has given them a faculty of vision which enables them to see correctly.*

* Throughout this chapter we are concerned with the practical intellect alone. He has already stated in cap. 6 that the intuitive reason is the basis of the speculative intellect; here he says that it is also the basis of the practical intellect. We have to distinguish here three different employments of the practical faculty:

(1) (if we invert the order), undemonstrated assertion, viz. that under the circumstances this is the right thing to do (§ 6): here the judgment is altogether intuitive; *i.e.* no grounds are given.

(2) demonstration (improperly so called, more properly calculation) that this is the right thing to do; *e.g.* this act is to be done because it is just: here the intuitive reason supplies the minor premise of the practical syllogism (this act is just), and also (indirectly) the major (whatever is just is good), *i.e.* it supplies the data—the several particular intuitions from which the general proposition is elicited: *ἐν ταῖς πρακτικαῖς*, sc. *ἀποδείξεσι* (practical calculations), § 4; *cf.* *τῶν ἀποδείξεων*, § 6, and *οἱ συλλογισμοὶ τῶν πρακτῶν*, 12, 10.

(3) deduction or demonstration (also improperly so called) of general truths in morals and politics: *κατὰ τὰς ἀποδείξεις*, § 4: here also the data from which deduction starts can only be apprehended by intuitive perception or reason: *cf.* I. 4, 7, 7, 20. The difference between (2) and (3) is plainly shown *supra* 8, 2, where *πολιτική* in the wider sense (= *νομοθετική*) which deals with laws, is distinguished from *πολιτική* in the narrower sense which has to do with decrees: *cf.* also I. 2, 7, and X. 9, 14.

We have said, then, what prudence is, and what wisdom is, and what each deals with, and that each is the virtue of a different part of the soul. 7

Of the uses of wisdom and prudence. How prudence is related to cleverness.

12. But here an objection may be raised. "What is the use of them?" it may be asked. "Wisdom does not consider what tends to make man happy (for it does not ask how anything is brought about). Prudence indeed does this, but why do we need it? Prudence is the faculty which deals with what is just and noble and good for man, *i.e.* with those things which it is the part of the good man to do; but the knowledge of them no more makes us apter to do them, if (as has been said) the [moral] virtues are habits, than it does in the case of what is healthy and wholesome—healthy and wholesome, that is, not in the sense of conducing to, but in the sense of issuing from, a healthy habit; for a knowledge of medicine and gymnastics does not make us more able to do these things. 1

"But if it be meant that a man should be prudent, not in order that he may do these acts, but in order that he may become able to do them, then prudence will be no use to those who *are* good, nor even to those who are not. For it will not matter whether they have prudence themselves, or take the advice of others who have it. It will be enough to do in these matters as we do in regard to health; for if we wish to be in health, we do not go and learn medicine. 2

"Again, it seems to be a strange thing that prudence, though inferior to wisdom, must yet govern it, since in every field the practical faculty bears sway and issues orders." 3

We must now discuss these points; for hitherto we have been only stating objections.

4 First, then, we may say that both prudence and wisdom must be desirable in themselves, since each is the virtue of one of the parts of the soul, even if neither of them produces anything.

5 Next, they *do* produce something.

On the one hand, wisdom produces happiness, not in the sense in which medicine produces health, but in the sense in which health produces health;* that is to say, wisdom being a part of complete virtue, its possession and exercise make a man happy.

6 On the other hand [in the sphere of action], man performs his function perfectly when he acts in accordance with both prudence and moral virtue; for while the latter ensures the rightness of the end aimed at, the former ensures the rightness of the means thereto.

The fourth † part of the soul, the vegetative part, or the faculty of nutrition, has no analogous excellence; for it has no power to act or not to act.

7 But as to the objection that prudence makes us no more apt to do what is noble and just, let us take the matter a little deeper, beginning thus:—

* *i.e.* in the sense in which a healthy state of the body (*ὑγίεια* as a *ἕξις* in Aristotle's language) produces healthy performance of the bodily functions (*ὑγίεια* as an *ἐνέργεια*).

† The other three are sense, reason, desire (*αἴσθησις*, *νοῦς*, *ὄρεξις*): *cf. supra*, cap. 2. The excellences or best states of the desires have already been described as the moral virtues. Wisdom and prudence are the excellences of the reason or intellect (*νοῦς* in its widest meaning). Sense (*αἴσθησις*) does not need separate treatment, as it is here regarded as merely subsidiary to reason and desire; for human life is (1) speculative, (2) practical, and no independent place is allowed to the artistic life. The fourth part therefore alone remains.

We allow, on the one hand, that some who do just acts are not yet just; *e.g.* those who do what the laws enjoin either unwillingly or unwittingly, or for some external motive and not for the sake of the acts themselves (though they do that which they ought and all that a good man should do). And, on the other hand, it seems that when a man does the several acts with a certain disposition he is good; *i.e.* when he does them of deliberate purpose, and for the sake of the acts themselves.

Now, the rightness of the purpose is secured by 8
[moral] virtue, but to decide what is proper to be done in order to carry out the purpose belongs not to [moral] virtue, but to another faculty. But we must dwell a little on this point and try to make it quite clear.

There is a faculty which we call cleverness 9
(*δεινότης*)—the power of carrying out the means to any proposed end, and so achieving it. If then the end be noble, the power merits praise; but if the end be base, the power is the power of the villain. So we apply the term clever both to the prudent man and the villain.*

Now, this power is not identical with prudence, 10
but is its necessary condition. But this power, the "eye of the soul" as we may call it, does not attain its perfect development † without moral virtue, as we said before, and as may be shown thus:—

All syllogisms or deductive reasonings about what is to be done have for their starting point [principle or major premise] "the end or the supreme good

* Reading *τοὺς πανούργους*.

† As *φρόνησις*, prudence.

is so and so" (whatever it be; any definition of the good will do for the argument). But it is only to the good man that this presents itself as the good; for vice perverts us and causes us to err about the principles of action. So it is plain, as we said, that it is impossible to be prudent without being morally good.

1 **13.** This suggests a further consideration of moral virtue; for the case is closely analogous to this—I mean that just as prudence is related to cleverness, being not identical with it, but closely akin to it, so is fully developed moral virtue related to natural virtue. *How prudence is related to moral virtue*

All admit that in a certain sense the several kinds of character are bestowed by nature. Justice, a tendency to temperance, courage, and the other types of character are exhibited from the moment of birth. Nevertheless, we look for developed goodness as something different from this, and expect to find these same qualities in another form. For even in children and brutes these natural virtues are present, but without the guidance of reason they are plainly hurtful. So much at least seems to be plain—that just as a strong-bodied creature devoid of sight stumbles heavily when it tries to move, because it
2 cannot see, so is it with this natural virtue; but when it is enlightened by reason it acts surpassingly well; and the natural virtue (which before was only like virtue) will then be fully developed virtue.

We find, then, that just as there are two forms of the calculative faculty, viz. cleverness and prudence, so there are two forms of the moral qualities, viz. natural virtue and fully developed virtue, and that the latter is impossible without prudence.

On this account some people say that all the virtues are forms of prudence, and in particular Socrates held this view, being partly right in his inquiry and partly wrong—wrong in thinking that all the virtues are actually forms of prudence, but right in saying that they are impossible without prudence. 3

This is corroborated by the fact that nowadays every one in defining virtue would, after specifying its field, add that it is a formed faculty or habit in accordance with right reason, "right" meaning "in accordance with prudence." 4

Thus it seems that every one has a sort of inkling that a formed habit or character of this kind (*i.e.* in accordance with prudence) is virtue.

Only a slight change is needed in this expression. Virtue is not simply a formed habit *in accordance with* right reason, but a formed habit *implying* right reason.* But right reason in these matters is prudence. 5

So whereas Socrates held that the [moral] virtues are forms of reason (for he held that they are all modes of knowledge), we hold that they imply reason.

It is evident, then, from what has been said that it is impossible to be good in the full sense without prudence, or to be prudent without moral virtue. And in this way we can meet an objection which may be urged. "The virtues," it may be said, "are found apart from each other; a man who is strongly 6

* μετὰ λόγου: the agent must not only be guided by reason, but by his own reason, not another's.

predisposed to one virtue has not an equal tendency towards all the others, so that he will have acquired this virtue while he still lacks that." We may answer that though this may be the case with the natural virtues, yet it cannot be the case with those virtues for which we call a man good without any qualifying epithet. The presence of the single virtue of prudence implies the presence of all the moral virtues.

And thus it is plain, in the first place, that, even if it did not help practice, we should yet need prudence as the virtue or excellence of a part of our nature; and, in the second place, that purpose cannot be right without both prudence and moral virtue; for the latter makes us desire the end, while the former makes us adopt the right means to the end.

Nevertheless, prudence is not the mistress of wisdom and of the better part of our nature [the reason], any more than medicine is the mistress of health. Prudence does not employ wisdom in her service, but provides means for the attainment of wisdom—does not rule it, but rules in its interests. To assert the contrary would be like asserting that statesmanship rules the gods, because it issues orders about all public concerns [including the worship of the gods.]

BOOK VII.

CHAPTERS 1–10. CHARACTERS OTHER THAN VIRTUE AND VICE.

Of continence and incontinence, heroic virtue and brutality. Of method. Statement of opinions about continence.

1. At this point we will make a fresh start and say that the undesirable forms of moral character are three in number, viz. vice, incontinence, brutality. In the case of two of these it is plain what the opposite is: virtue is the name we give to the opposite of vice, and continence to the opposite of incontinence; but for the opposite of the brutal character it would be most appropriate to take that excellence which is beyond us, the excellence of a hero or a god,—as Homer makes Priam say of Hector that he was surpassingly good—

> "Nor seemed the child
> Of any mortal man, but of a god."

If, then, superlative excellence raises men into gods, as the stories tell us, it is evident that the opposite of the brutal character would be some such superlative excellence. For just as neither virtue nor vice belongs to a brute, so does neither belong to a god; to the latter belongs something higher than virtue, to the former something specifically different from vice.

But as it is rare to find a godlike man (to employ the phrase in use among the Spartans; for when they admire a man exceedingly they call him σεῖος * ἀνήρ), so also is the brutal character rare among men. It occurs most frequently among the barbarians; it is also produced sometimes by disease and organic injuries; and, thirdly, we apply the name as a term of reproach to those who carry vice to a great pitch.†

However, we shall have to make some mention of this disposition further on,‡ and we have already discussed vice; so we will now speak of incontinence and softness and luxuriousness, and also of continence and hardiness—for we must regard these as the names of states or types of character that are neither identical with virtue and vice respectively nor yet generically different.

And here we must follow our usual method, and, after stating the current opinions about these affections, proceed first to raise objections, and then to establish, if possible, the truth of all the current opinions on the subject, or, if not of all, at least of the greater number and the most important. For if the difficulties can be resolved and the popular notions thus confirmed, we shall have attained as much certainty as the subject allows.

It is commonly thought (1) that continence and hardiness are good and laudable, while incontinence and softness are bad and blamable; and, again (2),

* *σεῖος* is a dialectical variety for *θεῖος*, godlike.

† (1) Some men are born brutal; (2) others are made so; (3) others make themselves so.

‡ *Infra*, cap. 5.

that a continent man is identical with one who abides
by his calculations, and an incontinent man with
one who swerves from them; and (3) that the incontinent man, knowing that an act is bad, is impelled
to do it by passion, while the continent man, knowing
that his desires are bad, is withheld from following
them by reason. Also (4) it is commonly thought
that the temperate man is continent and hardy: but
while some hold that conversely the latter is always
temperate, others think that this is not always so;
and while some people hold that the profligate is
incontinent, and that the incontinent man is profligate, and use these terms indiscriminately, others
make a distinction between them. Again (5), with 7
regard to the prudent man, sometimes people say it
is impossible for him to be incontinent; at other times
they say that some men who are prudent and clever
are incontinent. Lastly (6), people are called incontinent even in respect of anger and honour and
gain. These, then, are the common sayings or current
opinions.

Statement of difficulties as to how one can know right and do wrong.

2. But in what sense, it may be objected, can a 1
man judge rightly when he acts incontinently?

Some people maintain that he cannot act so if
he really knows what is right; for it would be
strange, thought Socrates, if, when real knowledge
were in the man, something else should master him
and hale him * about like a slave. Socrates, indeed,
contested the whole position, maintaining that there
is no such thing as incontinence: when a man
acts contrary to what is best, he never, according to

* Reading αὐτόν.

Socrates, has a right judgment of the case, but acts so by reason of ignorance.

Now, this theory evidently conflicts with experience; and with regard to the passion which sways the incontinent man, if it really is due to ignorance, we must ask what kind of ignorance it is due to. For it is plain that, at any rate, he who acts incontinently does not fancy that the act is good till the passion is upon him.

There are other people who in part agree and in part disagree with Socrates. They allow that nothing is able to prevail against knowledge, but do not allow that men never act contrary to what *seems* best; and so they say that the incontinent man, when he yields to pleasure, has not knowledge, but only opinion.

But if, in truth, it be only opinion and not knowledge, and if it be not a strong but a weak belief or judgment that opposes the desires (as is the case when a man is in doubt), we pardon a man for not abiding by it in the face of strong desires; but, in fact, we do not pardon vice nor anything else that we call blamable.

Are we, then, to say that it is prudence that opposes desire [in those cases when we blame a man for yielding]? For it is the strongest form of belief. Surely that would be absurd: for then the same man would be at once prudent and incontinent; but no one would maintain that a prudent man could voluntarily do the vilest acts. Moreover, we have already shown that prudence is essentially a faculty that issues in act; for it is concerned with the ultimate thing [the thing to be done], and implies the possession of all the moral virtues.

Again, if a man cannot be continent without 6
having strong and bad desires, the temperate man will not be continent, nor the continent man temperate; for it is incompatible with the temperate character to have either very violent or bad desires.

They must, however, be both strong and bad in the continent man: for if they were good, the habit that hindered from following them would be bad, so that continence would not be always good; if they were weak and not bad, it would be nothing to respect; and if they were bad, but at the same time weak, it would be nothing to admire.

Again, if continence makes a man apt to abide by 7
any opinion whatsoever, it is a bad thing—as, for instance, if it makes him abide by a false opinion: and if incontinence makes a man apt to abandon any opinion whatsoever, there will be a kind of incontinence that is good, an instance of which is Neoptolemus in the Philoctetes of Sophocles; for he merits praise for being prevented from persevering in the plan which Ulysses had persuaded him to adopt, by the pain which he felt at telling a lie.

Again, the well-known argument of the sophists, 8
though fallacious, makes a difficulty: for, wishing to establish a paradoxical conclusion, so that they may be thought clever if they succeed, they construct a syllogism which puzzles the hearer; for his reason is fettered, as he is unwilling to rest in the conclusion, which is revolting to him, but is unable to advance, since he cannot find a flaw in the argument. Thus it 9

may be argued * that folly combined with incontinence is virtue:—by reason of his incontinence a man does the opposite of that which he judges to be good; but he judges that the good is bad and not to be done; the result is that he will do the good and not the bad.

10 Again, he who pursues and does what is pleasant from conviction, and deliberately chooses these things, would seem [if this doctrine be true] to be better than he who does so, not upon calculation, but by reason of incontinence. For the former is more curable, as his convictions might be changed; but to the incontinent man we may apply the proverb which says, "If water chokes you, what will you wash it down with?" For if he were convinced that what he does is good, a change in his convictions might stop his doing it; but, as it is, though he is convinced that something else is good, he nevertheless does this.

11 Again, if incontinence and continence may be displayed in *anything*, who is the man whom we call incontinent simply? For though no one man unites all the various forms of incontinence, there yet are people to whom we apply the term without any qualification.

12 Something of this sort, then, are the objections that suggest themselves; and of these we must remove some and leave others; † for the resolution of a difficulty is the discovery of the truth.

* This is the sophistical paradox alluded to.

† Of these objections, as well as of the opinions which called them forth, it is to be expected that some should prove groundless, and that others should be established and taken up into the answer.

Solution: to know has many senses; in what sense such a man knows.

3. We have, then, to inquire (1) whether the incontinent man acts with knowledge or not, and what knowledge means here; then (2) what is to be regarded as the field in which continence and incontinence manifest themselves—I mean whether their field be all pleasures and pains, or certain definite classes of these; then (3), with regard to the continent and the hardy man, whether they are the same or different; and so on with the other points that are akin to this inquiry. 1

(But we ought to begin by inquiring whether the species of continence and the species of incontinence of which we are here speaking are to be distinguished from other species by the field of their manifestation or by their form or manner—I mean whether a man is to be called incontinent in this special sense merely because he is incontinent or uncontrolled by reason in certain things, or because he is incontinent in a certain manner, or rather on both grounds; and in connection with this we ought to determine whether or no this incontinence and this continence may be displayed in all things. And our answer to these questions will be that the man who is called simply incontinent, without any qualification, does not display his character in all things, but only in those things in which the profligate manifests himself; nor is it simply an uncontrolled disposition with regard to them that makes him what he is (for then incontinence would be the same as profligacy), but a particular kind of uncontrolled disposition. For the profligate is carried along of his own deliberate choice or purpose, holding that what 2 is pleasant at the moment is always to be pursued; while the incontinent man thinks otherwise, but pursues it all the same.)* [Let us now turn to question (1).]

3 As to the argument that it is true opinion and not knowledge against which men act incontinently, it really makes no difference here; for some of those who merely have opinions are in no doubt at all, but fancy that they have exact knowledge.

4 If then it be said that those who have opinion more readily act against their judgment because of the weakness of their belief, we would answer that there is no such difference between knowledge and opinion; for some people have just as strong a belief in their mere opinions as others have in

* This section (§ 2) seems to me not an alternative to § 1; but a correction of it, or rather a remark to the effect that the whole passage (both § 1 and the discussion introduced by it) ought to be rewritten, and an indication of the way in which this should be done. Of considerable portions of the Nicomachean Ethics we may safely say that the author could not have regarded them as finished in the form in which we have them. It is possible that the author made a rough draft of the whole work, or of the several parts of it, which he kept by him and worked upon,—working some parts up to completion; sometimes rewriting a passage without striking out the original version, or even indicating which was to be retained (*e.g.* the theory of pleasure); more frequently adding an after-thought which required the rewriting of a whole passage, without rewriting it (*e.g.*, to take one instance out of many in Book V., τὸ ἀντιπεπονθός is an after-thought which strictly requires that the whole book should be rewritten); sometimes (as here) making a note of the way in which a passage should be rewritten. Suppose, if need be, that the work, left in this incomplete state, was edited and perhaps further worked upon by a later hand, and we have enough, I think, to account for the facts.

what they really know, of which Heraclitus is an instance.*

But we use the word know (ἐπίστασθαι) in two 5
different senses: he who has knowledge which he is not now using is said to know a thing, and also he who is now using his knowledge. Having knowledge, therefore, which is not now present to the mind, about what one ought not to do, will be different from having knowledge which is now present. Only in the latter sense, not in the former, does it seem strange that a man should act against his knowledge.

Again, since these reasonings involve two kinds 6
of premises [a universal proposition for major and a particular for minor], there is nothing to prevent a man from acting contrary to his knowledge though he has both premises, if he is now using the universal only, and not the particular; for the particular is the thing to be done.

Again, different kinds of universal propositions may be involved: one may concern the agent himself, another the thing; for instance, you may reason (1) "all men are benefited by dry things, and I am a man;" and (2) "things of this kind are dry;" but the second minor, "this thing is of this kind," may be unknown or the knowledge of it may be dormant.†

These distinctions, then, will make a vast difference,

* Alluding to the Heraclitean doctrine of the union of opposites, which Aristotle rather unfairly interprets as a denial of the law of contradiction. *Cf.* Met. iii. 7, 1012^a 24.

† *i.e.* not effective, οὐκ ἐνεργεῖ: in § 10 ἐνεργεῖ is used again of the minor which when joined to the major is effective.

so much so that it does not seem strange that a man should act against his knowledge if he knows in one way, though it does seem strange if he knows in another way.

7 But, again, it is possible for a man to "have knowledge" in yet another way than those just mentioned: we see, I mean, that "having knowledge without using it" includes different modes of having, so that a man may have it in one sense and in another sense not have it; for instance, a man who is asleep, or mad, or drunk. But people who are under the influence of passion are in a similar state; for anger, and sexual desire and the like do evidently alter the condition of the body, and in some cases actually produce madness. It is plain, then, that the incontinent man must be allowed to have knowledge in the same sort of way as those who are asleep, mad, or drunk.*

8 But to repeat the words of knowledge is no proof that a man really has knowledge [in the full sense of having an effective knowledge]; for even when they are under the influence of these passions people repeat demonstrations and sayings of Empedocles,

* Action in spite of knowledge presents no difficulty (1) if that knowledge be not present at the time of action, § 5, or (2) if, though the major (or majors) be known and present, the minor (or one of the minors) be unknown or absent, § 6. But (3) other cases remain which can only be explained by a further distinction introduced in § 7; *i.e.* a man who has knowledge may at times be in a state in which his knowledge, though present, has lost its reality—in which, though he may repeat the old maxims, they mean no more to him than to one who talks in his sleep. § 7, I venture to think, is (like § 2) not a repetition or an alternative version, but an after-thought, which requires the rewriting of the whole passage.

just as learners string words together before they understand their meaning—the meaning must be ingrained in them, and that requires time. So we must hold that the incontinent repeat words in the same sort of way that actors do.

Again, one may inquire into the cause of this 9
phenomenon [of incontinence] by arguments based upon its special nature,* as follows:—You may have (1) a universal judgment, (2) a judgment about particular facts which fall at once within the province of sense or perception; but when the two are joined together,† the conclusion must in matters of speculation be assented to by the mind, in matters of practice be carried out at once into act; for instance, if you judge (1) "all sweet things are to be tasted," (2) "this thing before me is sweet"—a particular fact, —then, if you have the power and are not hindered, you cannot but at once put the conclusion ["this is to be tasted"] into practice.

Now, when you have on the one side the 10
universal judgment forbidding you to taste, and on the other side the universal judgment, "all sweet things are pleasant,"‡ with the corresponding particular, "this thing before me is sweet" (but it is the particular judgment which is effective), and appetite is present—then, though the former train of reasoning bids you avoid this, appetite moves you [to

* φυσικῶς, by arguments based upon the special nature of the subject-matter, opposed to λογικῶς, by arguments of a general nature; accordingly, in what follows both the elements of reason and desire are taken into account.

† In a practical syllogism.

‡ Notice that ἡδὺ here corresponds to γενέσθαι δεῖ above.

take it]; for appetite is able to put the several bodily organs in motion.

And thus it appears that it is in a way under the influence of reason, that is to say of opinion, that people act incontinently—opinion, too, that is, not in itself, but only accidentally, opposed to right reason.
11 For it is the desire, not the opinion, that is opposed to right reason.*

And this is the reason why brutes cannot be incontinent; they have no universal judgments, but only images and memories of particular facts.

12 As to the process by which the incontinent man gets out of this ignorance and recovers his knowledge, the account of it will be the same as in the case of a man who is drunk or asleep, and will not be peculiar to this phenomenon; and for such an account we must go to the professors of natural science.

13 But since the minor premise † is an opinion or judgment about a fact of perception, and determines action, the incontinent man, when under the influence of passion, either has it not, or has it in a sense in which, as we explained, having is equivalent,

* The minor premise, "this is sweet," obviously is not "opposed to right reason;" but is not the major premise? In one of the two forms in which it here appears, viz. "all sweet things are pleasant," it certainly is not so opposed; it merely states a fact of experience which the continent or temperate man assents to as much as the incontinent. In its other form, however, "all sweet things are to be tasted," the judgment is "opposed to right reason;" but it is so because desire for an object condemned by reason has been added; and thus it may be said that it is not the opinion, but the desire, which is opposed to right reason. It is a defect in the exposition here that the difference between these two forms of the major premise is not more expressly noticed.

† Of the syllogism which would forbid him to taste.

not to knowing in the full sense, but to repeating words as a drunken man repeats the sayings of Empedocles.

And thus, since the minor premise is not universal,
and is thought to be less a matter of knowledge than
the universal judgment [or major premise], it seems
that what Socrates sought to establish really is the
case; * for when passion carries a man away, what is 14
present to his mind is not what is regarded as knowledge in the strict sense, nor is it such knowledge
that is perverted by his passion, but sensitive knowledge merely. †

Of incontinence in the strict and in the metaphorical sense.

4. So much, then, for the question whether the 1
incontinent man knows or not, and in what sense it
is possible to act incontinently with knowledge. We
next have to consider whether a man can be
incontinent simply, or only incontinent in some
particular way, ‡ and, if the former be the case, what
is the field in which the character is manifested.

It is evident that it is in the matter of pleasures and pains that both continent and hardy and incontinent and soft men manifest their characters.

Of the sources of pleasure, some are necessary, and 2
others are desirable in themselves but admit of
excess: "necessary" are the bodily processes, such

* Reading full stop after 'Εμπεδοκλέους and comma after ὅρου.

† Or the perception of the particular fact. After all Socrates is right: the incontinent man does not really know; the fact does not come home to him in its true significance: he says it is bad, but says it as an actor might, without feeling it; what he realizes is that it is pleasant.

‡ As a man may be greedy (ἁπλῶς), or greedy for a particular kind of food.

as nutrition, the propagation of the species, and generally those bodily functions with which we said that profligacy and temperance have to do; others, though not necessary, are in themselves desirable, such as victory, honour, wealth, and other things ot the kind that are good and pleasant.*

Now, those who go to excess in these latter in spite of their own better reason are not called incontinent simply, but with a qualifying epithet, as incontinent with respect to money, or gain, or honour, or anger — not simply, since they are different characters, and only called incontinent in virtue of a resemblance—just as the victor in the last Olympic games was called a man; for though the meaning of the name as applied to him was but slightly different from its common meaning, still it was different.†

And this may be proved thus: incontinence is blamed, not simply as a mistake, but as a kind of vice, either of vice simply, or of some particular vice; but those who are thus incontinent [in the pursuit of wealth, etc.] are not thus blamed.

But of the characters that manifest themselves in the matter of bodily enjoyments, with which we say the temperate and the profligate are concerned, he

* Called also ἁπλῶς ἀγαθά, "good in themselves," as in V. 1, 9 (*cf.* V. 2, 6), and ἐκτὸς ἀγαθά, "external goods," as in I. 8, 2.

† As we do not know the facts to whieh Aristotle alludes we can only conjecture his meaning. It may be that the man in question had certain physical peculiarities, so that though he "passed for a man" he was not quite a man in the common meaning of the name. So Locke asks (Essay iv. 10, 13), "Is a changeling a man or a beast?"

who goes to excess in pursuing what is pleasant and avoiding what is painful, in the matter of hunger and thirst, and heat and cold, and all things that affect us by touch or taste, and who does this not of deliberate choice, but contrary to his deliberate choice and reasoning, is called incontinent—not with the addition that he is incontinent with respect to this particular thing, as anger, but simply incontinent.

A proof of this is that people are also called soft 4
in these latter matters, but not in any of the former [honour, gain, etc.].

And on this account we group the incontinent with the profligate and the continent and the temperate (but do not class with them any of those who are metaphorically called continent and incontinent), because they are in a way concerned with the same pleasures and pains. They are, in fact, concerned with the same matters, but their behaviour is different; for whereas the other three deliberately choose what they do, the incontinent man does not.

And so a man who, without desire, or with only a moderate desire, pursues excess of pleasure, and avoids even slight pains, would more properly be called profligate than one who is impelled so to act by violent desires; for what would the former do if the violent passions of youth were added, and if it were violent pain to him to forego the satisfaction of his natural appetites?

But some of our desires and pleasures are to be 5
classed as noble and good (for some of the things that please us are naturally desirable), while others are

the reverse of this, and others are intermediate between the two, as we explained before,*—such things as money, gain, victory, and honour falling within the first class. With regard both to these, then, and to the intermediate class, men are blamed not for being affected by them, or desiring them, or caring for them, but only for doing so in certain ways and beyond the bounds of moderation. So we blame those who are moved by, or pursue, some good and noble object to an unreasonable extent, as, for instance, those who care too much for honour, or for their children or parents: for these, too, are noble objects, and men are praised for caring about them; but still one might go too far in them also, if one were to fight even against the gods, like Niobe, or to do as did Satyrus, who was nicknamed Philopator from his affection for his father—for he seemed to carry his affection to the pitch of folly.

In these matters, then, there is no room for vice or wickedness for the reason mentioned, viz. that all these are objects that are in themselves desirable, though excess in them is not commendable, and is to be avoided.

Similarly, in these matters there is no room for incontinence strictly so called (for incontinence is not only to be avoided, but is actually blamable), but because of the similarity of the state of mind we do here use the term incontinence with a qualification, saying "incontinent in this or in that," just as we apply the term "bad physician" or "bad actor" to a

* As in § 2 only two classes are given, it is probable that these words are an interpolation, and that § 5 and 6 (which pave the way for the next chapter) were intended to replace § 2. The intermediate class of § 5 is the necessary of § 2.

man whom we should not call bad simply or without a qualifying epithet. Just as in the latter case, then, the term badness or vice is applied, not simply, but with a qualification, because each of these qualities is not a vice strictly, but only analogous to a vice, so in this case also it is plain that we must understand that only to be strictly incontinence (or continence) which is manifested in those matters with which temperance and profligacy are concerned, while that which is manifested with regard to anger is only metaphorically called so; and therefore we call a man "incontinent in anger," as "in honour" or "in gain," adding a qualifying epithet.

Of incontinence in respect of brutal or morbid appetites.

5. While some things are naturally pleasant (of 1
which some are pleasant in themselves, others pleasant to certain classes of animals or men), other things, though not naturally pleasant, come to be pleasant (1) through organic injuries, or (2) through custom, or again (3) through an originally bad nature; and in each of these three classes of things a corresponding character is manifested.

For instance [taking (3) first], there are the brutal 2
characters, such as the creature in woman's shape that is said to rip up pregnant females and devour the embryos, or the people who take delight, as some of the wild races about the Black Sea are said to take delight, in such things as eating raw meat or human flesh, or giving their children to one another to feast upon; or, again, in such things as are reported of Phalaris.

These, then, are what we call brutal natures 3
[corresponding to (3)]: but in other cases the dis-

position is engendered by disease or madness; for instance, there was the man who slew and ate his mother, and that other who devoured the liver of his fellow-slave [and these correspond to (1)].

Other habits are either signs of a morbid state, or the result of custom [and so come either under (1) or under (2)]; *e.g.* plucking out the hair and biting the nails, or eating cinders and earth, or, again, the practice of unnatural vice; for these habits sometimes come naturally,* sometimes by custom, as in the case of those who have been ill treated from their childhood.

Whenever nature is the cause of these morbid habits, no one would think of applying the term incontinence, any more than we should call women incontinent for the part they play in the propagation of the species; nor should we apply the term to those who, by habitual indulgence, have brought themselves into a morbid state.†

Habits of this kind, then, fall without the pale of vice, just as the brutal character does; but when a man who has these impulses conquers or is conquered by them, this is not to be called [continence or] incontinence strictly, but only metaphorically, just as the man who behaves thus in the matter of his angry passions cannot be strictly called in-

* *i.e.* here "by disease:" φύσις bears three different senses in the space of a few lines—(1) in § 1, beginning, natural = in accordance with the *true* nature of the thing, the thing as it ought to be; (2) in § 1, end, natural = what a man is born with, as opposed to subsequent modifications of this; (3) in § 3 natural includes what my body does by powers in it over which I have no control, *e.g.* modifications of my nature produced by disease.

† Because incontinence is a human weakness; these acts are brutal or morbid.

continent. For even folly, and cowardice, and profligacy, and ill temper, whenever they are carried beyond a certain pitch, are either brutal or morbid.
When a man is naturally so constituted as to be 6
frightened at anything, even at the sound of a mouse, his cowardice is brutal [inhuman]; but in the well-known case of a man who was afraid of a weasel, disease was the cause. And of irrational human beings, those who by nature are devoid of reason, and live only by their senses, are to be called brutal, as some races of remote barbarians, while those in whom the cause is disease (*e.g.* epilepsy) or insanity are to be called morbidly irrational.

Again, a man may on occasion have one of these 7
impulses without being dominated by it, as, for instance, if Phalaris on some occasion desired to eat the flesh of a child, or to indulge his unnatural lusts, and yet restrained himself; and, again, it is possible not only to have the impulse, but to be dominated by it.

To conclude, then: as in the case of vice there is 8
a human vice that is called vice simply, and another sort that is called with a qualifying epithet "brutal" or "morbid vice" (not simply vice), so also it is plain that there is a sort of incontinence that is called brutal, and another that is called morbid incontinence, while that only is called incontinence simply which can be classed with human profligacy.

We have thus shown that incontinence and con- 9
tinence proper have to do only with those things with which profligacy and temperance have to do, and that in other matters there is a sort of incon-

tinence to which the name is applied metaphorically and with a qualifying epithet.

Incontinence in anger less blamed than in appetite.

6. The next point we have to consider is that incontinence in anger is less disgraceful than incontinence in appetite.

The angry passions seem to hear something of what reason says, but to mis-hear it, like a hasty servant who starts off before he has heard all you are saying, and so mistakes his errand, or like a dog that barks so soon as he hears a noise, without waiting to find out if it be a friend. Just so our angry passions, in the heat and haste of their nature, hearing something but not hearing what reason orders, make speed to take vengeance. For when reason or imagination announces an insult or slight, the angry passion infers, so to speak, that its author is to be treated as an enemy, and then straightway boils up; appetite, on the other hand, if reason or sense do but proclaim "this is pleasant," rushes to enjoy it. Thus anger, in some sort, obeys reason, which appetite does not. The latter, therefore, is the more disgraceful; for he who is incontinent in anger succumbs in some sort to reason, while the other succumbs not to reason, but to appetite.

Again, when impulses are natural, it is more excusable to follow them (for even with our appetites it is more pardonable to follow them when they are common to all men, and the more pardonable the commoner they are); but anger and ill temper are more natural than desire for excessive and unnecessary pleasures, as we see in the story of the man who excused himself for beating his father. "He beat his own father," he said, "and that father beat his, and my son here," pointing to his child, "will beat me when he is a man; for it runs in the family." And there is that other story of the man who was being dragged out of the house by his son, and bade him stop at the doorway; for he had dragged his own father so far, but no further.

Again, the more a man is inclined to deliberate 3
malice, the more unjust he is. Now, the hot-tempered man is not given to deliberate malice, nor is anger of that underhand nature, but asserts itself openly. But of appetite we may say what the poets say of Aphrodite: "Craft-weaving daughter of Cyprus;" or what Homer says of her "embroidered girdle,"

"Whose charm doth steal the reason of the wise." *

If then this incontinence be more unjust, it is more disgraceful than incontinence in anger, and is to be called incontinence simply, and a sort of vice.

Again, when a man commits an outrage, he does 4
not feel pain in doing it, but rather pleasure, while he who acts in anger always feels pain as he is acting. If then the acts which rouse the justest indignation are the more unjust, it follows that incontinence in appetite is more unjust [than incontinence in anger]; for such outrage is never committed in anger.†

Thus it is plain that incontinence in appetite is 5
more disgraceful than incontinence in anger, and that

* Il., xiv. 214, 217.

† *e.g.* cruelty in the heat of battle rouses less indignation than ill-treatment of women afterwards. For a similar reason profligacy was said (III. 12) to be worse than cowardice.

continence and incontinence proper have to do with bodily appetites and pleasures.

5 But now let us see what differences we find in these bodily appetites and pleasures.

As we said at the outset, some of them are human and natural in kind and degree; others are signs of a brutal nature; others, again, are the result of organic injury or disease.

Now, it is with the first of these only that temperance and profligacy have to do: and for this reason we do not call beasts either temperate or profligate, except it be metaphorically, if we find a whole class of animals distinguished from others by peculiar lewdness and wantonness and voracity; for there is no purpose or deliberate calculation in what they do, but they are in an unnatural state, like madmen.

7 Brutality is less dangerous than vice, but more horrible; for the noble part is not corrupted here, as in a man who is merely vicious in a human way, but is altogether absent. To ask which is worse, then, would be like comparing inanimate things with animate: the badness of that which lacks the originating principle is always less mischievous; and reason [which the brutal man lacks] is here the originating principle. (To compare these, then, would be like comparing injustice with an unjust man: each is in its own way the worse.*) For a bad man

* This comparison is rendered superfluous by the preceding one (which probably was meant to be substituted for it), and is not very apt as it stands. We should rather expect πρὸς τὸ ἄδικον: the sense would then be, "injustice is morally worse than an unjust act which does not proceed from an unjust character, but the latter may be a worse evil;" *e.g.* humanity has suffered more by well-meaning persecutors than by the greatest villains. Cf. V. 11, 8.

would do ten thousand times as much harm as a brute.

Incontinence yields to pleasure, softness to pain. Two kinds of incontinence, the hasty and the weak.

7. With regard to the pleasures and pains of touch 1
and taste, and the corresponding desires and aversions, which we before marked out as the field of profligacy and temperance, it is possible to be so disposed as to succumb to allurements which most people resist, or so as to resist allurements to which most people succumb. When they are exhibited in the matter of pleasures, the former of these characters is called incontinent and the latter continent; when they are exhibited in the matter of pains, the former is called soft and the latter hardy. The character of the general run of men falls between these two, inclining perhaps rather to the worse.

But since some pleasures are necessary, while 2
others are not, and since the necessary pleasures are necessary in certain quantities only, but not in too great nor yet in too small quantities, and since the same is true of appetites and of pains, he who pursues pleasures that fall beyond the pale of legitimate pleasures, or pursues any pleasures to excess,* is called profligate, if he pursues them of deliberate

* Dropping the second ἢ or substituting εἰ for it. If we take it thus, the distinction may be illustrated by the distinction which opinion in England draws between opium-smoking and tobacco-smoking. Opium-smoking is commonly regarded by us as a ὑπερβολή, as a pleasure that in any degree is beyond the pale of legitimate pleasures; a man who is too much given to tobacco-smoking is regarded as pursuing καθ' ὑπερβολάς (in excess) a pleasure which in moderation is legitimate. If we adopt Bywater's conjecture ᾗ ὑπερβολαί the sense will be, "he who pursues excessive pleasures as such, that is of deliberate purpose."

purpose for their own sake and not for any result which follows from them; for such a man must be incapable of remorse—must be incurable therefore; for he who feels no remorse is incurable. In the opposite extreme is he who falls short of the mean (while he who observes the mean is temperate). So with the man who avoids bodily pains, not because he is momentarily overcome, but of deliberate purpose.

3 But those who act thus without deliberate purpose may do so either to gain pleasure or to escape the pain of desire, and we must accordingly distinguish these from one another.

But all would allow that a man who does something disgraceful without desire, or with only a moderate desire, is worse than if he had a violent desire; and that if a man strike another in cool blood he is worse than if he does it in anger; for what would he do if he were in a passion? The profligate man, therefore, is worse than the incontinent.

Of the characters mentioned, then, we must distinguish softness from profligacy.

4 The continent character is opposed to the incontinent, and the hardy to the soft; for hardiness implies that you endure, while continence implies that you overcome, and enduring is different from overcoming, just as escaping a defeat is different from winning a victory; so continence is better than hardiness.

5 But he that gives way to what the generality of men can and do resist is soft and luxurious (for luxury, too, is a kind of softness),—the sort of man that suffers his cloak to trail along the ground rather

than be at the pains to pull it up; that plays the invalid, and yet does not consider himself wretched, though it is a wretched man that he imitates.

Similarly with continence and incontinence. If 6
a man give way to violent and excessive pleasures or pains, we do not marvel, but are ready to pardon him if he struggled, like Philoctetes when bitten by the viper in the play of Theodectes, or Cercyon in the Alope of Carcinus; or like people who, in trying to restrain their laughter, burst out into a violent explosion, as happened to Xenophantus. But we do marvel when a man succumbs to and cannot resist what the generality of men are able to hold out against, unless the cause be hereditary disposition or disease (*e.g.* softness is hereditary in the Scythian kings, and the female is naturally softer than the male).

The man that is given up to amusement is gene- 7
rally thought to be profligate, but in fact he is soft; for amusement is relaxation, since it is a rest from labour; and among those who take too much relaxation are those who are given up to amusement.

There are two kinds of incontinence, the hasty and 8
the weak. Some men deliberate, but, under the influence of passion, do not abide by the result of their deliberations; others are swayed by passion because they do not deliberate; for as it is not easy to tickle a man who has just been tickling you, so there are people who when they see what is coming, and are forewarned and rouse themselves and their reason, are able to resist the impulse, whether it be pleasant or painful. People of quick sensibility or of a melan-

cholic temperament are most liable to incontinence of the hasty sort; such people do not wait to hear the voice of reason, because, in the former case through the rapidity, in the latter case through the intensity of their impressions, they are apt to follow their imagination.

Incontinence compared with vice and virtue.

8. Again, a profligate man, as we said, is not given to remorse, for he abides by his deliberate purpose; but an incontinent man is always apt to feel remorse. So the case is not as it was put in one of the difficulties we enumerated,* but the former is incurable, the latter is curable. For full-formed vice [profligacy] seems to be like such diseases as dropsy or consumption, incontinence like epilepsy; for the former is chronic, the latter intermittent badness.

Indeed, we may roundly say that incontinence is generically different from vice; for the vicious man knows not, but the incontinent man knows, the nature of his acts.†

But of these incontinent characters, those who momentarily lose their reason are not so bad as those who retain their reason but disobey it;‡ for the latter give way to a slighter impulse, and cannot, like the former, be said to act without deliberation. For an incontinent man is like one who gets drunk quickly and with little wine, *i.e.* with less than most men.

* *Cf. supra*, **2**, 10, 11.

† The incontinent man, when the fit is over and the better part of him reasserts itself (*cf.* § 5), recognizes the badness of his act; but the vicious man, though he is aware that his acts are called bad, dissents from the judgments of society (*cf.* **9**, 7), and so may be said not to know: *cf.* III. **1**, 12.

‡ The weak (ἀσθενεῖς) are worse than the hasty (προπετεῖς): *cf. supra*, **7**, 8.

We have seen that incontinence is not vice, but 3
perhaps we may say that it is in a manner vice. The difference is that the vicious man acts with deliberate purpose, while the incontinent man acts against it. But in spite of this difference their acts are similar; as Demodocus said against the Milesians, "The Milesians are not fools, but they act like fools." So an incontinent man is not unjust, but will act unjustly.

It is the character of the incontinent man to 4
pursue, without being convinced of their goodness, bodily pleasures that exceed the bounds of moderation and are contrary to right reason; but the profligate man is convinced that these things are good because it is his character to pursue them: the former, then, may be easily brought to a better mind, the latter not. For virtue preserves, but vice destroys the principle; but in matters of conduct the motive [end or final cause] is the principle [beginning or efficient cause] of action, holding the same place here that the hypotheses do in mathematics.* In mathematics no reasoning or demonstration can instruct us about these principles or starting points; so here it is not reason but virtue, either natural or acquired by training, that teaches us to hold right opinions about the principle of action. A man of this character, then, is temperate, while a man of opposite character is profligate.

But there is a class of people who are apt to be 5
momentarily deprived of their right senses by passion, and who are swayed by passion so far as not to act

* *i.e.* the definitions; not the axioms, since in Aristotle's language a ὑπόθεσις, strictly speaking, involves the assumption of the existence of a corresponding object.

according to reason, but not so far that it has become part of their nature to believe that they ought to pursue pleasures of this kind without limit. These are the incontinent, who are better than the profligate, and not absolutely bad; for the best part of our nature, the principle of right conduct, still survives in them.

To these are opposed another class of people who are wont to abide by their resolutions, and not to be deprived of their senses by passion at least. It is plain from this, then, that the latter is a good type of character, the former not good.

Continence and incontinence not identical with keeping and breaking a resolution.

9. Now, who is to be called continent? he who abides by any kind of reason and any kind of purpose, or he who abides by a right purpose? And who is to be called incontinent? he who abandons any kind of purpose and any kind of reason, or he who abandons a true reason and a right purpose?—a difficulty which we raised before.* Is it not the case that though "accidentally" it may be any kind, yet "essentially" it is a true reason and a right purpose that the one abides by and the other abandons? For if you choose or pursue A for the sake of B, you pursue and choose B "essentially," but A "accidentally." But by "essentially" (καθ' αὑτό) we mean "absolutely" or "simply" (ἁπλῶς); so that we may say that in a certain sense it may be any kind of opinion, but absolutely or simply it is a true opinion that the one abides by and the other abandons.

But there is another class of persons that are apt

* *Cf. supra*, 2, 7–9.

to stick to their opinions (I mean those whom we call stubborn or obstinate), because they are averse to persuasion and not readily induced to change their mind. These bear some resemblance to the continent, as the prodigal does to the liberal, and the foolhardy to the courageous, but in many respects are different. For it is changing his mind at the prompting of passion or appetite that the continent man dislikes; he is ready enough on occasion to yield to reason: but it is to reason especially that the obstinate man will not listen, while he often conceives a passion, and is led about by his pleasures.

The opinionated, the ignorant, and the boorish are 3
all obstinate—the opinionated from motives of pleasure and pain; for they delight in the sense of victory when they hold out against argument, and are pained if their opinion comes to naught like a decree that is set aside. They resemble the incontinent man, therefore, rather than the continent.

Sometimes also people abandon their resolutions 4
from something else than incontinence, as, for instance, Neoptolemus in the Philoctetes of Sophocles. It may be said, indeed, that pleasure was his motive in abandoning his resolution: but it was a noble pleasure; for truth was fair in his eyes, but Ulysses had persuaded him to lie. For he who acts with pleasure for motive is not always either profligate, or worthless, or incontinent, but only when his motive is a base pleasure.

Again, as there are people whose character it is to 5
take too little delight in the pleasures of the body, and who swerve from reason in this direction, those who

come between these and the incontinent are the continent. For while the incontinent swerve from reason because of an excess, and these because of a deficiency, the continent man holds fast and is not turned aside by the one or the other.

But if continence be a good thing, the characters that are opposed to it must be bad, as in fact they evidently are; only, since the other extreme is found but rarely and in few cases, incontinence comes to be regarded as the only opposite of continence, just as profligacy comes to be regarded as the only opposite of temperance.

6 We often apply names metaphorically; and so we come to speak metaphorically of the continence of the temperate man. For it is the nature both of the continent and of the temperate man never to do anything contrary to reason for the sake of bodily pleasures; but whereas the former has, the latter has not bad desires, and whereas the latter is of such a nature as to take no delight in what is contrary to reason, the former is of such a nature as to take delight in, but not to be swayed by such things.

7 The incontinent and the profligate also resemble each other, though they are different: both pursue bodily pleasures, but the latter pursues them on principle,* while the former does not.

Prudence is not, but cleverness is compatible with incontinence.

1 **10.** It is impossible for the same man to be at once prudent and incontinent; for we have shown that a man cannot be prudent without being at the same time morally good.

* Literally, thinking that he ought (οἰόμενος δεῖν); *i.e.* adopting them as his end.

Moreover, a man is not prudent simply because 2
he knows—he must also be apt to act according to his knowledge; but the incontinent man is not apt to act according to his knowledge (though there is nothing to prevent a man who is clever at calculating means from being incontinent; and so people sometimes think a man prudent and yet incontinent, because this cleverness is related to prudence in the manner before * explained, resembling prudence as an intellectual faculty, but differing from it by the
absence of purpose): nor indeed does he know as 3
one who knows and is now using his knowledge, but as one may know who is asleep or drunk.

He acts voluntarily (for in a manner he knows what he is doing and with what object), and yet is not bad: for his purpose is good; so he is only half bad. Moreover, incontinent men are not unjust,† for they are not deliberately malicious—some of them being apt to swerve from their deliberate resolutions, others of melancholic temper and apt to act without deliberating at all. An incontinent man, then, may be compared to a state which always makes excellent decrees and has good laws, but never carries them out; as Anaxandrides jestingly says—

"So willed the state that takes no heed of laws."

The bad man, on the contrary, may be compared to a 4
state that carries out its laws, but has bad laws.

* *Cf. supra*, VI. 12, 9.

† Though they do what is unjust or wrong. It must be remembered that above (V. 1, 12–end) it was laid down that *all* vicious action, when viewed in relation to others, is unjust (in the wider sense of the term).

Both incontinence and continence imply something beyond the average character of men; for the one is more steadfast than most men can be, the other less.

Of the several kinds of incontinence, that of the melancholic temper is more curable than that of those who make resolutions but do not keep them, and that which proceeds from custom than that which rests on natural infirmity: it is easier to alter one's habit than to change one's nature. For the very reason why habits are hard to change is that they are a sort of second nature, as Euenus says—

> "Train men but long enough to what you will,
> And that shall be their nature in the end."

We have now considered the nature of continence and incontinence, of hardiness and softness, and the relation of these types of character to each other.

CHAPTERS 11—14. OF PLEASURE.

11. The consideration of pleasure and pain also falls within the scope of the political philosopher, since he has to construct the end by reference to which we call everything good or bad.

We must now discuss pleasure. Opinions about it.

Moreover, this is one of the subjects we are bound to discuss; for we said that moral virtue and vice have to do with pleasures and pains, and most people say that happiness implies pleasure, which is the reason of the name μακάριος, blessed, from χαίρειν, to rejoice.

Now, (1) some people think that no pleasure is

good, either essentially or accidentally, for they say that good and pleasure are two distinct things; (2) others think that though some pleasures are good most are bad; (3) others, again, think that even though all pleasures be good, yet it is impossible that the supreme good can be pleasure.

(1) It is argued that pleasure cannot be good, (*a*) 4
because all pleasure is a felt transition to a natural state, but a transition or process is always generically different from an end, *e.g.* the process of building is generically different from a house; (*b*) because the temperate man avoids pleasures; (*c*) because the prudent man pursues the painless, not the pleasant; (*d*) because pleasures impede thinking, and that in proportion to their intensity (for instance, the sexual pleasures: no one engaged therein could think at all); (*e*) because there is no art of pleasure, and yet every good thing has an art devoted to its production; (*f*) because pleasure is the pursuit of children and brutes.

(2) It is argued that not all pleasures are good, 5
because some are base and disgraceful, and even hurtful; for some pleasant things are unhealthy.

(3) It is argued that pleasure is not the supreme good, because it is not an end, but a process or transition.—These, then, we may take to be the current opinions on the subject.

Answers to arguments against goodness of pleasure. Ambiguity of good and pleasant. Pleasure not a transition, but unimpeded activity.

12. But that these arguments do not prove that 1
pleasure is not good, or even the highest good, may be shown as follows.

In the first place, since "good" is used in two senses ("good in itself" and "relatively good"), natures and faculties will be called good in two senses, and so also will motions and processes: and when they are called bad, this sometimes means that they are bad in themselves, though for particular persons not bad but desirable; sometimes that they are not desirable even for particular persons, but desirable occasionally and for a little time, though in themselves not desirable; while some of them are not even pleasures, though they seem to be—I mean those that involve pain and are used medicinally, such as those of sick people.

In the second place, since the term good may be applied both to activities and to faculties, those activities that restore us to our natural faculties [or state] are accidentally pleasant.

But in the satisfaction of the animal appetites that which is active is not that part of our faculties * or of our nature which is in want, but that part which is in its normal state; for there are pleasures which involve no previous pain or appetite, such as those of philosophic study, wherein our nature is not conscious of any want.

This is corroborated by the fact that while our natural wants are being filled we do not take delight in the same things which delight us when that process has been completed: when the want has been filled we take delight in things that are pleasant in themselves, while it is being filled in their opposites; for we then take delight in sharp and bitter things, none of which are naturally pleasant or pleasant in them-

* *Cf. infra*, **14**, 7. I have frequently in this chapter rendered ἕξις by faculty, in order to express the opposition to ἐνέργεια, activity or exercise of faculty; but no single word is satisfactory.

selves. The pleasures, then, which these things give are not real pleasures; for pleasures are related to one another as the things that produce them.

Again, it does not necessarily follow, as some 3
maintain, that there is something else better than pleasure, as the end is better than the process or transition to the end: for a pleasure is not a transition, nor does it always even imply a transition; but it is an activity [or exercise of faculty], and itself an end: further, it is not in becoming something, but in doing something that we feel pleasure: and, lastly, the end is not always something different from the process or transition, but it is only when something is being brought to the completion of its nature that this is the case.

For these reasons it is not proper to say that pleasure is a felt transition, but rather that it is an exercise of faculties that are in their natural state, substituting "unimpeded" for "felt."

Some people, indeed, think that pleasure is a transition, just because it is in the full sense good, supposing that the exercise of faculty is a transition; but it is in fact something different.*

But to say that pleasures are bad because some 4
pleasant things are unhealthy, is like saying that health is bad because some healthy things are bad for money-making. Both are bad in this respect, but that

* The argument in full would be thus: pleasure is good; but good is exercise of faculty (ἐνέργεια), and this is a process or transition (γένεσις); ∴ pleasure is a transition. But according to Aristotle the highest ἐνέργεια involves no transition or motion at all (*cf.* 14, 8), and in every true ἐνέργεια, even when a transition is involved, the end is attained at every moment. *Cf.* Met. ix. 6. 1048b.

does not make them bad: even philosophic study is sometimes injurious to health.

5 As to pleasure being an impediment to thinking, the fact is that neither prudence nor any other faculty is impeded by the pleasure proper to its exercise, but by other pleasures; the pleasure derived from study and learning will make us study and learn more.

6 That there should be no art devoted to the production of any kind of pleasure, is but natural; for art never produces an activity, but only makes it possible: the arts of perfumery and cookery, however, are usually considered to be arts of pleasure.

7 As to the arguments that the temperate man avoids pleasure, that the prudent man pursues the painless life, and that children and brutes pursue pleasure, they may all be met in the same way, viz. thus:—

As we have already explained in what sense all pleasures are to be called good in themselves, and in what sense not good, we need only say that pleasures of a certain kind are pursued by brutes and by children, and that freedom from the corresponding pains is pursued by the prudent man—the pleasures, namely, that involve appetite and pain, *i.e.* the bodily pleasures (for these do so), and excess in them, the deliberate pursuit of which constitutes the profligate. These pleasures, then, the temperate man avoids; but he has pleasures of his own.

Pleasure is good, and the pleasure that consists in the highest activity is

13. But all admit that pain is a bad thing and undesirable; partly bad in itself, partly bad as in some sort an impediment to activity. But that which is opposed to what is undesirable, in that respect in

THE good. All admit that happiness is pleasant. Bodily pleasures not the only pleasures.

which it is undesirable and bad, is good. It follows, then, that pleasure is a good thing. And this argument cannot be met, as Speusippus tried to meet it, by the analogy of the greater which is opposed to the equal as well as to the less; for no one would say that pleasure is essentially a bad thing.*

2 Moreover, there is no reason why a certain kind of pleasure should not be the supreme good, even though some kinds be bad, just as there is no reason why a certain kind of knowledge should not be, though some kinds be bad. Nay, perhaps we ought rather to say that since every formed faculty admits of unimpeded exercise, it follows that, whether happiness be the exercise of all these faculties, or of some one of them, that exercise must necessarily be most desirable when unimpeded: but unimpeded exercise of faculty is pleasure: a certain kind of pleasure, therefore, will be the supreme good, even though most pleasures should turn out to be bad in themselves.

And on this account all men suppose that the happy life is a pleasant one, and that happiness involves pleasure: and the supposition is reasonable; for no exercise of a faculty is complete if it be impeded; but happiness we reckon among complete things; and so, if he is to be happy, a man must have the goods of the body and external goods and good fortune, in order that the exercise of his faculties may not

* The argument is, "Pleasure is good because it is the opposite of pain, which is evil." "No," says Speusippus; "it is neither pleasure nor pain, but the neutral state, which is opposite to both, that is good." "No," replies Aristotle, "for then pleasure will be bad."

3 be impeded. And those who say that though a man be put to the rack and overwhelmed by misfortune, he is happy if only he be good, whether they know it or not, talk nonsense.

4 Because fortune is a necessary condition, some people consider good fortune to be identical with happiness; but it is not really so, for good fortune itself, if excessive, is an impediment, and is then, perhaps, no longer to be called good fortune; for good fortune can only be defined by its relation to happiness.

5 Again, the fact that all animals and men pursue pleasure is some indication that it is in some way the highest good:

> "Not wholly lost can e'er that saying be
> Which many peoples share."

6 But as the nature of man and the best development of his faculties neither are nor are thought to be the same for all, so the pleasure which men pursue is not always the same, though all pursue pleasure. Yet, perhaps, they do in fact pursue a pleasure different from that which they fancy they pursue and would say they pursue—a pleasure which is one and the same for all. For all beings have something divine implanted in them by nature.

But bodily pleasures have come to be regarded as the sole claimants to the title of pleasure, because they are oftenest attained and are shared by all; these then, as the only pleasures they know, men fancy to be the only pleasures that are.

7 But it is plain that unless pleasure—that is, unimpeded exercise of the faculties—be good, we can no

longer say that the happy man leads a pleasant life; for why should he need it if it be not good? Nay, he may just as well lead a painful life: for pain is neither bad nor good, if pleasure be neither; so why should he avoid pain? The life of the good man, then, would be no pleasanter than others unless the exercise of his faculties were pleasanter.

Of the bodily pleasures, and the distinction between naturally and accidentally pleasant.

14. Those who say that though some pleasures 1
are very desirable — to wit, noble pleasures — the pleasures of the body, with which the profligate is concerned, are not desirable, should consider the nature of these pleasures of the body. Why [if they 2
are bad] are the opposite pains bad? for the opposite of bad is good. Are we to say that the "necessary" pleasures are good in the sense that what is not bad is good? or are they good up to a certain point?

Those faculties and those motions or activities which do not admit of excess beyond what is good,* do not admit of excessive pleasure; but those which admit of excess admit also of excessive pleasure. Now, bodily goods admit of excess, and the bad man is bad because he pursues this excess, not merely because he pursues the necessary pleasures; for men always take some delight in meat, and drink, and the gratification of the sexual appetite, but not always as they ought. But with pain the case is reversed: it is not excess of pain merely that the bad man avoids, but pain generally; [which is not inconsistent with the proposition that pain is bad,] for the

* Virtuous faculties and activities (II. 6, 20) do not admit of excess, because by their very nature they are right and occupy the mean; too much of them would be a contradiction in terms.

opposite of excessive pleasure is not painful, except to the man who pursues the excess.*

3 But we ought to state not only the truth, but also the cause of the error; for this helps to produce conviction, as, when something has been pointed out to us which would naturally make that seem true which is not, we are more ready to believe the truth. And so we must say why it is that the bodily pleasures seem more desirable.

4 First of all, then, it is because of its efficacy in expelling pain, and because of the excessiveness of the pain to which it is regarded as an antidote, that men pursue excessive pleasure and bodily pleasure generally. But these remedies produce an intense feeling, and so are pursued, because they appear in strong contrast to the opposite pain.

(The reasons why pleasure is thought to be not good are two, as we said before: (1) some pleasures are the manifestation of a nature that is bad either from birth, as with brutes, or by habit, as with bad men: (2) the remedial pleasures imply want; and it is better to be in a [natural] state than in a transition to such a state; but these pleasures are felt while a want in us is being filled up, and therefore they are only accidentally good.†)

* Pain generally (ὅλως) is bad, to be avoided.

Objection: The pain of foregoing certain excessive pleasures is not to be avoided.

Answer: The opposite of these excessive pleasures, *i.e.* the foregoing them, is not painful to the virtuous man, but only to him who sets his heart upon them, *i.e.* to a vicious or incontinent man.

† As these words disturb the order of the argument, I have, following Ramsauer, put them in brackets; but I see no sufficient reason for regarding them as spurious.

Again, these pleasures are pursued because of 5
their intensity by those who are unable to take delight in other pleasures; thus we see people make themselves thirsty on purpose. When the pleasures they pursue are harmless, we do not blame them (though when they are hurtful the pursuit is bad); for they have no other sources of enjoyment, and the neutral state is painful to many because of their nature: for an animal is always labouring, as physical science teaches, telling us that seeing and hearing is labour and pain, only we are all used to it, as the
saying is. And thus in youth, because they are 6
growing, men are in a state resembling drunkenness; and youth is pleasant. But people of a melancholic nature are always wanting something to restore their balance; for their bodies are always vexing them because of their peculiar temperament, and they are always in a state of violent desire. But pain is expelled either by the opposite pleasure or by any pleasure, if it be sufficiently strong; and this is the reason why such men become profligate and worthless.

But pleasures that have no antecedent pain do not
admit of excess. These are the pleasures derived from 7
things that are naturally and not merely accidentally pleasant. I call those things accidentally pleasant that have a restorative effect; for as the restoration cannot take place unless that part of the system which remains healthy be in some way active, the restoration itself seems pleasant: but I call those things naturally pleasant that stimulate the activity of a healthy system.*

* *Cf. supra*, 12, 2.

I am sick and take medicine, hungry and take food (which

8 But nothing can continue to give us uninterrupted pleasure, because our nature is not simple, but contains a second element which makes us mortal beings;* so that if the one element be active in any way, this is contrary to the nature of the other element, but when the two elements are in equilibrium, what we do seems neither painful nor pleasant; for if there were a being whose nature were simple, the same activity would be always most pleasant to him. And on this account God always enjoys one simple pleasure; for besides the activity of movement, there is also activity without movement, and rest admits of truer pleasure than motion. But change is "the sweetest of all things," as the poet says, because of a certain badness in us: for just as it is the bad man who is especially apt to change, so is it the bad nature that needs change; for it is neither simple nor good.

seems to be here included under medicine); but neither the drug nor the food can of themselves cure me and restore the balance of my system—they must be assimilated (for the body is not like a jar that can be filled merely by pouring water from another jar), *i.e.* part of my system must remain in its normal state and operate in its normal manner. But this operation, this *ἐνέργεια τῆς κατὰ φύσιν ἕξεως*, is pleasure (by the definition given above, **12**, 3), and in ignorance of the process we transfer the pleasure to the medicine and call it pleasant. The weakness of this account is that it overlooks the fact that, though the medicine cannot itself cure without the operation of *τῆς κατὰ φύσιν ἕξεως*, yet on the other hand this *ἕξις*, this faculty, cannot operate in this manner without this stimulus; so that there seems to be no reason why the medicine, as setting up an *ἐνέργεια τῆς κατὰ φύσιν ἕξεως*, should not itself be called *φύσει ἡδύ*. But the whole passage rests on the assumption that there can be activity without stimulus, *i.e.* without want—an assumption which has become inconceivable to us.

* *Cf.* X. 7, 8.

We have now considered continence and incon- 9
tinence, and pleasure and pain, and have explained what each is, and how some of them are good and some bad. It remains to consider friendship.

BOOK VIII.

FRIENDSHIP OR LOVE.

Uses of friendship. Differences of opinion about it.

1. AFTER the foregoing, a discussion of friendship will naturally follow, as it is a sort of virtue, or at least implies virtue, and is, moreover, most necessary to our life. For no one would care to live without friends, though he had all other good things. Indeed, it is when a man is rich, and has got power and authority, that he seems most of all to stand in need of friends; for what is the use of all this prosperity if he have no opportunity for benevolence, which is most frequently and most commendably displayed towards friends? or how could his position be maintained and preserved without friends? for the greater it is, the more is it exposed to danger. In poverty and all other misfortunes, again, we regard our friends as our only refuge. We need friends when we are young to keep us from error, when we get old to tend upon us and to carry out those plans which we have not strength to execute ourselves, and in the prime of life to help us in noble deeds—"two together" [as Homer says]; for thus we are more efficient both in thought and in action.

Love seems to be implanted by nature in the parent towards the offspring, and in the offspring towards the parent, not only among men, but also among birds and most animals; and in those of the same race towards one another, among men especially —for which reason we commend those who love their fellow-men. And when one travels one may see how man is always akin to and dear to man.

Again, it seems that friendship is the bond that 4
holds states together, and that lawgivers are even more eager to secure it than justice. For concord bears a certain resemblance to friendship, and it is concord that they especially wish to retain, and dissension that they especially wish to banish as an enemy. If citizens be friends, they have no need of justice, but though they be just, they need friendship or love also; indeed, the completest realization of justice * seems to be the realization of friendship or love also.

Moreover, friendship is not only an indispensable, 5
but also a beautiful or noble thing: for we commend those who love their friends, and to have many friends is thought to be a noble thing; and some even think that a good man is the same as a friend †

But there are not a few differences of opinion 6
about the matter. Some hold that it is a kind of likeness, and that those who are like one another are friends; and this is the origin of "Like to like," and "Birds of a feather flock together," ‡ and other similar sayings. Others, on the contrary, say that "two of a trade never agree." §

* τῶν δικαίων τὸ μάλιστα, *sc.* τὸ ἐπιεικές: *cf.* V. 10, and VI. 11, 2.

† *Cf.* Plato, Rep., 334.

‡ Literally, "Crow to crow."

§ Literally, "say that all who thus resemble one another are to

Others go deeper into these questions, and into the causes of the phenomena; Euripides, for instance says—

> "The parched earth loves the rain,
> And the high heaven, with moisture laden, loves
> Earthwards to fall."

Heraclitus also says, "Opposites fit together," and "Out of discordant elements comes the fairest harmony," and "It is by battle that all things come into the world." Others, and notably Empedocles, take the opposite view, and say that like desires like.

Of these difficulties, all that refer to the constitution of the universe may be dismissed (for they do not properly concern our present inquiry); but those that refer to human nature, and are intimately connected with man's character and affections, we will discuss —as, for instance, whether friendship can exist in all men, or whether it is impossible for men to be friends if they are bad, and whether there be one form of friendship or rather many. For those who suppose that there is only one kind of friendship, because it admits of degrees, go upon insufficient grounds. Things that differ in kind may differ also in degree. (But we have already spoken about this point.*)

Three motives of friendship. Friendship defined.

2. Perhaps these difficulties will be cleared up if we first ascertain what is the nature of the lovable. For it seems that we do not love *anything*, but only the lovable, and that the lovable is either good or pleasant or useful. But useful would appear

one another like potters," alluding to the saying of Hesiod,—

Καὶ κεραμεὺς κεραμεῖ κοτέει καὶ τέκτονι τέκτων—

"Potter quarrels with potter, and carpenter with carpenter."

* See Ramsauer.

to mean that which helps us to get something good, or some pleasure; so that the good and the pleasant only would be loved as ends.

Now, do men love what is good, or what is good 2
for themselves? for there is sometimes a discrepancy between these two.

The same question may be asked about the pleasant.

It seems that each man loves what is good for himself, and that, while the good is lovable in itself, that is lovable to each man which is good for him. It may be said that each man loves not what is really good for him, but what seems good for him. But this will make no difference; for the lovable we are speaking of will then be the apparently lovable.

The motives of love being thus threefold, the love 3
of inanimate things is not called friendship. For there is no return of affection here, nor any wish for the good of the object: it would be absurd to wish well to wine, for instance; at the most, we wish that it may keep well, in order that we may have it. But it is commonly said that we must wish our friend's good for his own sake. One who thus wishes the good of another is called a well-wisher, when the wish is not reciprocated; when the well-wishing is mutual, it is called friendship.

But ought we not to add that each must be aware 4
of the other's well-wishing? For a man often wishes well to those whom he has never seen, but supposes to be good or useful men; and one of these may have the same sentiments towards him. These two, then, are plainly well-wishers one of another; but how

could one call them friends when each is unaware of the other's feelings?

In order to be friends, then, they must be well-wishers one of another, *i.e.* must wish each other's good from one of the three motives above mentioned, and be aware of each other's feelings.

Three kinds of friendship, corresponding to the three motives. Perfect friendship is that whose motive is the good.

3. But these three motives are specifically different from one another; the several affections and friendships based upon them, therefore, will also be specifically different. The kinds of friendship accordingly are three, being equal in number to the motives of love; for any one of these may be the basis of a mutual affection of which each is aware.

Now, those who love one another wish each other's good in respect of that which is the motive of their love. Those, therefore, whose love for one another is based on the useful, do not love each other for what they are, but only in so far as each gets some good from the other.

It is the same also with those whose affection is based on pleasure; people care for a wit, for instance, not for what he is, but as the source of pleasure to themselves.

Those, then, whose love is based on the useful care for each other on the ground of their own good, and those whose love is based on pleasure care for each other on the ground of what is pleasant to themselves, each loving the other, not as being what he is, but as useful or pleasant.

These friendships, then, are "accidental;" for the object of affection is loved, not as being the person or character that he is, but as the source of some good

or some pleasure. Friendships of this kind, therefore, 3
are easily dissolved, as the persons do not continue unchanged; for if they cease to be pleasant or useful to one another, their love ceases. But the useful is nothing permanent, but varies from time to time. On the disappearance, therefore, of that which was the motive of their friendship, the friendship itself is dissolved, since it existed solely with a view to that.

Friendship of this kind seems especially to be 4
found among elderly men (for at that time of life men pursue the useful rather than the pleasant) and those middle-aged and young men who have a keen eye to what is profitable. But friends of this kind do not generally even live together; for sometimes they are by no means pleasant (nor indeed do they want such constant intercourse with others, unless they are useful); for they make themselves pleasant only just so far as they have hopes of getting something good thereby.

With these friendships is generally classed the kind of friendship that exists between host and guest.*

The friendship of young men is thought to be 5
based on pleasure; for young men live by impulse, and, for the most part, pursue what is pleasant to themselves and what is immediately present. But the things in which they take pleasure change as they advance in years. They are quick to make friendships, therefore, and quick to drop them; for

* A family of importance in a Greek state was usually connected by ties of hospitality with other families in other states: persons so connected were not φίλοι, not strictly friends, since they lived apart; but ξένοι, for which there is no English equivalent.

their friendship changes as the object which pleases them changes; and pleasure of this kind is liable to rapid alteration.

Moreover, young men are apt to fall in love; for love is, for the most part, a matter of impulse and based on pleasure: so they fall in love, and again soon cease to love, passing from one state to the other many times in one day.

Friends of this kind wish to spend their time together and to live together; for thus they attain the object of their friendship.

6 But the perfect kind of friendship is that of good men who resemble one another in virtue. For they both alike wish well to one another as good men, and it is their essential character to be good men. And those who wish well to their friends for the friends' sake are friends in the truest sense; for they have these sentiments towards each other as being what they are, and not in an accidental way: their friendship, therefore, lasts as long as their virtue, and that is a lasting thing.

Again, each is both good simply and good to his friend; for it is true of good men that they are both good simply and also useful to one another.

In like manner they are pleasant too; for good men are both pleasant in themselves and pleasant to one another: for every kind of character takes delight in the acts that are proper to it and those that resemble these; but the acts of good men are the same or similar.

7 This kind of friendship, then, is lasting, as we might expect, since it unites in itself all the con-

ditions of true friendship. For every friendship has for its motive some good or some pleasure (whether it be such in itself or relatively to the person who loves), and is founded upon some similarity: but in this case all the requisite characteristics belong to the friends in their own nature; for here there is similarity and the rest, viz. what is good simply and pleasant simply, and these are the most lovable things: and so it is between persons of this sort that the truest and best love and friendship is found.

It is but natural that such friendships should be 8
uncommon, as such people are rare. Such a friendship, moreover, requires long and familiar intercourse. For, as the proverb says, it is impossible for people to know one another till they have consumed the requisite quantity of salt together. Nor can they accept one another as friends, or be friends, till each show and approve himself to the other as worthy to be loved. Those who quickly come to 9
treat one another like friends may wish to be friends, but are not really friends, unless they not only are lovable, but know each other to be so; a wish to be friends may be of rapid growth, but not friendship.

This kind of friendship, then, is complete in respect of duration and in all other points, and that which each gets from the other is in all respects identical or similar, as should be the case with friends.

The others are imperfect copies of this.

4. The friendship of which pleasure is the motive 1
bears some resemblance to the foregoing; for good men, too, are pleasant to each other. So also does that of which the useful is the motive; for good men are useful also to one another. And in these cases,

too, the friendship is most likely to endure when that which each gets from the other is the same (*e.g.* pleasure), and not only the same, but arising from the same source—a friendship between two wits, for instance, rather than one between a lover and his beloved. For the source of pleasure in the latter case is not the same for both: the lover delights to look upon his beloved, the beloved likes to have attentions paid him; but when the bloom of youth is gone, the friendship sometimes vanishes also; for the one misses the beauty that used to please him, the other misses the attentions. But, on the other hand, they frequently continue friends, *i.e.* when their intercourse has brought them to care for each other's characters, and they are similar in character.

2 Those who in matters of love exchange not pleasure but profit, are less truly and less permanently friends. The friendship whose motive is profit ceases when the advantage ceases; for it was not one another that they loved, but the profit.

For pleasure, then, or for profit it is possible even for bad men to be friends with one another, and good men with bad, and those who are neither with people of any kind, but it is evident that the friendship in which each loves the other for himself is only possible between good men; for bad men take no delight in each other unless some advantage is to be gained.

3 The friendship of good men, again, is the only one that can defy calumny; for people are not ready to accept the testimony of any one else against him whom themselves have tested. Such friendship also implies mutual trust, and the certainty that neither

would ever wrong the other, and all else that is implied in true friendship; while in other friendships there is no such security.

For since men also apply the term friends to 4
those who love one another for profit's sake, as happens with states (for expediency is thought to be the ground on which states make alliances), and also to those who love one another for pleasure's sake, as children do, perhaps we too ought to apply the name to such people, and to speak of several kinds of friendship—firstly, in the primary and strict sense of the word, the friendship of good men as such; secondly, the other kinds that are so called because of a resemblance to this: for these other people are called friends in so far as their relation involves some element of good, which constitutes a resemblance; for the pleasant,
too, is good to those who love pleasant things. But 5
these two latter kinds are not apt to coincide, nor do the same people become friends for the sake both of profit and pleasure; for such accidental properties are not apt to be combined in one subject.

Now that we have distinguished these several 6
kinds of friendship, we may say that bad men will be friends for the sake of pleasure or profit, resembling one another in this respect, while good men, when they are friends, love each other for what they are, *i.e.* as good men. These, then, we say, are friends simply; the others are friends accidentally and so far as they resemble these.

Intercourse necessary to the maintenance of friendship.

5. But just as with regard to the virtues we 1
distinguish excellence of character or faculty from excellence manifested, so is it also with friendship:

when friends are living together, they take pleasure in, and do good to, each other; when they are asleep or at a distance from one another, they are not acting as friends, but they have the disposition which, if manifested, issues in friendly acts; for distance does not destroy friendship simply, but the manifestation of friendship. But if the absence be prolonged, it is thought to obliterate even friendship; whence the saying—

> "Full many a friendship hath ere now been loosed
> By lack of converse."

2 Old men do not seem apt to make friends, nor morose men; for there is little in them that can give pleasure: but no one can pass his days in intercourse with what is painful or not pleasant; for our nature seems, above all things, to shun the painful and seek the pleasant.

3 Those who accept each other's company, but do not live together, seem to be rather well-wishers than friends. For there is nothing so characteristic of friendship as living together:* those who need help seek it thus, but even those who are happy desire company; for a solitary life suits them least of all men. But people cannot live together unless they are pleasant to each other, nor unless they take delight in the same things, which seems to be a necessary condition of comradeship.

4 The truest friendship, then, is that which exists between good men, as we have said again and again.

* To a Greek, of course, this does not necessarily imply living under the same roof, as it does to us with our very different conditions of life.

For that, it seems, is lovable and desirable which is good or pleasant in itself, but to each man that which is good or pleasant to him; and the friendship of good men for one another rests on both these grounds.

But it seems that while love is a feeling, friend- 5
ship is a habit or trained faculty. For inanimate things can equally well be the object of love, but the love of friends for one another implies purpose, and purpose proceeds from a habit or trained faculty. And in wishing well for their sakes to those they love, they are swayed not by feeling, but by habit. Again, in loving a friend they love what is good for themselves; for he who gains a good man for his friend gains something that is good for himself. Each then, loves what is good for himself, and what he gives in good wishes and pleasure is equal to what he gets; for love and equality, which are joined in the popular saying φιλότης ἰσότης, are found in the highest degree in the friendship of good men.

6. Morose men and elderly men are less apt 1
to make friends in proportion as they are harsher in temper, and take less pleasure in society; for delight in society seems to be, more than anything else, characteristic of friendship and productive of it. So young men are quick to make friends, but not old men (for people do not make friends with those who do not please them), nor morose men. Such people may, indeed, be well-wishers, for they wish each other good and help each other in need; but they are by no means friends, since they do not live with nor delight in each other, which things are thought to be, more than anything else, characteristic of friendship.

2 It is impossible to have friendship, in the full sense of the word, for many people at the same time, just as it is impossible to be in love with many persons at once (for it seems to be something intense, but intense feeling implies a single object); and it is not easy for one man to find at one time many very agreeable persons, perhaps not many good
3 ones. Moreover, they must have tested and become accustomed to each other, which is a matter of great difficulty. But in the way of profit or pleasure, it is quite possible to find many * agreeable persons; for such people are not rare, and their services can be rendered in a short time.

4 Of these other kinds, that which more nearly resembles true friendship is that whose motive is pleasure, when each renders the same service to the other, and both take pleasure in one another, or in the same things, such as young men's friendships are wont to be; for a generous spirit is commoner in them than in others. But the friendship whose motive is utility is the friendship of sordid souls. Those who are happy do not need useful, but pleasant friends; it is people to live with that they want, and though they may for a short time put up with what is painful, yet no one could endure anything continually, not even the good itself, if it were painful to him; so they require that their friends shall be pleasant. But they ought, we may say, to require that they shall be good as well as pleasant, and good for them; then all the characteristics of a friend will be combined.

* Reading πολλούς.

People in exalted positions seem to make distinct 5
classes of friends. They have some who are useful, and others who are pleasant, but seldom any that unite both these qualities; for they do not seek for people who are at once agreeable and virtuous, or people who can be useful to them in noble actions, but they seek for witty persons to satisfy their craving for pleasure, while for other purposes they choose men who are clever at carrying out their instructions: but these two qualities are seldom united in one person.

The good man, indeed, as we have already said, 6
is both pleasant and useful; but such a man does not make friends with a man in a superior station, unless he allows himself inferior in virtue:* only thus does he meet the good man on equal terms, being inferior in one respect in the same ratio as he is superior in another. But great men are by no means wont to behave in this manner.

In the friendships hitherto spoken of the persons 7
are equal, for they do the same and wish the same for each other, or else exchange equal quantities of different things, as pleasure for profit. (We have already explained that the latter less deserve the name of friendship, and are less lasting than the former kind. We may even say that, being at once

* The words ἂν μὴ καὶ τῇ ἀρετῇ ὑπερέχηται literally mean "unless he also be surpassed in virtue." Who is "he"? Not the former, for ὁ σπουδαῖος, *the* ideally good man, cannot be surpassed in virtue; therefore the latter—the great man, the tyrant, king or prince. The whole passage displays a decided *animus* against princes (perhaps, as Stahr suggests, a reminiscence of experiences in the Macedonian court).

both like it and unlike it, they seem both to be and not to be friendships. On the ground of their resemblance to the friendship that is based on virtue, they seem to be friendships; for one involves pleasure, the other profit, both of which belong to true friendship; but, again, inasmuch as it is beyond calumny and is lasting, while they are liable to rapid change and different in many other respects, they seem not to be friendships because of their unlikeness to it.)

1 7. But, besides these, there is another kind of friendship, in which the persons are unequal, as that of a father for a son, and generally of an elder for a younger person, or of a man for a woman, or of a ruler of any kind for a subject.

Of friendship between unequal persons and its rule of proportion. Limits within which this is possible.

These also are different from one another; for that of parent for child is not the same as that of ruler for subject, nor even that of father for son the same as that of son for father, nor that of man for woman the same as that of woman for man. For each of these classes has a different excellence and a different function, and the grounds of their affection are different; therefore their love and their friendship
2 also are different. What each does for the other, then, is not the same, nor should they expect it to be the same; but when children give to their parents what they owe to those who begat them, and parents on their part give what they owe to their children, then such friendship will be lasting, and what it ought to be. But in all friendships based on inequality, the love on either side should be proportional—I mean that the better of the two (and the more useful,

and so on in each case) should receive more love than he gives; for when love is proportioned to desert, then there is established a sort of equality, which seems to be a necessary condition of friendship.

But there seems to be a difference between the 3
equality that prevails in the sphere of justice and that which prevails in friendship: for in the sphere of justice the primary sense of "equal" [or "fair," ἴσον] is "proportionate to merit," and "equal in quantity" is only the secondary sense; but in friendship "equal in quantity" is the primary, and "proportionate to merit" the secondary sense.*

This is plainly seen in cases where there comes to 4
be a great distance between the persons in virtue, or
vice, or wealth, or in any other respect; for they no
longer are, nor expect to be, friends. It is most
plainly seen in the case of the gods; for they have
the greatest superiority in all good things. But it is
seen also in the case of princes; for here also those
who are greatly inferior do not claim their friendship; nor do people of no consideration expect to be
friends with the best and wisest in the state. It is 5
impossible accurately to determine the limits within
which friendship may subsist in such cases: many
things may be taken away, and it may remain; but

* The general rule of justice is that what different people receive is different, being proportionate to their respective merits (τὸ κατ' ἀξίαν ἴσον, or ἰσότης λόγων: *cf.* V. 3, 6, 5, 6 and 17); in exceptional cases, when the merits of the persons are the same, what they receive is equal (τὸ κατ' ἀξίαν becomes τὸ κατὰ ποσὸν ἴσον). But friendship in the primary sense is friendship between equals, so that the general rule here is that both give and take equal amounts of love, etc.; in the exceptional case of inequality between the persons, the amounts must be proportionate.

again, if a person be very far removed, as God is, it can no longer be.

6 This has suggested the objection that, after all, a friend does not wish his friend the greatest of all goods, that he should become a god; for then he would lose a friend—that is, a good; for a friend is a good thing. If then we were right in saying that a friend wishes good to his friend for his (the friend's) sake, we must add, "the friend remaining what he is:" so far as is compatible with his being a man, he will wish him the greatest good—but perhaps not everything that is good; for every man wishes good most of all to himself.

1 8. Most people seem, from a desire for honour, to wish to be loved rather than to love, and on this account most men are fond of flatterers; for a flatterer is an inferior friend, or pretends to be so and to love more than he is loved: but being loved is thought to come near to being honoured, and that most men strive for. *Of loving and being loved*

2 But they seem to desire honour not for its own sake, but accidentally: it is expectation that makes most men delight in being honoured by those in authority; for they hope to get from them anything they may want: they delight in this honour, therefore, as a token of good things to come. On the other hand, those who desire the honour or respect of good men and men who know, are anxious to confirm their own opinion of themselves; they rejoice, therefore, in the assurance of their worth which they gain from confidence in the judgment of those who declare it.

But men delight in being loved for its own sake; wherefore it would seem that being loved is better than being honoured, and that friendship is desirable for its own sake.

Friendship, however, seems to lie in the loving, 3
rather than in the being loved. This is shown by the delight that mothers take in loving; for some give their children to others to rear, and love them since they know them, but do not look for love in return, if it be impossible to have both, being content to see their children doing well, and loving them, though they receive from them, in their ignorance, nothing of what is due to a mother.

Since friendship lies more in loving [than in being 4
loved], and since we praise those who love their friends, it would seem that the virtue of a friend is to love, so that when people love each other in proportion to their worth, they are lasting friends, and theirs is a lasting friendship.

This is also the way in which persons who are 5
unequal can be most truly friends; for thus they will make themselves equal: but equality and similarity tend to friendship, and most of all the similarity of those who resemble each other in virtue; for such men, being little liable to change, continue as they were in themselves and to one another, and do not ask anything unworthy of one another, or do anything unworthy for one another—nay, rather restrain one another from anything of the sort; for it is characteristic of a good man neither to go wrong himself, nor to let his friend go wrong.

Bad men on the other hand [as friends] have no

stability: for they do not even continue like themselves; but for a short space they become friends, rejoicing in each other's wickedness.

Those, however, who are useful and agreeable to one another continue friends longer, *i.e.* so long as they continue to furnish pleasure or profit.

The friendship whose motive is utility seems, more than any other kind, to be a union of opposites, as of rich and poor, ignorant and learned; for when a man wants a thing, in his desire to get it he will give something else in exchange. And perhaps we might include the lover and his beloved, the beautiful and the ugly person, in this class. And this is the reason why lovers often make themselves ridiculous by claiming to be loved as they love; if they were equally lovable they might perhaps claim it, but when there is nothing lovable about them the claim is absurd.

But perhaps nothing desires its opposite as such but only accidentally, the desire being really for the mean which is between the two; for this is good. For the dry, for instance, it is good not to become wet, but to come to the intermediate state, and so with the hot, and with the rest of these opposites. But we may dismiss these questions; for, indeed, they are somewhat foreign to our present purpose.

Every society has its own form of friendship as of justice. All societies are summed up in civil society.

9. It seems, as we said at the outset, that the subject-matter and occasion of friendship and of justice are the same. Every community or association, it is thought, gives some occasion for justice, and also for friendship; at least, people address as friends their partners in a voyage or campaign, and so on with other associations. To what extent soever they are partners, to that extent is there occasion for friendship; for to that extent is there occasion for justice.

Moreover, "friends' goods are common property," says the proverb rightly; for friendship implies community. Brothers, indeed, and comrades have all 2
things in common: other friends have certain definite things in common, some more and some less; for friendships also differ in degree. But what justice requires is also different in different cases; it does not require from parents towards children, for instance, the same as from brothers towards one another, nor from comrades the same as from fellow-citizens, and so on through the other kinds of friendship.

Injustice also assumes different forms in these 3
several relations, and increases according to the degree of friendship; *e.g.* it is a grosser wrong to rob a comrade than a fellow-citizen, and to refuse help to a brother than to a stranger, and to strike one's father than to strike any other man. The claims of justice, in fact, are such as to increase as friendship increases, both having the same field and growing *pari passu*.

But all kinds of association or community seem to 4
be, as it were, parts of the political community or association of citizens. For in all of them men join together with a view to some common interest, and in pursuit of some one or other of the things they need for their life. But the association of citizens seems both originally to have been instituted and to continue for the sake of common interests; for this is what legislators aim at, and that which is for the common interest of all is said to be just.

Thus all other associations seem to aim at some particular advantage, *e.g.* sailors work together for a successful voyage, with a view to making money or something of that sort; soldiers for a successful campaign, whether their ulterior end be riches, or victory, or the founding of a state; and so it is with the members of a tribe or a deme. Some associations, again, seem to have pleasure for their object, as when men join together for a feast or a club dinner; for the object here is feasting and company. But all these associations seem to be subordinate to the association of citizens; for the association of citizens seems to have for its aim, not the interests of the moment, but the interests of our whole life, even when its members celebrate festivals and hold gatherings on such occasions, and render honour to the gods, and provide recreation and amusement for themselves.* For the ancient festivals and assemblies seem to take place after the gathering in of the harvest, being of the nature of a dedication of the first-fruits, as it was at these seasons that people had most leisure.

All associations, then, seem to be parts of the association of citizens; and the several kinds of friendship will correspond to the several kinds of association.

10. Now, of constitutions there are three kinds, and an equal number of perverted forms, which are, so to speak, corruptions of these. Constitutions proper are kingly government and aristocracy; and, thirdly, there

* It is the institution of the state which gives a permanent significance to these amusements of a day.

is a form of government based upon an assessment of property, which should strictly be called timocracy, though most people are wont to speak of it as constitutional government simply.

Of these, kingly government is the best and timocracy the worst. The perversion of kingly government is tyranny: both are monarchies, but there is a vast difference between them; for the tyrant seeks his own interest, the king seeks the interest of his subjects. For he is not properly a king who is not self-sufficient and superabundantly furnished with all that is good; such a man wants nothing more; his own advantage, then, will not be his aim, but that of his subjects. A man of another character than this could only be the sort of king that is chosen by lot.*

Tyranny is the opposite of kingly rule, because the tyrant seeks his own good; and of this government it is quite obvious † that it is the worst of all: we may add that the opposite of the best must be the worst.

Kingly government degenerates into tyranny; for tyranny is a vicious form of monarchy: the bad king, then, becomes a tyrant.

Aristocracy degenerates into oligarchy through the vice of the rulers, who, instead of distributing public property and honours according to merit, take all or most of the good things for themselves, and give the offices always to the same people, setting the greatest store by wealth; you have, then, a small

* As the ἄρχων βασιλεύς at Athens.

† Lit. "more evident," sc. than that kingly rule is the best.

number of bad men in power, in place of the best men.

Lastly, timocracy degenerates into democracy: and indeed they border closely upon each other; for even timocracy is intended to be government by the multitude, and all those who have the property qualification are equal.

Democracy is the least bad [of the corrupt forms], for it is but a slight departure from the corresponding form of constitution.

These, then, are the ways in which the several constitutions are most apt to change; for these are the directions in which the change is slightest, and encounters the least resistance.

Likenesses of these forms of government and patterns of them, so to speak, may be found in families. For instance, the association of father and sons has the form of kingly rule; for the father cares for his children. This, also, is the reason why Homer addresses Zeus as father; for kingly government aims at being a paternal government. But in Persia the association of father and son is tyrannical; for fathers there use their sons as slaves. The association of master and slave is also tyrannical; for it is the interest of the master that is secured by it. But this seems to be a legitimate kind of tyranny, while the Persian kind seems to be wrong; for different beings require different kinds of government.

The association of man and wife seems to be aristocratic: for the husband bears rule proportionate to his worth, *i.e.* he rules in those matters which are his province; but he entrusts to his wife those matters that properly belong to her. But when the man lords it in all things, he perverts this relation into an oligarchical one; for he then takes rule where he is not entitled to it, and not only in those matters in which he is better. Sometimes, on the other hand, the wife rules because she is an heiress. In these cases authority is not proportionate to merit, but is given on the ground of wealth and influence, just as in oligarchies.

The association of brothers resembles a timocracy; 6
for they are equal except in so far as they differ in age. On this account, if they differ very widely in age, their friendship can no longer be a brotherly friendship.

A democratic form of association is chiefly found in those households which have no master (for there all are on a footing of equality), or where the head of the house is weak, and every one does what he likes.

Of the corresponding forms of friendship.

11. In each of these forms of government friend- 1
ship has place to the same extent as justice. In the first place, the king shows his friendship for his subjects * by transcendent benefits; for he does good to his subjects, seeing that he is good, and tends them with a view to their welfare, as a shepherd tends his sheep,—whence Homer calls Agamemnon "shepherd of peoples."

The friendship of a father for his child is of a 2
similar kind, though the benefits conferred are still greater. For the father is the author of the child's existence, which seems the greatest of all benefits,

* Scarcely consistent with 7, 4; but *cf.* 7, 1.

and of his nurture and education; and we also ascribe these to our forefathers generally: and thus it is in accordance with nature that fathers should rule their children, forefathers their descendants, kings their subjects.

These friendships involve the superiority of one side to the other; and on this account parents receive honour as well [as service].* Moreover, what justice requires here is not the same on both sides, but that which is proportionate to their worth; for this is the rule of friendship also [as well as of justice].

The friendship, again, of man and wife is the same as that which has place in an aristocracy; for both benefit in proportion to their merit, the better getting more good, and each what is fitting; but this is the rule of justice also.

The friendship of brothers resembles that of comrades, for they are equal and of like age; but those with whom that is the case for the most part have the same feelings and character. And the friendship in a timocracy is of the same type as this; for the citizens here wish to be equal and fair; so they take office in turn, and share it equally: their friendship, then, will follow the same rule.

In the corrupt forms, as there is but little room for justice, so there is but little room for friendship, and least of all in the worst; in a tyranny there is little or no friendship. For where ruler and subject have nothing in common, there cannot be any friend-

* We pay taxes to the king, and tend our parents in their old age; but, as this is no adequate repayment of what they have done for us, we owe them honour besides.

ship, any more than there can be any justice,—*e.g.* when the relation is that of a workman to his tools, or of the soul to the body, or of master to slave. The tools and the body and the slave are all benefited by those who use them; but our relations with inanimate objects do not admit of friendship or justice; nor our relations with a horse or an ox; nor our relations with a slave as such. For there is nothing in common between master and slave. The slave is a living tool; the tool is a lifeless slave. As a slave, 7
then, his master's relations with him do not admit of friendship, but as a man they may: for there seems to be room for some kind of justice in the relations of any man to any one that can participate in law and contract,—and if so, then for some kind of friendship, so far, that is to say, as he deserves the name man.

And so friendships and justice are found to some 8
small extent even in tyrannies, but to a greater extent in democracies than in any other of the corrupt forms; for there the citizens, being equal, have many things in common.

Of the friendship of kinsmen and comrades.

12. All friendship, as we have already said, implies 1
association; but we may separate from the rest the friendship of kinsmen and that of comrades. The friendships of fellow-citizens, of fellow-tribesmen, of fellow-sailors, etc., seem, as opposed to these, to have more to do with association; for they appear to be founded upon some sort of compact. The friendship of host and guest might also be included in this class.

Kinsmen's friendship seems to include several 2
species, but to be dependent in all its forms upon the

friendship of parent and child. For parents love their children as part of themselves; children love their parents as the source of their being. But parents know their children better than the children know that these are their parents, and that which gives birth is more closely attached to that which proceeds from it, than the offspring is to that which gave it life: for that which proceeds from us belongs to us, as a tooth or a hair, or anything of that sort, to its owner; but we do not belong to it at all, or belong to it in a less degree.

Again, there is a difference in respect of time; for parents love their offspring from the moment of their birth, but children love their parents only after the lapse of time, when they have acquired understanding or sense.

These considerations also show why mothers love their children more than fathers do.

3 Parents, then, love their children as themselves (for what proceeds from them is as it were a second self when it is severed), but children love their parents as the source of their being, and brothers love each other because they proceed from the same source: for the identity of their relation to this source constitutes an identity between them; so that they say that they are of the same blood and stock, etc. And so they are in a way identical, though they are separate persons.

4 But friendship between brothers is greatly furthered by common nurture and similarity of age; for those of the same age naturally love one another, as the saying is, and those who are used to one another

naturally make comrades of one another, so that the friendship of brothers comes to resemble that of comrades.

Cousins and other kinsfolk become attached to each other for the same reason—I mean because they come of the same stock. But the attachment is more or less close according to the nearness or remoteness of the founder of the family.

The friendship of children for their parents (like 5
that of men for the gods) is friendship for what is good and superior to themselves, as the source of the greatest benefits, namely, of their life and nurture, and their education from their birth upwards.

Friendship of this kind brings with it more, both 6
of pleasure and profit, than that of strangers, in proportion as there is more community of life.

The friendship of brothers has all the characteristics of the friendship of comrades, and has them in a greater degree (provided they are good and generally resemble one another) inasmuch as they belong more to one another and love each other from their birth up, and have more similarity of character, as being of the same stock and brought up together and educated alike; moreover, they have had the longest and the surest experience of one another.

In all other kinsmen's friendships the same ele- 7
ments will be found in proportion to the relationship.

The friendship of man and wife seems to be natural; for human beings are by nature more apt to join together in couples than to form civil societies, inasmuch as the family is prior in time to the state and more indispensable, and the propagation of the species is a more fundamental characteristic of animal existence. The other animals associate for this purpose alone, but man and wife live together not merely for the begetting of children, but also to satisfy the needs of their life: for the functions of the man and the woman are clearly divided and distinct the one from the other; they supply each other's wants, therefore, both contributing to the common stock. And so this sort of friendship is thought to bring with it both pleasure and profit. But it will be based on virtue, too, if they be good; for each sex has its own virtue, and both will rejoice in that which is of like nature.

Children also seem to be a bond that knits man and wife together (which is a reason why childless unions are more quickly dissolved); for children are a good which both have in common, but that which people have in common holds them together.

8 To ask on what terms a man should live with his wife, and generally friend with friend, seems the same as to ask what justice requires in these cases; for what is required of a man towards his friend is different from what is required of him towards a stranger, a comrade, or a fellow-student.

1 13. There are three kinds of friendship, as we said at the outset, and in each kind there are both equal and unequal friendships; I mean that sometimes two equally good persons make friends, and sometimes a better and a worse,—and so with those who are pleasant to one another, and with those who are friends with a view to profit—sometimes rendering equal services to one another, and sometimes unequal.

Now, those who are equal should effect equality by loving one another, etc., equally, but those who are unequal should effect equality by making what each renders proportionate to the greater or less merit of the other.

But accusations and reproaches arise solely or 2
mostly in friendships whose motive is profit, as we should expect. For those whose friendship is based on virtue are eager to do good to each other (for this is the office of virtue and friendship); and between people who are thus vieing with one another no accusations or quarrels can arise; for a man cannot be embittered against one who loves him and does him a service, but, if he be of a gracious nature, requites him with a like service. And he who renders the greater service will not reproach his friend, since he gets what he desires;* for each desires what is good.

Such quarrels, again, are not apt to arise in friend- 3
ships whose motive is pleasure; for both get at the same time that which they desire, if they delight in each other's company; but if one were to accuse the other for not being agreeable to him, he would make himself ridiculous, seeing that he was under no compulsion to associate with him.

But the friendship whose motive is utility is 4
fruitful in accusations; for as the friends here use each other solely with a view to their own advantage, each always wants the larger share and thinks he has less than his due, and reproaches the other with not doing for him so much as he requires and deserves; though, in truth, it is impossible for the one who

* For he desires the good of his friend.

is doing a service to supply all that the other wants.

But it seems that as the rules of justice are twofold, the unwritten and those that are set down in laws, so the friendship whose motive is utility is of two kinds—one resting on disposition, the other on contract. And accusations are most apt to arise when the relation is understood in one sense at the commencement, and in the other sense at the conclusion.

That which rests on contract is that in which there are specified conditions, and it is of two kinds: one is purely commercial, on the principle of cash payments; the other is less exacting in point of time, though in it also there is a specified *quid pro quo*.

In the latter case, what is due is evident and cannot be disputed, but there is an element of friendliness in the deferment of payment; for which reason, in some states, there is no recovery by law in such cases, but it is held that when a man has given credit he must take the consequences.

That which rests on disposition has no specified conditions, but one gives another presents (or whatever else it may be) as a friend. But afterwards he claims as much or more in return, regarding what he gave not as a gift, but as a loan. And thus, wishing to terminate the relation in a different spirit from that in which he entered upon it, he will accuse the other.* And this is apt to happen because all or nearly

* In the papers of October 8, 1880, a suit is reported in which A tries in vain to recover from B certain goods given during courtship,—according to B as presents, according to A ἐπὶ ῥητοῖς, viz. on condition of marriage, which condition had not been fulfilled.

all men, though they wish for what is noble, choose what is profitable; and while it is noble to do a good service without expecting a return, it is profitable to receive a benefit.

In such cases, then, we should, if we have the power, make an equivalent return for benefits received (for we must not treat a man as a friend if he does not wish it: we should consider that we made a mistake at the beginning, and received a benefit from a person from whom we ought not to have accepted it—for he was not a friend and did not act disinterestedly—and so we ought to terminate the relation in the same way as if we had received a service for a stipulated consideration): and the return should be what we would have agreed * to repay if able; if we were unable, the donor would not even have expected repayment. So we may fairly say that we should repay if we have the power.

But we ought at the outset carefully to consider who it is that is doing us a service, and on what understanding, so that we may accept it on that understanding or else reject it.

It is a debatable question whether the requital is to be measured by, and to be made proportionate to, the value of the service to the recipient or to the benefactor. For the recipients are apt to say that they received what was but a small matter to their benefactors, and what they might just as well have got from others, depreciating the service done them; but the others, on the contrary, are apt to say that what they gave was the best they had, and what

* Reading ὃ ὡμολόγησεν.

could not be got from any one else, and that it was given in a time of danger or on some other pressing occasion.

11 Perhaps we may say that, if the friendship have profit for its motive, the benefit received should be taken as the measure; for it is the recipient who asks a service, which the other renders in expectation of an equal service in return: the amount of the assistance rendered, then, is determined by the extent to which the former is benefited, and he should repay as much as he received, or even more; for that would be the nobler course.

In friendships based on virtue, on the other hand, such accusations do not occur, but it would seem that the measure of the service is the purpose of him who does it; for virtue and moral character are determined by purpose.

1 14. Quarrels occur also in unequal friendships; for sometimes each claims the larger share, but when this happens the friendship is dissolved. For instance, the better of the two thinks he ought to have the larger share; "the good man's share is larger," he says: the more useful of the two makes the same claim; "it is allowed," he says, "that a useless person should not share equally; for friendship degenerates into gratuitous service unless that which each receives from the friendship be proportionate to the value of what he does." For such people fancy that the same rule should hold in friendship as in a commercial partnership, where those who put in more take a larger share. *Of the same in unequal friendships*

The needy man and the inferior man argue in the

contrary way; "it is the office of a good friend," they say, "to help you when you are in need; for what is the use of being friends with a good man or a powerful man, if you are to get nothing by it?"

It seems that the claims of both are right, and 2
that each ought to receive a larger share than the other, but not of the same things—the superior more honour, the needy man more profit; for honour is the tribute due to virtue and benevolence, while want receives its due succour in the pecuniary gain.

This seems to be recognized in constitutions too: 3
no honour is paid to him who contributes nothing to the common stock of good; the common stock is distributed among those who benefit the community, and of this common stock honour is a part. For he who makes money out of the community must not expect to be honoured by the community also; and no one is content to receive a smaller share in everything. To him, then, who spends money on public objects we pay due honour, and money to him whose services can be paid in money; for, by giving to each what is in proportion to his merit, equality is effected and friendship preserved, as we said before.

The same principles, then, must regulate the intercourse of individuals who are unequal; and he who is benefited by another in his purse or in his character, must give honour in return, making repayment in
that which he can command. For friendship exacts 4
what is possible rather than what is due: what is due is sometimes impossible, as, for instance, in the case of the honour due to the gods and to parents; for no one could ever pay all his debt to them; but

he who gives them such service as he can command is held to fulfil his obligation.

For this reason it would seem that a man may not disown his father, though a father may disown his son; for he who owes must pay: but whatever a son may do he can never make a full return for what he has received, so that he is always in debt. But the creditor is at liberty to cast off the debtor; a father, therefore, is at liberty to cast off his son. But, at the same time, it is not likely that any one would ever disown a son, unless he were a very great scoundrel; for, natural affection apart, it is but human not to thrust away the support that a son would give. But to the son, if he be a scoundrel, assisting his father is a thing that he wishes to avoid, or at least is not eager to undertake; for the generality of men wish to receive benefits, but avoid doing them as unprofitable. So much, then, for these questions.

BOOK IX.

FRIENDSHIP OR LOVE—*continued.*

1. In all dissimilar friendships * it is proportionate exchange that maintains equality and preserves the friendship (as we have already said), just as in the association of citizens, where the shoemaker, in exchange for his shoes, receives some return proportionate to his desert, and so on with the weaver and the rest. 1

Now, in these latter cases, a common measure is supplied by money; money is the standard to which everything is referred, and by which it is measured. 2

In sentimental friendships, on the other hand, the lover sometimes complains that while he loves excessively he gets no love in return, although, maybe, there is nothing lovable about him; often the beloved complains that whereas the other used to promise everything, he now performs nothing.

Complaints of this sort are wont to arise when, pleasure being the motive of the friendship with one person and profit with the other, they do not both get what they want. For the friendship, being based on 3

* Where the two friends have different motives.

these motives, is dissolved whenever they fail to obtain that for the sake of which they made friends; for it was not the other's self that each loved, but only something which he had, and which is not apt to endure; for which reason these friendships also are not apt to endure. But friendship based on character, being pure, is likely to last, as we said.

Sometimes, again, friends quarrel when they find they are getting something different from what they want; for failing to get what you want is like getting nothing. This may be illustrated by the story of the harper: a man promised him that the better he played, the more he should receive; but when, as dawn drew near, the harper claimed the fulfilment of his promise, the other replied that he had already paid him pleasure * for pleasure. Now, if this was what both wished, there would be nothing more to say: but if the one wanted pleasure and the other profit, and the one has what he wants, while the other has not, the bargain will not be fairly carried out; for it is what a man happens to want that he sets his heart on, and consents for the sake of it to render this particular service.

But whose business is it to fix the value of the service? his who first gives, or rather his who first receives?—for he who first gives seems to leave it to the other. This, they say, was the custom of Protagoras: when he had been giving lessons in any subject, he used to tell his pupil to estimate the value of the knowledge he had acquired, and so much he would take.

* Viz. the pleasure of anticipation

Some, however, think the rule should be, "Let a friend be content with his stated wage." *

But if a man, after being paid in advance, fulfils 6
none of his engagements, because he had promised
more than he could perform, he is rightly held chargeable; for he does not fulfil his contract. But the 7
sophists, perhaps, are compelled to adopt this plan [of
payment in advance]; for otherwise no one would
give anything for what they know.

He, then, who fails to do that for which he has
already been paid, is rightly chargeable. But when
there is no express agreement about the service
rendered, (*a*) when one voluntarily helps another for
that other's sake, no accusation can arise, as we said:
for this is the nature of friendship based on virtue.
The return must here be regulated by the purpose
of him who renders the first service; for it is purpose
that makes both friend and virtue. The same rule
would seem to apply also to the relations of a philosopher and his disciples; for desert cannot here be
measured in money, and no honour that could be paid
him would be an adequate return; but, nevertheless,
as in our relations to gods and parents, the possible
is accepted as sufficient. (*b*) If however, the first 8
gift has been made, not in this spirit, but on the understanding that there shall be some return, the return
should, if possible, be such as both deem proportionate
to desert: but if this cannot be, it would seem to
be not only necessary, but just, that the recipient of
the first benefit should assess it; for whatever be the
amount of the advantage he has received, or whatever

* μισθὸς δ' ἀνδρὶ φίλῳ εἰρημένος ἄρκιος ἔστω.—Hesiod.

he would have been willing to give for the pleasure, the other, in receiving the same amount, will receive as much as is due from him. For even in sales this is plainly what takes place; and in some states there is no recovery by law in voluntary contracts, as it is held that when you have given a man credit, you must conclude your bargain with him in the same spirit in which you began it. It is held to be fairer that the service should be valued by him who is trusted than by him who trusts. For most things are differently valued by those who have them and by those who wish to get them: what belongs to us, and what we give away, always seems very precious to us. Nevertheless, the return to be made must be measured by the value which is set upon the service by the receiver. But perhaps he ought to put it, not at what it seems to be worth when he has got it, but at the value he set upon it before he had it.

Of the conflict of duties.

2. There are some further questions that here suggest themselves, such as whether the father's claims to service ought to be unlimited, and the son should obey him in everything, or whether in sickness he should obey the physician, and in the election of a general should choose him who is skilled in war; and, similarly, whether one ought to help one's friend rather than a good man, and repay a benefactor rather than make a present to a comrade, if one cannot do both.

We may, perhaps, say that to lay down precise rules for all such cases is scarcely possible; for the different cases differ in all sorts of ways, according to the importance or unimportance, the nobility or

necessity of the act. But it is tolerably evident that 3
no single person's claims can override all others; and that, as a general rule, we ought to repay benefits received before we do a favour to a comrade—just as, if we had borrowed money, we ought to pay our creditors before we make presents to our comrades.

But it may be that even this rule will not hold 4
good in all cases; for instance, if a man has been ransomed from a band of brigands, ought he in turn to ransom his ransomer, whoever he may be, or repay him when he demands it, even though he be not captured, in preference to ransoming his father? For it would seem that a man ought to ransom his father even before himself.

As we said then, generally speaking, we should 5
repay what we owe: but if giving [instead of repaying] be more noble or meet a more pressing need, it is right to incline in this direction; for sometimes it is not even fair to repay the original service, *e.g.* when one man has helped another, knowing him to be a good man, while the latter in repaying him would be helping one whom he believes to be a bad man. And so a man is sometimes not bound to lend in turn to one who has lent him money: A may have lent to B in full expectation of being repaid, as B is an honourable man; but B may have no hope of being repaid by A, who is a rascal. If this be the real state of the case, the demand for a loan in return is not fair; but even if the facts be otherwise, yet, if they think thus of each other, their conduct would be regarded as natural.

As we have often said, statements concerning 6

human affections and actions must share the indefiniteness of their subject.

It is tolerably plain, then, that, on the one hand, the claims of all men are not the same, but that, on the other hand, the father's claims do not override all others, just as Zeus does not receive all our sacrifices;
7 the claims of parents, brothers, comrades, and benefactors are all different, and to each must be rendered that which is his own and his due.

And this is the way in which men appear to act: to a wedding they invite their kinsfolk; for they have a share in the family, and therefore in all acts relating thereto: and for the same reason it is held that kinsfolk have more claim than any others to be invited to funerals.

8 Parents would seem to have a special claim upon us for sustenance, as we owe it them, and as it is nobler to preserve the life of those to whom we are indebted for our own than to preserve ourselves.

Honour, also, we should pay to our parents, as to the gods; but not all honour: for the honour due to a father is not the same as that due to a mother; nor do we owe them the honour due to a wise man or a good general, but that which is due to a father and that which is due to a mother.

9 To all our elders, again, we should pay the honour due to their age, by rising up at their approach and by giving them the place of honour at the table, and so forth. But between comrades and brothers there should be freedom of speech and community in everything. And to kinsfolk and fellow-tribesmen and fellow-citizens, and all other persons, we should

always try to give their due, and to assign to each what properly belongs to him, according to the closeness of his connection with us, and his goodness or usefulness. When the persons are of one kind this 10
assignment is comparatively easy, but when they are of different kinds it is more difficult. We must not, however, on this account shirk the difficulty, but must distinguish as best we can.

Of the dissolution of friendships.

3. Another difficult question is, whether we should 1
or should not break off friendship with those who have ceased to be what they were.

We may, perhaps, say that those whose friendship is based on profit or pleasure naturally part when these cease; for it was these that they loved: when these are gone, therefore, it is to be expected that the love goes too. But complaints would be likely to arise if a man who loved another for profit or pleasure's sake pretended to love him for his character; for, as we said at the outset, quarrels between friends very frequently arise from a difference between the real and the supposed motives of the friendship. If, 2
then, a man deceives himself, and supposes that he is beloved for his character, though the other's behaviour gives no ground for the supposition, he has only himself to blame; but if he is deceived by the other's pretence, then there is a fair ground of complaint against such an impostor, even more than against those who counterfeit the coinage, inasmuch as it is a more precious thing that is tampered with.

But if a man admit another to his friendship as 3
a good man, and he becomes and shows himself to be a bad man, is he still to be loved? Perhaps we may

answer that it is impossible, as it is not everything that is lovable, but only the good. A bad man, then, is not lovable, and ought not to be loved: for we ought not to love what is bad, nor to make ourselves like what is worthless; but, as we said before, it is like that makes friends with like.

Is the friendship, then, to be immediately broken off? Perhaps not in all cases, but only in the case of those who are incurably bad: when their reformation is possible, we are more bound to help them in their character than their fortune, inasmuch as character is a nobler thing, and has more to do with friendship than fortune has. But a man who withdraws his friendship in such a case, would seem to do nothing unnatural; for it was not with such a man that he made friends: his friend has become another man, and as he cannot restore him, he stands aloof from him.

But suppose that the one remains what he was while the other gets better and becomes far superior in virtue: is the latter still to treat the former as a friend? Perhaps it is hardly possible that he should do so. We see this most plainly if the interval between the two be very considerable. Take, for instance, a boyish friendship: if one of the two remains a child in understanding, while the other has become a man in the fullest sense of the word, how can they any longer be friends, now that the things that will please them, and the sources of their joys and sorrows, are no longer the same? for not even in regard to each other's character will their tastes agree, and without this, we found, people cannot be friends, since they cannot live together. (But this point has been already discussed.)

Shall we, then, simply say that the latter should 5
regard the former as no more a stranger than if he had never been his friend? Perhaps we may go further than this, and say that he should not entirely forget their former intercourse, and that just as we hold that we ought to serve friends before strangers, so former friends have some claims upon us on the ground of past friendship, unless extraordinary depravity were the cause of our parting.

A man's relation to his friend like his relation to himself.

4. Friendly relations to others, and all the charac- 1
teristics by which friendship is defined, seem to be derived from our relations towards ourselves. A friend is sometimes described as one who wishes and does to another what is good or seems good for that other's sake, or as one who wishes his friend to exist and to live for his (the friend's) sake. (This is what mothers feel towards their children, and what friends who have had a difference feel for one another.) Others describe a friend as one who lives with another and chooses what he chooses, or as one who sympathizes with the griefs and joys of his friend. (This, also, is especially the case with mothers.) And, similarly, friendship is usually defined by some one or other of these characteristics.

Now, every one of these characteristics we find 2
in the good man's relations to himself (and in other men just so far as they suppose themselves to be good; but it seems, as we have said, that virtue and
the good man are in everything the standard): for 3
the good man is of one mind with himself, and

desires the same things with all his soul, and wishes for himself what both is and seems good, and does that (for it is characteristic of him to work out that which is good) for his own sake—for the sake, that is to say, of the rational part of him, which seems to be a man's self. And he wishes his self to live and be preserved, and especially that part of his self by which he thinks: for existence is good to the good
4 man. But it is for himself that each wishes the good; no one would choose to have all that is good (as *e.g.* God is in complete possession of the good) on condition of becoming some one else, but only on condition of still being just himself.* But his reason would seem to be a man's self, or, at least, to be so in a truer sense than any other of his faculties.

5 Such a man also wishes to live with himself; for his own company is pleasant to him. The memory of his past life is sweet, and for the future he has good hopes; and such hopes are pleasant. His mind, moreover, is well stored with matter for contemplation: and he sympathizes with himself in sorrow and in joy; for at all seasons the same things give him pain and pleasure, not this thing now, and then another thing,—for he is, so to speak, not apt to change his mind.

Since, then, all these characteristics are found in the good man's relations to himself, and since his relations to his friend are the same as his relations to himself (for his friend is his second self), friendship is described by one or other of these characteristics,

* Omitting ἐκεῖνο τὸ γενόμενον, after Bywater, *Journal of Philology*, vol. xvii. p. 71.

and those are called friends in whom these characteristics are found.

The question whether friendship towards one's self 6
is or is not possible may be dismissed at present; but that it is possible so far as one has two or more selves would seem to follow from what has been already said, and also from the fact that the extreme of friendship for another is likened to friendship for one's self.

But the characteristics we have mentioned appear 7
to be found in the generality of men, though they are not good.* Perhaps we may say that so far as they are agreeable to themselves, and believe they are good, so far do they share these characteristics. People who are utterly worthless and impious never have them, nor
do they even seem to have them. But we might almost 8
say roundly that they are wanting in all who are not good; for such men are not at one with themselves: they desire one thing while they wish another, as the incontinent do, for instance (for, instead of what they hold to be good, they choose what is pleasant though injurious). Others, again, through cowardice or laziness, shrink from doing that which they believe is the best for them; while those who have done many terrible things out of wickedness, hate life, and wish to get rid of it, and sometimes actually destroy themselves.

Bad men try to find people with whom to spend 9
their time, and eschew their own company; for there is much that is painful in the past on which they

* φαῦλος here as elsewhere includes all who are not good, the incontinent as well as the vicious.

look back and in the future to which they look forward when they are by themselves, but the company of others diverts them from these thoughts. As there is nothing lovable in them, they have no friendly feelings towards themselves.

He who is not good, then, cannot sympathize with himself in joy or sorrow; for his soul is divided against itself: one part of him, by reason of its viciousness, is pained at being deprived of something, while another part of him is pleased; one part pulls this way, another that, tearing him to pieces, as it were, between them.
10 Or if it be impossible to be pained and pleased at the same time, yet, at any rate, after a short interval he is pained that he was pleased, and wishes that he had never partaken of this pleasure; for those who are not good are full of remorse.

Thus we may say roundly that he who is not good has no friendly feelings even for himself, as there is nothing lovable in him. If, then, to be in this state is utterly miserable, we ought to strain every nerve to avoid vice, and try to be good; for thus we may be friendly disposed towards ourselves, and make friends with others.

Friendship and good-will.

1 5. Well-wishing seems to be friendly, but is not friendship: for we may wish well to those who are unknown to us, and who are not aware that we wish them well; but there can be no friendship in such cases. But this we have already said.

Neither is well-wishing the same as love; for it has none of the intense emotion and the desire which accompany love.

Love, moreover, implies intimate acquaintance,

while well-wishing may spring up in a moment; it does so, for instance, when athletes are competing for a prize: we may wish well to a competitor, and be eager for his success, though we would not do anything to help him; for, as we said, we suddenly become well-wishers and conceive a sort of superficial affection in such cases.

The truth seems to be that well-wishing is the 3
germ of friendship, in the same way as pleasure in the sight of a person is the germ of love: for no one falls in love unless he is first pleased by visible beauty; but he who delights in the beauty of a person is not one whit in love on that account, unless he also feels the absence and desires the presence of that person. Just so it is impossible for people to be friends unless they first become well-wishers, but people who wish each other well are not a whit on that account friends; for they merely wish good to those whose well-wishers they are, but would never help them in any enterprise, or put themselves out for them. One might say, then—extending the meaning of the term—that well-wishing is an undeveloped friendship, which with time and intimate acquaintance may become friendship proper,—not that friendship whose motive is profit, nor that whose motive is pleasure; for well-wishing is no element in them. He who has received a benefit does indeed give his good wishes in return to his benefactor, and it is but just that he should; but he who wishes that another may prosper, in the hope of good things to be got by his means, does not seem really to wish well to the other, but rather to himself, just as he is not

really a friend if he serves him with an eye to profit.

But, generally speaking, well-wishing is grounded upon some kind of excellence or goodness, and arises when a person seems to us beautiful or brave, or endowed with some other good quality, as we said in the case of the athletes.

Friendship and unanimity

6. Unanimity [or unity of sentiment] also seems to be an element in friendship; and this shows that it is not mere agreement in opinion, for that is possible even between people who know nothing of each other.

Nor do we apply the term to those who agree in judgment upon *any* kind of subject, *e.g.* upon astronomy (for being of one mind in these matters has nothing to do with friendship); but we say that unanimity prevails in a state when the citizens agree in their judgments about what is for the common interest, and choose the same course, and carry out the decision of the community. It is with regard to practical matters, therefore, that people are said to be of one mind, especially with regard to matters of importance and things that may be given to both persons, or to all the persons concerned; for instance, a state is said to be of one mind when all the citizens are agreed that the magistracies shall be elective, or that an alliance be made with Sparta, or that Pittacus be governor, Pittacus himself being willing to accept the office. But when each wishes the government for himself, like the brothers in the Phœnissæ of Euripides, then they are at discord: for being of one mind means that each not merely thinks of the same thing (whatever it be), but thinks of it under the same conditions—as, for instance, if both the populace and the upper classes agree that the best men shall govern; for thus they all get what they want.

Unanimity, then, seems to be, as it is called, the kind of friendship that prevails in states; for it has to do with what is for the common interest, and with things that have a considerable influence upon life.

This kind of unanimity is found in good men; 3
for they are of one mind with themselves and with each other, standing, so to speak, always on the same ground: for the wishes of such people are constant, and do not ebb and flow like the Euripus; they wish what is just and for the common interest, and make united efforts to attain it. But people who are not 4
good cannot be of one mind, just as they cannot be friends except for a little space or to a slight extent, as they strive for more than their share of profit, but take less than their share of labours and public services: but every man, while wishing to do this himself, keeps a sharp eye upon his neighbour, and prevents him from doing it; for if they are not thus on their guard, the community is ruined. The result is that they are at discord, striving to compel one another to do what is just, but not willing to do it themselves.

Why benefactors love more than they are loved.

7. Benefactors seem to love those whom they have 1
benefited more than those who have received benefits love those who have conferred them; and as this appears irrational, people seek for the cause of this phenomenon.

Most people think the reason is that the one is in

the position of a debtor, the other in the position of a creditor; and that, therefore, just as in the case of a loan the debtor wishes his creditor were out of the way, while the lender, on the other hand, is anxious that his debtor may be preserved, so here the benefactor desires the existence of him whom he has benefited in hopes of receiving favours in return, while the other is not at all anxious to repay.

Epicharmus, indeed, might perhaps say that this is only the view of "those who have bad places at the play," * but it seems to be true to life; for the generality of men have short memories, and are more eager to receive benefits than to confer them.

But it would seem that the real cause is something that lies deeper in the nature of things, and that the case of creditors does not even resemble this: for creditors have no real affection for their debtors, but only a wish that they may be preserved in order that they may repay; but those who have conferred benefits have a real love and affection for those whom they have benefited, even though they are not, and are never likely to be, of any service.

The same phenomenon may be observed in craftsmen; for every craftsman loves the work of his own hands more than it would love him if it came to life. But perhaps poets carry it furthest; for they love their own poems to excess, and are as fond of them as if they were their children.

Now, the case of the benefactors seems to resemble theirs; those whom they have benefited they have made, so to speak: that which they have made, then,

* Epicharmus was a Sicilian dramatist.

they love more than the work loves its maker. And the reason of this is that we all desire existence and love it: but it is in the exercise of our faculties, or in the realization of ourselves, that our existence lies (for it lies in living and doing): but * that which a man makes is, in a way, a realization of his self; therefore he loves it, because he loves existence.

But this is in accordance with the nature of things; for it is a law of nature that what a thing is as yet potentially is exhibited in realization by that which it makes or does.

Moreover, the manifestation of his action is beau- 5
tiful to the benefactor, so that he delights in the person that makes it manifest; but to him who has received the benefit there is nothing beautiful in the benefactor, but at the most something useful; and such an object is less pleasing and less lovable.

Again, we take pleasure in realizing ourselves in 6
the present, in hopes for the future, and in memories of the past; but that in which we are realizing ourselves is the most pleasant, and likewise the most lovable. Now, for the benefactor what he has done endures (for that which is beautiful is lasting), while for him who has received the benefit the advantage soon passes away.

Again, the memory of beautiful deeds is pleasant, of profitable actions not at all pleasant, or not so pleasant; but with expectation the reverse seems to be the case.

Again, loving seems like doing something, being loved like having something done to you: but those

* Reading Ἐνεργείᾳ δ' ὁ ποιήσας τὸ ἔργον ἐστί πως.

who have the better part in the transaction naturally feel and show more love.

Again, we all have more affection for what we have achieved with toil, as those who have made money love it more than those who have inherited it; but receiving a benefit seems to involve no labour, while conferring one seems to be troublesome. And for this reason mothers have more affection for their children than fathers; for they have more trouble in giving them birth, and fuller assurance that they are their own. But this would seem to be a characteristic of benefactors also.

In what sense it is right to love one's self.

8. Another question which is raised is, whether we ought most to love ourselves or others.

We blame, it is said, those who love themselves most, and apply the term self-loving to them as a term of reproach: and, again, he who is not good is thought to have regard to himself in everything that he does, and the more so the worse he is; and so we accuse him of doing nothing disinterestedly. The good man on the other hand, it is thought, takes what is noble as his motive, and the better he is the more is he guided by this motive, and by regard for his friend, neglecting his own interest.

But this theory disagrees with facts, nor is it surprising that it should. For it is allowed that we ought to love him most who is most truly a friend, and that he is most truly a friend who, in wishing well to another, wishes well to him for his (the other's) sake, and even though no one should ever know. But all these characteristics, and all the others which go to make up the definition of a friend, are found in the highest degree in a man's relations to himself; for we have already seen how it is from our relations to ourselves that all our friendly relations to others are derived. Moreover, all the proverbs point to the same conclusion—such as "Friends have one soul," "Friends have all things in common," "Equality makes friendship," "The knee is nearer than the shin." All these characteristics are found in the highest degree in a man's relations to himself; for he is his own best friend: and so he must love himself better than any one else.

People not unnaturally are puzzled to know which of these two statements to adopt, since both appeal to them. Perhaps the best method of dealing 3
with conflicting statements of this kind is first to make out the difference between them, and then to determine how far and in what sense each is right. So here, if we first ascertain what self-loving means in each statement, the difficulty will perhaps be cleared up.

Those who use self-loving as a term of reproach 4
apply the name to those who take more than their due of money, and honour, and bodily pleasures; for the generality of men desire these things, and set their hearts upon them as the best things in the world, so that they are keenly competed for. Those, then, who grasp at more than their share of these things indulge their animal appetites and their passions generally—in a word, the irrational part of their nature. But this is the character of the generality of men; and hence the term self-loving has come to be used in this bad sense from the fact that

the greater part of mankind are not good. It is with justice, then, that we reproach those who are self-loving in this sense.

That it really is to those who take more than their due of these things that the term is usually applied by the generality of men, may easily be shown; for if what a man always set his heart upon were that he, rather than another, should do what is just or temperate, or in any other way virtuous—if, in a word, he were always claiming the noble course of conduct, no one would call him self-loving and no one would reproach him.

And yet such a man would seem to be more truly self-loving. At least, he takes for himself that which is noblest and most truly good, and gratifies the ruling power in himself, and in all things obeys it. But just as the ruling part in a state or in any other system seems, more than any other part, to be the state or the system, so also the ruling part of a man seems to be most truly the man's self. He therefore who loves and gratifies this part of himself is most truly self-loving.

Again, we call a man continent or incontinent,* according as his reason has or has not the mastery, implying that his reason is his self; and when a man has acted under the guidance of his reason he is thought, in the fullest sense, to have done the deed himself, and of his own will.

It is plain, then, that this part of us is our self, or is most truly our self, and that the good man more

* ἐγκρατής, continent, in whom the true masters the false self; ἀκρατής, incontinent, in whom the true self is mastered.

than any other loves this part of himself. He, then, more than any other, will be self-loving, in another sense than the man whom we reproach as self-loving, differing from him by all the difference that exists between living according to reason and living according to passion, between desiring what is noble and desiring what appears to be profitable.

Those who beyond other men set their hearts on 7
noble deeds are welcomed and praised by all; but if all men were vieing with each other in the pursuit of what is noble, and were straining every nerve to act in the noblest possible manner, the result would be that both the wants of the community would be perfectly satisfied, and at the same time each individually would win the greatest of all good things —for virtue is that.

The good man, therefore, ought to be self-loving; for by doing what is noble he will at once benefit himself and assist others: but the bad man ought not; for he will injure both himself and his neighbours by following passions that are not good.

Thus, with the bad man there is a discrepancy 8
between what he ought to do and what he does: but with the good man what he ought to do is what he does; for reason always chooses that which is best for itself; and the good man obeys the voice of reason.

Again, it is quite true to say of the good man 9
that he does many things for the sake of his friends and of his country, and will, if need be, even die for them. He will throw away money and honour, and, in a word, all the good things for which men compete,

claiming for himself that which is noble; for he will prefer a brief period of intense pleasure to a long period of mild pleasure, one year of noble life to many years of ordinary life, one great and noble action to many little ones. This, we may perhaps say, is what he gets who gives his life for others: and so he chooses for himself something that is noble on a grand scale.

Such a man will surrender wealth to enrich his friend: for while his friend gets the money, he gets what is noble; so he takes the greater good for himself.

10 His conduct will be the same with regard to honours and offices: he will give up all to his friend; for this he deems noble and praiseworthy.

Such a man, then, is not unreasonably considered good, as he chooses what is noble in preference to everything else.

But, again, it is possible to give up to your friend an opportunity for action. and it may be nobler to cause your friend to do a deed than to do it yourself.

11 It is plain, then, that in all cases in which he is praised the good man takes for himself a larger share of what is noble. And in this sense, as we have said, a man ought to be self-loving, but not in the sense in which the generality of men are self-loving.

1 **9.** Another disputed question is whether a happy man needs friends or not. *Why a happy man needs friends.*

It is said that those who are blessed and self-sufficient have no need of friends; for they are already supplied with good things: as self-sufficient, then they need nothing more, while a friend is an *alter ego* who procures for you what you cannot procure yourself; whence the saying—

"When the god favours you, what need of friends?"

But it seems strange, while endowing the happy 2
man with all good things, to deny him friends, which are thought to be the greatest of all external goods.

And if it is more characteristic of a friend to confer than to receive benefits, and if it is characteristic of a good man and a virtuous character to do good to others, and if it is nobler to confer benefits on friends than on strangers, the good man will need friends to receive benefits from him.

And so people ask whether friends are more needed in prosperity or adversity, considering that in adversity we want some one to help us, and in prosperity some one that we may help.

Again, it is surely absurd to make the happy man 3
a solitary being: for no one would choose to have all conceivable good things on condition of being alone; for man is a social being, and by nature adapted to share his life with others. The happy man, then, must have this good, since he has whatever is naturally good for man. But it is obvious that it is better to live with friends and good people, than with strangers and casual persons. The happy man, then, must have friends.

What, then, do those who maintain the former 4
opinion mean? and in what sense are they right? Is it that the generality of men think that friends means useful people? Friends in this sense certainly the happy or blessed man will not need, as he already has

whatever is good. And, again, he will have no need, or but little need, of the friendship that is based on pleasure; for his life is pleasant and does not require adventitious pleasure. Because he does not need this kind of friends then, people come to think he does not need friends at all.

5 But I think we may say that this opinion is not true. For we said at the outset that happiness is a certain exercise of our faculties; but the exercise of our faculties plainly comes to be in time, and is not like a piece of property acquired once for all. But if happiness consists in living and exercising our faculties; and if the exercise of the good man's faculties is good and pleasant in itself, as we said at the outset; and if the sense that a thing belongs to us is also a source of pleasure, but it is easier to contemplate others than ourselves, and others' acts than our own—then * the acts of the good men who are his friends are pleasant to the good man (for both the natural sources of pleasure are united in them). † The happy or blessed man, therefore, will need such friends, since he desires to contemplate acts that are good and belong to him, and such are the acts of a good man who is his friend.

Again, it is thought that the happy man's life must be pleasant. Now, if he is solitary, life is hard for him; for it is very difficult to be continuously
active by one's self, but not so difficult along with
6 others, and in relation to others. With friends, then,
the exercise of his faculties will be more continuous,
being pleasant in itself. And this is what ought

* Reading δὴ. See Stewart. † (1) They are good, (2) they belong to him.

to be the case with the blessed man; for the good man, as such, delights in acts of virtue and is vexed by acts of vice, just as a musician is pleased by good music and pained by bad.

Again, he would get a sort of practice in virtue by 7
living with good men, as Theognis says.*

But if we look a little deeper into the nature of things, a good friend appears to be naturally desirable to the good man:—

What is naturally good, we have already said, is good and pleasant in itself to the good man.

Now, life is defined in the case of animals by the power of feeling, in the case of man by the power of feeling or thought: but the power involves reference to its exercise; and it is in this exercise that the reality lies: life, then, in its reality, seems to be feeling or thinking.

Life, again, is one of the things that are good and pleasant in themselves; for it is determinate or formed, and the determinate or formed is of the nature of the good; but that which is naturally [or in itself] good is good to the good man. (And hence life
seems to be pleasant to all men. But by life we must 8
not understand a bad or corrupt life, or a life of pain; for such a life is formless, as are all its constituents. We shall endeavour, presently, to throw some light on the nature of pain.)

Life itself, then, is good and pleasant (as appears 9
also from the fact that all desire it, and especially the good and the blessed; for life is most desirable to them, and their life is the most blessed).

* *Cf.* the last words of this book.

But he who sees feels that he sees, and he who hears feels that he hears, and he who walks feels that he walks; and similarly, whatever else we do, there is something that perceives that we are putting forth power, so that whether we feel or think, we must be conscious of feeling or thinking.

But to be conscious of feeling or thinking is to be conscious of existence; for our existence, we found, is feeling or thinking.

But consciousness of life is a thing that is pleasant in itself; for life is naturally good, and to be conscious of the presence of a good thing is pleasant.

Life, then, is desirable, and most of all desirable to the good man, because his existence is good to him, and pleasant; for he is pleased by the consciousness of that which is good in itself.

10 But the good man stands in the same relation to his friend as to himself, for his friend is another self: just as his own existence, then, is desirable to each, so, or nearly so, is his friend's existence desirable.

But existence, we found, is desirable because of the consciousness that one's self is good, such a consciousness being pleasant in itself.

The good man, then, should be conscious of the existence of his friend also, and this consciousness will be given by living with him and by rational converse with him (for this would seem to be the proper meaning of living together, when applied to man, and not merely feeding in the same place, which it means when applied to beasts).

Putting all this together, then, if his own existence is desirable in itself to the good man, being naturally good and pleasant, and if his friend's existence is also desirable to him in nearly the same way, it follows that a friend is a desirable thing for him. But that which is desirable for him he ought to have, or in that respect he will be incomplete. Our conclusion, therefore, is that he who is to be happy must have good friends.

Of the proper number of friends.

10. Are we to make as many friends as possible? 1
or, as in the case of guest-friendship * we approve of the saying, "neither a host of guest-friends nor yet none," shall we say that in the case of friendship also it is best neither to be friendless nor yet to have too many friends?

With regard to friends who are chosen with a 2
view to being useful, the saying would seem to be perfectly appropriate; for it would be troublesome to repay the services of a large number, and indeed life is not long enough to enable us to do it. Of such friends, therefore, a larger number than is sufficient for one's own life would be superfluous and a hindrance to noble living; so we do not want more than that number.

Again, of friends chosen with a view to pleasure a small number is enough, as a small proportion of sweets is enough in our diet.

But are we to have as many good men for friends 3
as we can, or is there any limit of numbers in friendship, as there is in a state? for you could not make a state out of ten men, and if you had a hundred thousand your state would cease to be a state. But perhaps the right number of citizens is not one fixed

* *Cf.* note on viii. 3, 4.

number, but any number within certain limits. And
so with friends there is a limit to their number, and
that is, we may say, the largest number that one can
live with (for living together is, as we saw, one of the
4 most essential characteristics of friendship); but it is
quite evident that it is impossible to live with and
spread one's self abroad among a large number.

Moreover, a man's friends must be friends with one another, if all are to spend their time together; but this is difficult with a large number.

5 Again, it becomes hard for him to sympathize duly with the joys and sorrows of a large number; for then he is likely to have at the same time to rejoice with one and to grieve with another. Perhaps, then, the best plan is not to try to have as many friends as possible, but so many as are sufficient for a life in common; and indeed it would be impossible to have an ardent friendship with a great number.

And, for the same reason, it is impossible to be in love with many persons at once; for it seems that love is a sort of superlative friendship, and that this is only possible towards one person, and an ardent friendship towards a few only.

6 And this seems, in fact, to happen: we do not find a number of people bound together by the sort of friendship that exists between comrades, but the friendships that the poets celebrate are friendships of two persons. And the man of many friends, who is hail-fellow-well-met with everybody, seems to be really friends with no one (in any other way than as fellow-citizens are friends)—I mean the man whom we call obsequious.

After the manner of fellow-citizens, indeed, it is possible to be friends with a great number, and yet not to be obsequious, but to be a truly good man; but that kind of friendship which is based on virtue and on regard for the friend's self one cannot have for many, but must be well satisfied if one can find even a few such persons.

Friends needed both in prosperity and adversity.

11. Is it in prosperity or adversity that we most 1
need friends? For under both circumstances we have recourse to them: in misfortune we need help, in prosperity we need people to live with and to do good to; for we wish to do good.

In adversity, it may be answered, the need is more pressing; we then require useful friends: but friendship is a nobler thing in prosperity; we then seek out good men for friends; for it is more desirable to do good to and to live with such people.

The mere presence of friends is sweet, even in 2
misfortune; for our grief is lightened when our friends share it. And so it might be asked whether they literally take a share of it as of a weight, or whether it is not so, but rather that their presence, which is sweet, and the consciousness of their sympathy, make our grief less. But whether this or something else be the cause of the relief, we need not further inquire; the fact is evidently as we said.

But their presence seems to be complex in its
effects. On the one hand, the mere sight of friends 3
is pleasant, especially when we are in adversity, and contributes something to assuage our grief; for a friend can do much to comfort us both by sight and speech, if he has tact: he knows our character, and

4 what pleases and what pains us. But, on the other hand, to see another grieving over our misfortunes is a painful thing; for every one dislikes to be the cause of sorrow to his friends. For this reason he who is of a manly nature takes care not to impart his grief to his friends, shrinking from the pain that would give them, unless this is quite outweighed by the relief it would give him;* and generally he does not allow others to lament with him, as he is not given to lamentations himself; but weak women and effeminate men delight in those who lament with them, and love them as friends and sympathizers. (But evidently we ought in all circumstances to take the better man for our model.)

5 In prosperity, again, the presence of friends not only makes the time pass pleasantly, but also brings the consciousness that our friends are pleased at our good fortune. And for this reason it would seem that we should be eager to invite our friends to share our prosperity, for it is noble to be ready to confer benefits,—but slow to summon them to us in adversity, for we ought to be loth to give others a share of our evil things: whence comes the saying, "That I am in sorrow is sorrow enough." But we should be least unwilling to call them in when they will be likely to relieve us much without being greatly troubled themselves.

6 But, on the other hand, when our friends are in trouble, we should, I think, go to them unsummoned and readily (for it is a friend's office to serve his friend, and especially when he is in need and does not

* See a few lines on end of § 5.

claim assistance, for then it is nobler and pleasanter to both): when they are in prosperity, we should go readily to help them (for this is one of the uses of a friend), but not so readily to share their good things; for it is not a noble thing to be very ready to receive a benefit. But we may add that we ought to be careful that our refusal shall not seem ungracious, as sometimes happens.

The presence of friends, then, in conclusion, is manifestly desirable on all occasions.

Friendship is realized in living together.

12. Lovers delight above all things in the sight 1
of each other, and prefer the gratification of this sense to that of all the others, as this sense is more concerned than any other in the being and origin of love. In like manner, we may venture to say, do friends find living together more desirable than anything else: for friendship is essentially community, and a man stands to his friend in the same relation in which he stands to himself; but with regard to himself the consciousness of existence is desirable; therefore the same consciousness with regard to his friend is desirable; but it is in a common life that they attain this consciousness; therefore they naturally desire a life in common.

Again, whatever that be which a man holds to 2
constitute existence, or for the sake of which he chooses to live, in that he wishes to pass his time together with his friends; and thus some drink together, others gamble, others practise gymnastics, or hunt, or study philosophy together—in each case spending their time together in that which they love most of all things in life; for, wishing to live in

common with their friends, they do those things and take part together in those things which, as they think, constitute life in common.

3 Thus the friendship of those who are not good comes to be positively bad; for, having no stability of character, they confirm each other in things that are not good, and thus become positively bad as they become more like one another. But the friendship of good men is good, and grows with their intercourse; and they seem to become better as they exercise their faculties and correct each other's deficiencies: for each moulds himself to the likeness of that which he approves in the other; whence the saying, "From good men thou shalt learn good things." *

4 So much, then, for friendship. We will now pass to the consideration of pleasure.

* ἐσθλῶν μὲν γὰρ ἄπ' ἐσθλὰ μαθήσεαι.—Theognis.

BOOK X.

CHAPTERS 1–5. PLEASURE.

Reasons for discussing pleasure.

1. OUR next business, I think, should be to treat 1
of pleasure. For pleasure seems, more than anything else, to have an intimate connection with our nature; which is the reason why, in educating the young, we use pleasure and pain as the rudders of their course. Moreover, delight in what we ought to delight in, and hatred of what we ought to hate, seem to be of the utmost importance in the formation of a virtuous character; for these feelings pervade the whole of life, and have power to draw a man to virtue and happiness, as we choose what pleases, and shun what pains us.

And it would seem that the discussion of these 2
matters is especially incumbent on us, since there is much dispute about them. There are people who say that the good is pleasure, and there are people who say, on the contrary, that pleasure is altogether bad—some, perhaps, in the conviction that it is really so, others because they think it has a good effect on men's lives to assert that pleasure is a bad thing, even though it be not; for the generality

of men, they say, incline this way, and are slaves to their pleasures, so that they ought to be pulled in the opposite direction: for thus they will be brought into the middle course.

But I cannot think that it is right to speak thus. For assertions about matters of feeling and conduct carry less weight than actions; and so, when assertions are found to be at variance with palpable facts, they fall into contempt, and bring the truth also into discredit. Thus, when a man who speaks ill of pleasure is seen at times to desire it himself, he is thought to show by the fact of being attracted by it that he really considers all pleasure desirable; for the generality of men are not able to draw fine distinctions. It seems, then, that true statements are the most useful, for practice as well as for theory; for, being in harmony with facts, they gain credence, and so incline those who understand them to regulate their lives by them. But enough of this: let us now go through the current opinions about pleasure.

Arguments of Eudoxus that pleasure is the good.

2. Eudoxus thought pleasure was the good, because he saw that all beings, both rational and irrational, strive after it; but in all cases, he said, that which is desirable * is the good, and that which is most desirable is best: the fact, then, that all beings incline to one and the same thing indicates that this is the best thing for all (for each being finds out what is good for itself—its food, for instance); but that which is good for all, and which all strive after, is the good.

The statements of Eudoxus were accepted rather

* τὸ αἱρετόν covers, as no English word can, the transition from desired to desirable.

because of the excellence of his character than on their own account; for he seemed to be a remarkably temperate man; and so people thought that it was not from love of pleasure that he spoke thus, but that what he said really was the fact.

Eudoxus also thought that his point could be proved no less clearly by the argument from the opposite of pleasure:—pain is, in itself, an object of aversion to all beings; therefore its opposite is desirable for all. 2

Again, he argued, that is most desirable which we choose, not on account of something else, but for its own sake: but this is admitted to be the case with pleasure; for we never ask a man for his motive in taking pleasure, it being understood that pleasure is in itself desirable.

Again, he argued that any good thing whatsoever is made more desirable by the addition of pleasure, *e.g.* just or temperate conduct; but it can only be by the good that the good is increased.

Now, this last argument seems indeed to show that pleasure is a good thing, but not that it is one whit better than any other good thing; for *any* good thing is more desirable with the addition of another good thing than by itself. 3

Nay, Plato actually employs a similar argument to show that pleasure is not the good. "The pleasant life," he says, "is more desirable with wisdom than without: but if the combination of the two be better, pleasure itself cannot be the good; for no addition can make the good more desirable." And it is equally evident that, if any other thing be made more desir-

able by the addition of one of the class of things that are good in themselves, that thing cannot be the good.
4 What good is there, then, which is thus incapable of addition, and at the same time such that men can participate in it? For that is the sort of good that we want.

But those who maintain, on the contrary, that what all desire is not good, surely talk nonsense. What all men think, that, we say, is true. And to him who bids us put no trust in the opinion of mankind, we reply that we can scarce put greater trust in his opinion. If it were merely irrational creatures that desired these things, there might be something in what he says; but as rational beings also desire them, how can it be anything but nonsense? Indeed, it may be that even in inferior beings there is some natural principle of good stronger than themselves, which strives after their proper good.

5 Again, what the adversaries of Eudoxus say about his argument from the nature of the opposite of pleasure, does not seem to be sound. They say that, though pain be bad, yet it does not follow that pleasure is good; for one bad thing may be opposed to another bad thing, and both to a third thing which is different from either.* Now, though this is not a bad remark, it does not hold true in the present instance. For if both were bad, both alike ought to be shunned, or if neither were bad, neither should be shunned, or, at least, one no more than the other: but, as it is, men evidently shun the one as bad and

* The neutral state, neither pleasure nor pain, which they hold to be good.

choose the other as good; they are, in fact, therefore, opposed to one another in this respect.

Argument that it is not a quality; that it is not determined; that it is a motion or coming into being. Pleasures differ in kind.

3. Again, even though pleasure is not a quality, 1
it does not follow that it is not a good thing. The
exercise of virtue, happiness itself, is not a quality.

It is objected, again, that the good is determinate, 2
while pleasure is indeterminate, because it admits of
a more and a less.

Now, if they say this because one may be more or less pleased, then the same thing may be said of justice and the other virtues; for it is plain that, with regard to them, we speak of people as being and showing themselves more or less virtuous: some men are more just and more brave than others, and it is possible to act more or less justly and temperately.

But if they mean that one pleasure may be more
or less of a pleasure than another, I suspect that they
miss the real reason when they say it is because
some are pure and some are mixed. Why should it 3
not be the same with pleasure as with health, which,
though something determinate, yet allows of more
and less? For the due proportion of elements
[which constitutes health] is not the same for all, nor
always the same for the same person, but may vary
within certain limits without losing its character,
being now more and now less truly health. And it
may be the same with pleasure.

Again, assuming that the good is complete, while 4
motion and coming into being are incomplete, they try
to show that pleasure is a motion and a coming into
being.

But they do not seem to be right even in saying

that it is a motion : for every motion seems necessarily to be quick or slow, either absolutely, as the motion of the universe, or relatively; but pleasure is neither quick nor slow. It is, indeed, possible to be quickly pleased, as to be quickly angered; the feeling, however, cannot be quick, even relatively, as can walking and growing, etc. The passage to a state of pleasure, then, may be quick or slow, but the exercise of the power, *i.e.* the feeling of pleasure, cannot be quick.

5 Again, how can pleasure be a coming into being?

It seems that it is not possible for anything to come out of just anything, but what a thing comes out of, that it is resolved into. Pain, then, must be the dissolution of that whose coming into being is plea-
6 sure. Accordingly, they maintain that pain is falling short of the normal state, pleasure its replenishment.

But these are bodily processes. If, then, pleasure be the replenishment of the normal state, that in which the replenishment takes place, *i.e.* the body, must be that which is pleased. But this does not seem to be the case. Pleasure, therefore, is not a replenishment, but while the process of replenishment is going on we may be pleased, and while the process of exhaustion is going on we may be pained.*

This view of pleasure seems to have been suggested by the pleasures and pains connected with nutrition; for there it is true that we come into a state of want, and, after previous pain, find pleasure in replenish-
7 ment. But this is not the case with all pleasures; for there is no previous pain involved in the pleasures

* Adopting Spengel's conjecture, κενούμενος for τεμνόμενος.

of the mathematician, nor among the sensuous pleasures in those of smell, nor, again, in many kinds of sights and sounds, nor in memories and hopes. What is there, then, of which these pleasures are the becoming? Here there is nothing lacking that can be replenished.

To those, again, who [in order to show that 8
pleasure is not good] adduce the disgraceful kinds of pleasure we might reply that these things are not pleasant. Though they be pleasant to ill-conditioned persons, we must not therefore hold them to be pleasant *except* to them; just as we do not hold that to be wholesome, or sweet, or bitter, which is wholesome, sweet, or bitter to the sick man, or that to be white which appears white to a man with ophthalmia.

Or, again, we might reply that these pleasures 9
are desirable, but not when derived from these sources, just as it is desirable to be rich, but not at the cost of treachery, and desirable to be in health, but not at the cost of eating any kind of abominable food.

Or we might say that the pleasures are specifically 10
different. The pleasures derived from noble sources are different from those derived from base sources, and it is impossible to feel the just man's pleasure without being just, or the musical man's pleasure without being musical, and so on with the rest.

The distinction drawn between the true friend 11
and the flatterer seems to show either that pleasure is not good, or else that pleasures differ in kind. For the former in his intercourse is thought to have the good in view, the latter pleasure; and while we blame

the latter, we praise the former as having a different aim in his intercourse.

12 Again, no one would choose to live on condition of having a child's intellect all his life, though he were to enjoy in the highest possible degree all the pleasures of a child; nor choose to gain enjoyment by the performance of some extremely disgraceful act, though he were never to feel pain.

There are many things, too, which we should care for, even though they brought no pleasure, as sight, memory, knowledge, moral and intellectual excellence. Even if we grant that pleasure necessarily accompanies them, this does not affect the question; for we should choose them even if no pleasure resulted from them.

13 It seems to be evident, then, that pleasure is not the good, nor are all pleasures desirable, but that some are desirable, differing in kind, or in their sources, from those that are not desirable. Let this be taken then as a sufficient account of the current opinions about pleasure and pain.

1 4. As to the nature or quality of pleasure, we shall more readily discover it if we make a fresh start as follows:— *Pleasure defined: its relation to activity.*

Vision seems to be perfect or complete at any moment; for it does not lack anything which can be added afterwards to make its nature complete. Pleasure seems in this respect to resemble vision; for it is something whole and entire, and it would be impossible at any moment to find a pleasure which would become complete by lasting longer.

2 Therefore pleasure is not a motion; for every

motion requires time and implies an end (*e.g.* the motion of building), and is complete when the desired result is produced—either in the whole time therefore, or in this final moment of it. But during the progress of the work all the motions are incomplete, and specifically different from the whole motion and from each other; the fitting together of the stones is different from the fluting of the pillar, and both from the building of the temple. The building of the temple is complete; nothing more is required for the execution of the plan. But the building of the foundation and of the triglyph are incomplete; for each is the building of a part only. These motions, then, are specifically different from one another, and it is impossible to find a motion whose nature is complete at any moment—it is complete, if at all, only in the whole time.

It is the same also with walking and the other 3
kinds of locomotion. For though all locomotion is a motion from one place to another, yet there are distinct kinds of locomotion, as flying, walking, leaping, etc. Nay, not only so, but even in walking itself there are differences, for the whence and whither are not the same in the entire course and in a portion of the course, or in this portion and in that, nor is crossing this line the same as crossing that; for you do not cross a line simply, but a line that is in a given place, and this line is in a different place from that. I must refer to my other works * for a detailed dis-

* Physics, Book iii. f.: *cf.* especially viii. 8, 264 *b*, 27, quoted by Ramsauer, who founds on it an ingenious emendation of this passage.

cussion of motion; but it seems that it is not complete at any moment, but that its several parts are incomplete, and that they are specifically different from one another, the whence and whither being a specific difference.

4 Pleasure, on the other hand, is complete in its nature at any moment. It is evident, therefore, that these two must be distinct from each other, and that pleasure must be one of the class of whole and complete things. And this would also seem to follow from the fact that though duration is necessary for motion, it is not necessary for pleasure—for a momentary pleasure is something whole and entire.

From these considerations it is plain that they are wrong in saying that pleasure is a motion or a coming into being. For these terms are not applied to every thing, but only to those things that are divisible into parts and are not wholes. We cannot speak of the coming into being of vision, or of a mathematical point, or of unity; nor is any one of them a motion or a coming into being. And these terms are equally inapplicable to pleasure; for it is something whole and entire.

5 Every sense exercises itself upon its proper object, and exercises itself completely when it is in good condition and the object is the noblest of those that fall within its scope (for the complete exercise of a faculty seems to mean this; and we may assume that it makes no difference whether we speak of the sense, or of the sensitive subject as exercising itself): of each sense, then, we may say that the exercise is best when on the one side you have the finest condition,

and on the other the highest of the objects that fall within the scope of this faculty.

But this exercise of the faculty will be not only the most complete, but also the pleasantest: for the exercise of every sense is attended with pleasure, and so is the exercise of reason and the speculative faculty; and it is pleasantest when it is most complete, and it is most complete when the faculty is well-trained and the object is the best of those that fall under this faculty.

And, further, the pleasure completes the exercise 6
of the faculty. But the pleasure completes it in a different way from that in which the object and the faculty of sense complete it, when both are as they should be; just as health causes healthy activities in a different way from that in which the physician causes them.

(That the exercise of every sense is accompanied 7
by pleasure is evident: we speak of pleasant sights and pleasant sounds.

It is evident also that the pleasure is greatest when both the faculty and that upon which it is exercised are as good as they can be: when this is the case both with the object of sense and the sentient subject, there will always be pleasure, so long, that is, as you have the subject to act and the object to be acted upon.)

Now, the pleasure makes the exercise complete 8
not as the habit or trained faculty* does, being

* As already remarked, there is no one English word which includes these various senses of ἕξις, (1) habit of body, (2) moral habit or character, (3) intellectual habit or trained faculty.

already present in the subject, but as a sort of superadded completeness, like the grace of youth.*

So long, then, as both the object of thought or of sense and the perceptive or contemplative subject are as they ought to be, so long will there be pleasure in the exercise; for so long as the object to be acted upon and the subject that is able to act remain the same, and maintain the same relation to each other, the result must be the same.

9 How is it, then, that we are incapable of continuous pleasure? Perhaps the reason is that we become exhausted; for no human faculty is capable of continuous exercise. Pleasure, then, also cannot be continuous; for it is an accompaniment of the exercise of faculty. And for the same reason some things please us when new, but afterwards please us less. For at first the intellect is stimulated and exercises itself upon them strenuously, just as we strain our eyes to look hard at something; but after a time the exertion ceases to be so intense, and becomes relaxed; and so the pleasure also loses its keenness.

10 The desire for pleasure we should expect to be shared by all men, seeing that all desire to live.

For life is an exercise of faculties, and each man exercises the faculties he most loves upon the things he most loves; *e.g.* the musical man exercises his hearing upon melodies, and the studious man exer-

* At other periods of life the various organs of the body may perform their functions completely, but in youth this is accompanied by an inexpressible charm which all other ages lack.

The only analogy between pleasure and the doctor is that both "complete the activity" from outside: medicines alter the functions; pleasure, like beauty, does not alter them, but is an added perfection.

cises his intellect upon matters of speculation, and so on with the rest.

But pleasure completes the exercise of faculties, and therefore life, which men desire.

Naturally, therefore, men desire pleasure too; for each man finds in it the completion of his life, which is desirable.

But whether we desire life for the sake of plea- 11
sure, or pleasure for the sake of life, is a question which we may dismiss for the present. For the two seem to be joined together, and not to admit of separation: without exercise of faculties there is no pleasure, and every such exercise is completed by pleasure.

leasures ffer according to e activities he standard the good an.

5. And from this it seems to follow that pleasures 1
differ in kind, since specifically different things we believe to be completed by specifically different things. For this seems to be the case with the products both of nature and of art, as animals and trees, paintings, sculptures, houses, and furniture. Similarly, then, we believe that exercises of faculty which differ in kind are completed by things different in kind.

But the exercises of the intellectual faculties are 2
specifically different from the exercises of the senses, and the several kinds of each from one another; therefore the pleasures which complete them are also different.

The same conclusion would seem to follow from the close connection that exists between each pleasure and the exercise of faculty which it completes. For the exercise is increased by its proper pleasure; *e.g.* people are more likely to understand any matter, and to go to the bottom of it, if the exercise is pleasant to them. Thus, those who delight in geometry become geometricians, and understand all the propositions better than others; and similarly, those who are fond of music, or of architecture, or of anything else, make progress in that kind of work, because they delight in it. The pleasures, then, help to increase the exercise; but that which helps to increase it must be closely connected with it: but when things are specifically different from one another, the things that are closely connected with them must also be specifically different.

The same conclusion follows perhaps still more clearly from the fact that the exercise of one faculty is impeded by the pleasure proper to another; *e.g.* a lover of the flute is unable to attend to an argument if he hears a man playing, since he takes more delight in flute-playing than in his present business; the pleasure of the flute-player, therefore, hinders the exercise of the reason.

The same result follows in other cases, too, whenever a man is exercising his faculties on two things at a time; the pleasanter business thwarts the other, and, if the difference in pleasantness be great, thwarts it more and more, even to the extent of suppressing it altogether. Thus, when anything gives us intense delight, we cannot do anything else at all, and when we do a second thing, we do not very much care about the first; and so people who eat sweetmeats in the theatre do this most of all when the actors are bad.

Since its proper pleasure heightens the exercise of a faculty, making it both more prolonged and better, while pleasure from another source spoils it, it is evident that there is a great difference between these two pleasures. Indeed, pleasure from another source has almost the same effect as pain from the activity itself. For the exercise of a faculty is spoilt by pain arising from it; as happens, for instance, when a man finds it disagreeable and painful to write or to calculate; for he stops writing in the one case and calculating in the other, since the exercise is painful. The exercise of a faculty, then, is affected in opposite ways by its proper pleasure and its proper pain; and by "proper" I mean that which is occasioned by the exercise itself. But pleasure from another source, we have already said, has almost the same effect as its proper pain; *i.e.* it interferes with the exercise of the faculty, though not to the same extent.

Again, as the exercises of our faculties differ in 6
goodness and badness, and some are to be desired and some to be shunned, while some are indifferent, so do the several pleasures differ; for each exercise has its proper pleasure. The pleasure which is proper to a good activity, then, is good, and that which is proper to one that is not good is bad: for the desire of noble things is laudable, and the desire of base things is blamable; but the pleasures which accompany the exercises of our faculties belong to them even more than the desires do, since the latter are distinct both in time and in nature, while the former are almost coincident in time, and so hard to distinguish from them that it is a matter of debate whether the exercise be not identical with the pleasure.

It seems, however, that the pleasure is not the 7
same as the act of thinking or of feeling; that is im-

possible: but the fact that the two are inseparable makes some people fancy that they are identical.

As, then, the exercises of the faculties vary, so do their respective pleasures. Sight is purer than touch, hearing and smell than taste*: there is a corresponding difference, therefore, between their pleasures; and the pleasures of the intellect are purer than these pleasures of sense, and some of each kind are purer than others.

8 Each kind of being, again, seems to have its proper pleasure, as it has its proper function,—viz. the pleasure which accompanies the exercise of its faculties or the realization of its nature. And a separate consideration of the several kinds of animals will confirm this: the pleasures of a horse, a dog, and a man are all different—as Heraclitus says, a donkey would prefer hay to gold; for there is more pleasure in fodder than in gold to a donkey.

The pleasures of specifically different beings, then, are specifically different; and we might naturally suppose that there would be no specific difference between the pleasures of beings of the same species.
9 And yet there is no small difference, in the pleasures of men at least: what pleases this man pains that; what is grievous and hateful to one is pleasant and lovable to another. This occurs in the case of sweet

* Sight and touch are classed together on the one hand, and hearing, smell, and taste on the other, because, while the announcements of all the senses are, in the first instance, of secondary qualities (colours, sounds, etc.), it is mainly from the announcements of sight and touch that we advance to the knowledge of the mathematical properties or primary qualities (number, figure, motion, etc.).

things, too: a man in a fever has a different notion of what is sweet from a man in health; and a feeble man's notion of what is hot is different from that of a robust man. And the like occurs in other matters also.

But in all matters of this kind we hold that 10
things *are* what they appear to be to the perfect man.

Now, if this opinion is correct, as we hold it to be—if, that is, in every case the test is virtue, or the good man as such—then what appears to him to be pleasure will be pleasure, and what he delights in will be pleasant.

If what is disagreeable to him appears pleasant
to another, we need not be astonished; for there are
many ways in which men are corrupted and perverted: such things, however, are not pleasant, but
only pleasant to these men with their disposition. It 11
is plain, then, that we must not allow the confessedly
base pleasures to be pleasures at all, except to corrupt
men.

But of the pleasures that are considered good, which or what kind are to be called the proper pleasures of man? We cannot be in doubt if we know what are the proper exercises of his faculties; for the proper pleasures are their accompaniments. Whether, then, the exercise of faculties proper to the complete and happy man be one or many, the pleasures that complete that exercise will be called pleasures of man in the full meaning of the words, and the others in a secondary sense and with a fraction of that meaning, just as is the case with the exercises of the faculties.

CHAPTERS 6–9. CONCLUSION.

6. Now that we have discussed the several kinds of virtue and friendship and pleasure, it remains to give a summary account of happiness, since we assume that it is the end of all that man does. And it will shorten our statement if we first recapitulate what we have said above.

Happiness not amusement, but life.

We said that happiness is not a habit or trained faculty. If it were, it would be within the reach of a man who slept all his days and lived the life of a vegetable, or of a man who met with the greatest misfortunes. As we cannot accept this conclusion, we must place happiness in some exercise of faculty, as we said before. But as the exercises of faculty are sometimes necessary (*i.e.* desirable for the sake of something else), sometimes desirable in themselves, it is evident that happiness must be placed among those that are desirable in themselves, and not among those that are desirable for the sake of something else: for happiness lacks nothing; it is sufficient in itself.

Now, the exercise of faculty is desirable in itself when nothing is expected from it beyond itself.

Of this nature are held to be (1) the manifestations of excellence; for to do what is noble and excellent must be counted desirable for itself: and (2) those amusements which please us; for they are not chosen for the sake of anything else,—indeed, men are more apt to be injured than to be benefited by them, through neglect of their health and fortunes

Now, most of those whom men call happy have recourse to pastimes of this sort. And on this account

those who show a ready wit in such pastimes find favour with tyrants; for they make themselves pleasant in that which the tyrant wants, and what he wants is pastime. These amusements, then, are generally thought to be elements of happiness, because
princes employ their leisure in them. But such per- 4
sons, we may venture to say, are no criterion. For princely rank does not imply the possession of virtue or of reason, which are the sources of all excellent exercise of faculty. And if these men, never having tasted pure and refined pleasure, have recourse to the pleasures of the body, we should not on that account think these more desirable; for children also fancy that the things which they value are better than anything else. It is only natural, then, that as children differ from men in their estimate of what is valuable, so bad men should differ from good.

As we have often said, therefore, that is truly 5
valuable and pleasant which is so to the perfect man. Now, the exercise of those trained faculties which are proper to him is what each man finds most desirable; what the perfect man finds most desirable, therefore, is the exercise of virtue.

Happiness, therefore, does not consist in amuse- 6
ment; and indeed it is absurd to suppose that the end is amusement, and that we toil and moil all our life long for the sake of amusing ourselves. We may say that we choose everything for the sake of something else, excepting only happiness; for it is the end. But to be serious and to labour for the sake of amusement seems silly and utterly childish; while to amuse ourselves in order that we may be serious, as

Anacharsis says, seems to be right; for amusement is a sort of recreation, and we need recreation because we are unable to work continuously.

Recreation, then, cannot be the end; for it is taken as a means to the exercise of our faculties.

Again, the happy life is thought to be that which exhibits virtue; and such a life must be serious and cannot consist in amusement.

Again, it is held that things of serious importance* are better than laughable and amusing things, and that the better the organ or the man, the more important is the function; but we have already said that the function or exercise of that which is better is higher and more conducive to happiness.

Again, the enjoyment of bodily pleasures is within the reach of anybody, of a slave no less than the best of men; but no one supposes that a slave can participate in happiness, seeing that he cannot participate in the proper life of man. For indeed happiness does not consist in pastimes of this sort, but in the exercise of virtue, as we have already said.

Of the speculative life as happiness in the highest sense

7. But if happiness be the exercise of virtue, it is reasonable to suppose that it will be the exercise of the highest virtue; and that will be the virtue or excellence of the best part of us.

Now, that part or faculty—call it reason or what you will—which seems naturally to rule and take the lead, and to apprehend things noble and divine—

* *τὰ σπουδαῖα.* It is impossible to convey in a translation the play upon the words *σπουδή* and *σπουδαῖος*: *σπουδή* is earnestness; *σπουδαῖος* usually = good: here, however, *σπουδαῖος* carries both senses, earnest or serious, and good.

whether it be itself divine, or only the divinest part of us—is the faculty the exercise of which, in its proper excellence, will be perfect happiness.

That this consists in speculation or contemplation we have already said.

This conclusion would seem to agree both with 2
what we have said above, and with known truths.

This exercise of faculty must be the highest possible; for the reason is the highest of our faculties, and of all knowable things those that reason deals with are the highest.

Again, it is the most continuous; for speculation can be carried on more continuously than any kind of action whatsoever.

We think too that pleasure ought to be one of the 3
ingredients of happiness; but of all virtuous exercises it is allowed that the pleasantest is the exercise of wisdom.* At least philosophy † is thought to have pleasures that are admirable in purity and steadfastness; and it is reasonable to suppose that the time passes more pleasantly with those who possess, than with those who are seeking knowledge.

Again, what is called self-sufficiency will be most 4
of all found in the speculative life. The necessaries of life, indeed, are needed by the wise man as well as by the just man and the rest; but, when these have been provided in due quantity, the just man further needs persons towards whom, and along with whom, he may act justly; and so does the temperate and the courageous man and the rest; while the

* ἡ κατὰ τὴν σοφίαν ἐνέργεια, the contemplation of absolute truth.

† The search for this truth.

wise man is able to speculate even by himself, and the wiser he is the more is he able to do this. He could speculate better, we may confess, if he had others to help him, but nevertheless he is more self-sufficient than anybody else.

5 Again, it would seem that this life alone is desired solely for its own sake; for it yields no result beyond the contemplation, but from the practical activities we get something more or less besides action.

6 Again, happiness is thought to imply leisure; for we toil in order that we may have leisure, as we make war in order that we may enjoy peace. Now, the practical virtues are exercised either in politics or in war; but these do not seem to be leisurely occupations:—

War, indeed, seems to be quite the reverse of leisurely; for no one chooses to fight for fighting's sake, or arranges a war for that purpose: he would be deemed a bloodthirsty villain who should set friends at enmity in order that battles and slaughter might ensue.

But the politician's life also is not a leisurely occupation, and, beside the practice of politics itself, it brings power and honours, or at least happiness, to himself and his fellow-citizens, which is something different from politics; for we [who are asking what happiness is] also ask what politics is, evidently implying that it is something different from happiness.

7 If, then, the life of the statesman and the soldier, though they surpass all other virtuous exercises in nobility and grandeur, are not leisurely occupations,

and aim at some ulterior end, and are not desired merely for themselves, but the exercise of the reason seems to be superior in seriousness (since it contemplates truth), and to aim at no end beside itself, and to have its proper pleasure (which also helps to increase the exercise), and further to be self-sufficient, and leisurely, and inexhaustible (as far as anything human can be), and to have all the other characteristics that are ascribed to happiness, it follows that the exercise of reason will be the complete happiness of man, *i.e.* when a complete term of days is added; for nothing incomplete can be admitted into our idea of happiness.

8 But a life which realized this idea would be something more than human; for it would not be the expression of man's nature, but of some divine element in that nature—the exercise of which is as far superior to the exercise of the other kind of virtue [*i.e.* practical or moral virtue], as this divine element is superior to our compound human nature.*

If then reason be divine as compared with man, the life which consists in the exercise of reason will also be divine in comparison with human life. Nevertheless, instead of listening to those who advise us as men and mortals not to lift our thoughts above what is human and mortal, we ought rather, as far as possible, to put off our mortality and make every effort to live in the exercise of the highest of our faculties; for though it be but a small part of us, yet in power and value it far surpasses all the rest.

* *i.e.* our nature as moral agents, as compounds of reason and desire.

And indeed this part would even seem to constitute our true self, since it is the sovereign and the better part. It would be strange, then, if a man were to prefer the life of something else to the life of his true self.

Again, we may apply here what we said above—for every being that is best and pleasantest which is naturally proper to it. Since, then, it is the reason that in the truest sense is the man, the life that consists in the exercise of the reason is the best and pleasantest for man—and therefore the happiest.

Of the practical life as happiness in a lower sense, and of the relation between the two. Prosperity, how far needed.

8. The life that consists in the exercise of the other kind of virtue is happy in a secondary sense; for the manifestations of moral virtue are emphatically human [not divine]. Justice, I mean, and courage, and the other moral virtues are displayed in our relations towards one another by the observance, in every case, of what is due in contracts and services, and all sorts of outward acts, as well as in our inward feelings. And all these seem to be emphatically human affairs.

Again, moral virtue seems, in some points, to be actually a result of physical constitution, and in many points to be closely connected with the passions.

Again, prudence is inseparably joined to moral virtue, and moral virtue to prudence, since the moral virtues determine the principles of prudence,* while prudence determines what is right in morals.

But the moral virtues, being bound up with the

* *i.e.* the principles of morals cannot be proved, but are accepted without proof by the man whose desires are properly trained. *Cf. supra*, I. 4, 6.

passions, must belong to our compound nature; and the virtues of the compound nature are emphatically human. Therefore the life which manifests them, and the happiness which consists in this, must be emphatically human.

But the happiness which consists in the exercise of the reason is separate from the lower nature. (So much we may be allowed to assert about it: a detailed discussion is beyond our present purpose.)

Further, this happiness would seem to need but a 4
small supply of external goods, certainly less than the moral life needs. Both need the necessaries of life to the same extent, let us say; for though, in fact, the politician takes more care of his person than the philosopher, yet the difference will be quite inconsiderable. But in what they need for their activities there will be a great difference. Wealth will be needed by the liberal man, that he may act liberally; by the just man, that he may discharge his obligations (for a mere wish cannot be tested,—even unjust people pretend a wish to act justly); the courageous man will need strength if he is to execute any deed of courage; and the temperate man liberty of indulgence,—for how else can he, or the possessor of any other virtue, show what he is?

Again, people dispute whether the purpose or the 5
action be more essential to virtue, virtue being understood to imply both. It is plain, then, that both are necessary to completeness. But many things are needed for action, and the greater and nobler the action, the more is needed.

On the other hand, he who is engaged in specula- 6

tion needs none of these things for his *work;* nay, it may even be said that they are a hindrance to speculation: but as a man living with other men, he chooses to act virtuously; and so he will need things of this sort to enable him to behave like a man.

7 That perfect happiness is some kind of speculative activity may also be shown in the following way:—

It is always supposed that the gods are, of all beings, the most blessed and happy; but what kind of actions shall we ascribe to them? Acts of justice? Surely it is ridiculous to conceive the gods engaged in trade and restoring deposits, and so on. Or the acts of the courageous character who endures fearful things and who faces danger because it is noble to do so?* Or acts of liberality? But to whom are they to give? and is it not absurd to suppose that they have money or anything of that kind? And what could acts of temperance mean with them? Surely it would be an insult to praise them for having no evil desires. In short, if we were to go through the whole list, we should find that all action is petty and unworthy of the gods.

And yet it is universally supposed that they live, and therefore that they exert their powers; for we cannot suppose that they lie asleep like Endymion.

Now, if a being lives, and action cannot be ascribed to him, still less production, what remains but contemplation? It follows, then, that the divine life, which surpasses all others in blessedness, consists in contemplation.

* Reading *ἀνδρείου ὑπομένοντος . . κινδυνεύοντος* after Bywater. "Contributions," p. 69.

Of all modes of human activity, therefore, that which is most akin to this will be capable of the greatest happiness.

And this is further confirmed by the fact that the 8
other animals do not participate in happiness, being quite incapable of this kind of activity. For the life of the gods is entirely blessed, and the life of man is blessed just so far as he attains to some likeness of this kind of activity; but none of the other animals are happy, since they are quite incapable of contemplation.

Happiness, then, extends just so far as contemplation, and the more contemplation the more happiness is there in a life,—not accidentally, but as a necessary accompaniment of the contemplation: for contemplation is precious in itself.

Our conclusion, then, is that happiness is a kind of speculation or contemplation.

But as we are men we shall need external good 9
fortune also: for our nature does not itself provide all that is necessary for contemplation; the body must be in health, and supplied with food, and otherwise cared for. We must not, however, suppose that because it is impossible to be happy without external good things, therefore a man who is to be happy will want many things or much. It is not the superabundance of good things that makes a man independent, or enables him to act; and a man may do 10
noble deeds, though he be not ruler of land and sea. A moderate equipment may give you opportunity for virtuous action (as we may easily see, for private persons seem to do what is right not less, but rather

more, than princes), and so much as gives this opportunity is enough; for that man's life will be happy who has virtue and exercises it.

11 Solon too, I think, gave a good description of the happy man when he said that, in his opinion, he was a man who was moderately supplied with the gifts of fortune, but had done the noblest deeds, and lived temperately; for a man who has but modest means may do his duty.

Anaxagoras also seems to have held that the happy man was neither a rich man nor a prince; for he said that he should not be surprised if the happy man were one whom the masses could hardly believe to be so; for they judge by the outside, which is all they can appreciate.

12 The opinions of the wise, then, seem to agree with our theory. But though these opinions carry some weight, the test of truth in matters of practice is to be found in the facts of life; for it is in them that the supreme authority resides. The theories we have advanced, therefore, should be tested by comparison with the facts of life; and if they agree with the facts they should be accepted, but if they disagree they should be accounted mere theories.

13 But, once more, the man who exercises his reason and cultivates it, and has it in the best condition, seems also to be the most beloved of heaven. For if the gods take any care for men, as they are thought to do, it is reasonable to suppose that they delight in that which is best in man and most akin to themselves (*i.e.* the reason), and that they requite those who show the greatest love and reverence for it, as

caring for that which is dear to themselves and doing rightly and nobly. But it is plain that all these points are found most of all in the wise man. The wise man, therefore, is the most beloved of heaven; and therefore, we may conclude, the happiest.

In this way also, therefore, the wise man will be happier than any one else.

How is the end to be realized?

9. Now that we have treated (sufficiently, though 1
summarily) of these matters, and of the virtues, and also of friendship and pleasure, are we to suppose that we have attained the end we proposed? Nay, surely the saying holds good, that in practical matters the end is not a mere speculative knowledge of what is
to be done, but rather the doing of it. It is not 2
enough to know about virtue, then, but we must endeavour to possess it and to use it, or to take any other steps that may make us good.

Now, if theories had power of themselves to make 3
us good, "many great rewards would they deserve" as Theognis says, and such ought we to give; but in fact it seems that though they are potent to guide and to stimulate liberal-minded young men, and though a generous disposition, with a sincere love of what is noble, may by them be opened to the influence of virtue, yet they are powerless to turn the
mass of men to goodness. For the generality of men 4
are naturally apt to be swayed by fear rather than by reverence, and to refrain from evil rather because of the punishment that it brings than because of its own foulness. For under the guidance of their passions they pursue the pleasures that suit their nature and the means by which those pleasures may

be obtained, and avoid the opposite pains, while of that which is noble and truly pleasant they have not even a conception, as they have never tasted it.

5 What theories or arguments, then, can bring such men as these to order? Surely it is impossible, or at least very difficult, to remove by any argument what has long been ingrained in the character. For my part, I think we must be well content if we can get some modicum of virtue when all the circumstances are present that seem to make men good.

6 Now, what makes men good is held by some to be nature, by others habit [or training], by others instruction.

As for the goodness that comes by nature, it is plain that it is not within our control, but is bestowed by some divine agency on certain people who truly deserve to be called fortunate.

As for theory or instruction, I fear that it cannot
avail in all cases, but that the hearer's soul must be
prepared by training it to feel delight and aversion
on the right occasions, just as the soil must be pre-
7 pared if the seed is to thrive. For if he lives under
the sway of his passions, he will not listen to the
arguments by which you would dissuade him, nor
even understand them. And when he is in this state,
how can you change his mind by argument? To
put it roundly, passion seems to yield to force only,
8 and not to reason. The character, then, must be
already * formed, so as to be in some way akin to
virtue, loving what is noble and hating what is base.

But to get right guidance from youth up in the

* Before theory or instruction can be any use. *Cf.* I. 4, 6.

road to virtue is hard, unless we are brought up under suitable laws; for to live temperately and regularly is not pleasant to the generality of men, especially to the young. Our nurture, then, should be prescribed by law, and our whole way of life; for it will cease to be painful as we get accustomed to it.
And I venture to think that it is not enough to get 9
proper nurture and training when we are young, but that as we ought to carry on the same way of life after we are grown up, and to confirm these habits, we need the intervention of the law in these matters also, and indeed, to put it roundly, in our whole life. For the generality of men are more readily swayed by compulsion than by reason, and by fear of punishment than by desire for what is noble.

For this reason, some hold that the legislator 10
should, in the first instance, invite the people and exhort them to be virtuous because of the nobility of virtue, as those who have been well trained will listen to him; but that when they will not listen, or are of less noble nature, he should apply correction and punishment, and banish utterly those who are incorrigible. For the good man, who takes what is noble as his guide, will listen to reason, but he who is not good, whose desires are set on pleasure, must be corrected by pain like a beast of burden. And for this reason, also, they say the pains to be applied must be those that are most contrary to the pleasures which the culprit loves.

As we have said, then, he who is to be good must 11
be well nurtured and trained, and thereafter must continue in a like excellent way of life, and must never,

either voluntarily or involuntarily, do anything vile; and this can only be effected if men live subject to some kind of reason and proper regimen, backed by force.

12 Now, the paternal rule has not the requisite force or power of compulsion, nor has the rule of any individual, unless he be a king or something like one; but the law has a compulsory power, and at the same time is a rational ordinance proceeding from a kind of prudence or reason.* And whereas we take offence at individuals who oppose our inclinations, even though their opposition is right, we do not feel aggrieved when the law bids us do what is right.

13 But Sparta is the only, or almost the only, state where the legislator seems to have paid attention to the nurture and mode of life of the citizens. In most states these matters are entirely neglected, and each man lives as he likes, ruling wife and children in Cyclopean fashion.†

14 It would be best, then, that the regulation of these matters should be undertaken and properly carried out by the state; but as the state neglects it, it would seem that we should each individually help our own children or friends on the road to virtue, and should have the power or at least the will to do this.‡

Now, it would seem from what has been said that to enable one to do this the best plan would be to learn how to legislate. For state training is carried on by means of laws, and is good when the laws are

* *Cf.* VI. 8, 1–3. † *Cf.* Hom. Od. ix. 114.

‡ Transposing *καὶ δρᾶν αὐτὸ δύνασθαι* as suggested by Bywater: *cf.* I. 2, 8.

good; but it would seem to make no difference whether the laws be written or unwritten, nor whether they regulate the education of one person or many, any more than it does in the case of music, or gymnastics, or any other course of training. For as in the state that prevails which is ordained by law and morality, so in the household that which is ordained by the word of the father of the family and by custom prevails no less, or even more, because of the ties of kinship and of obligation; for affection and obedience are already implanted by nature in the members of the family.

Moreover, in spite of what has just been said, 15
individual treatment is better than treatment by masses, in education no less than in medicine. As a general rule, repose and fasting are good for a fever patient, but in a particular case they may not be good. A teacher of boxing, I suppose, does not recommend every one to adopt the same style. It would seem, then, that individuals are educated more perfectly under a system of private education; for then each gets more precisely what he needs.

But you will best be able to treat an individual case (whether you are a doctor, or a trainer, or anything else) when you know the general rule, "Such and such a thing is good for all men," or "for all of a certain temperament;" for science is said to deal, and does deal, with that which is common to a number of individuals.

I do not mean to deny that it may be quite pos- 16
sible to treat an individual well, even without any scientific knowledge, if you know precisely by ex-

perience the effect of particular causes upon him, just as some men seem to be able to treat themselves better than any doctor, though they would be quite unable to prescribe for another person.

But, nevertheless, I venture to say that if a man wishes to master any art, or to gain a scientific knowledge of it, he must advance to its general principles, and make himself acquainted with them in the proper method; for, as we have said, it is with universal propositions that the sciences deal.

17 And so I think that he who wishes to make men better by training (whether many or few) should try to acquire the art or science of legislation, supposing that men may be made good by the agency of law. For fairly to mould the character of any person that may present himself is not a thing that can be done by anybody, but (if at all) only by him who has knowledge, just as is the case in medicine and other professions where careful treatment and prudence are required.

18 Our next business, then, I think, is to inquire from whom or by what means we are to learn the science or art of legislation.

"As we learn the other arts," it will be said,—"*i.e.* from the politicians who practise it: for we found that legislation is a part of politics."

But I think the case is not quite the same with politics as with the other sciences and arts. For in other cases it is plain that the same people communicate the art and practise it, as physicians and painters do. But in the case of politics, while the sophists profess to teach the art, it is never they that practise it,

but the statesmen. And the statesmen would seem to act by some instinctive faculty, proceeding empirically rather than by reasoning. For it is plain that they never write or speak about these matters (though perhaps that were better than making speeches in the courts or the assembly), and have never communicated the art to their sons or to any of their friends.
And yet we might expect that they would have 19
done so if they could; for they could have left no better legacy to their country, nor have chosen anything more precious than this power as a possession for themselves, and, therefore, for those dearest to them.

Experience, however, seems, we must allow, to be of great service here; for otherwise people would never become statesmen by familiarity with politics. Those who wish for a knowledge of statesmanship, then, seem to need experience [as well as theory].

But those sophists who profess to teach states- 20
manship seem to be ludicrously incapable of fulfilling their promises: for, to speak roundly, they do not even know what it is or what it deals with. If they did know, they would not make it identical with rhetoric, or inferior to it, nor would they think it was easy to frame a system of laws when you had made a collection of the most approved of existing laws. "It is but a matter of picking out the best," they say, ignoring the fact that this selection requires understanding, and that to judge correctly is a matter of the greatest difficulty here, as in music. Those who have special experience in any department can pass a correct judgment upon the result, and under-

stand how and by what means it is produced, and what combinations are harmonious; but those who have no special experience must be content if they are able to say whether the result is good or bad—as, for instance, in the case of painting. Now, laws are the work or result, so to speak, of statesmanship. How then could a collection of laws make a man able to legislate, or to pick out the best of the collection?

21 Even the art of healing, it seems, can not be taught by compendia. And yet the medical compendia try to tell you not only the remedies, but how to apply them, and how to treat the several classes of patients, distinguishing them according to their temperament. But all this, though it may be serviceable to those who have experience, would seem to be quite useless to those who know nothing of medicine.

So also, I think we may say, collections of laws and constitutions may be very serviceable to those who are able to examine them with a discriminating eye, and to judge whether an ordinance is good or bad, and what ordinances agree with one another, but if people who have not the trained faculty go through such compendia, they cannot judge properly (unless indeed a correct judgment comes of itself), though they may perhaps sharpen their intelligence in these matters.

22 Since then our predecessors have left this matter of legislation uninvestigated, it will perhaps be better ourselves to inquire into it, and indeed into the whole question of the management of a state, in order that our philosophy of human life may be completed to the best of our power.

Let us try, then, first of all, to consider any valuable utterances that our predecessors have made upon this or that branch of the subject; and then, looking at our collection of constitutions, let us inquire what things tend to preserve or to destroy states, and what things tend to preserve or destroy the several kinds of constitution, and what are the causes of the good government of some states and the misgovernment of others: for when we have got an insight into these matters we shall, I think, be better able to see what is the best kind of constitution, and what is the best arrangement of each of the several kinds; that is to say, what system of laws and customs is best suited to each.

Let us begin then.*———

* The work to which this conclusion forms a preface is the Politics of Aristotle, still extant, but in an incomplete state.

INDEX.

Absolute, I. 6, 5
Action and end, I. 1; and life, I. 7; and virtue, II. 1-6; and will, III. 1-5; life of action, X. 8
Activity, highest, VII. 14, 8; X. 7-8; how related to pleasure, VII. 12-13; X. 4-5
Æschylus, III. 1, 17
Agamemnon, VIII. 11, 1
Agathon, VI. 4, 5
Agreeableness, IV. 6
Alcmæon, III. 1, 8
Alope, VII. 7, 6
Ambition, II. 7, 8; IV. 4
Amusement not the end, X. 6
Anacharsis, X. 6, 6.
Anaxagoras, VI. 7, 5; X. 8, 11
Anaxandrides, VII. 10, 3
Anger, II. 7, 10; IV. 5; acts done in, not involuntary, III. 1, 21
Aphrodite, VII. 6, 3
Apparent. See *Real*
Appetite, I. 13, 15 f.*; III. 2, 3-5; III. 10-12; VII.
Argives, III. 8, 16
Art, II. 6, 8 f.; VI. 4
Association, V. 1, 13; V. 5; VIII. 9
Athenians, IV. 3, 25

Being, I. 6, 3
Bias quoted, V. 1, 16
Boastfulness, IV. 7
Bodily goods, I. 8, 2; VII. 14; pleasures, III. 10; VII.; X. 3, 6 f.; X. 6, 4
Boorishness, II. 7, 13; IV. 8, 3. 10
Brasidas, V. 7, 1
Brutality, VII. 1. 5-6
Buffoonery, II. 7, 13; IV. 8, 10

Calculation, faculty of, VI. 1, 6; VI. 5 f.
Calypso, II. 9, 3
Carcinus, VII. 7, 6
Cercyon, VII. 7, 6
Chance, I. 9, 1. 5; III. 3, 5. 7; VI. 4, 5
Choice and will, III. 2. See *Purpose*
Civil society, VIII. 9
Cleverness, VI. 12, 9; VII. 10
Compulsion, III. 1, 3 f.
Conflicting duties, IX. 2
Consciousness, IX. 9, 7 f.
Constitutions, II. 1, 5; V. 7, 5; VIII. 10; X. 9, 21
Contemplation, the highest life, X. 7
Continence, VII. 1-10
Correction, justice in, V. 4
Courage, II. 7, 2; III. 6-9
Cretans, I. 13, 3
Cyclopean, X. 9, 13
Cyprus, VII. 6, 3

* *f means and following sections or chapters.*

Death, I. **10**; III. **6**, 3 f.; III. **9**, 4
Delian inscription, I. **8**, 14
Deliberation, III. **3**; VI. **1**, 6 f.; VI. **9**
Democracy, V. **3**, 7; VIII. **10**, 3. 6; VIII. **11**, 8
Demonstration, faculty of, VI. **1**, 6
Demonstrative science, VI. **3**
Desire, I. **2**, 1; I. **3**, 7; III. **3**, 19; III. **12**, 6; VI. **2**; VII. **1–10**
Diomede, III. **8**, 2
Distribution, justice in, V. **1**, 9; V. **2–3**
Divine life, VII. **14**, 8; X, **8**, 7

Education, I. **4**, 6; II. **1**; II. **3**, 2; V. **2**, 11; X. **9**
Emotion, II. **5**
Empedocles, VII. **3**, 8. 13; VIII. **1**, 6
End, the, I. **1–12**; X. **6–9**; and means, I. **1**; I. **2**; I. **7**; III. **2**, 9; III. **3**, 11 f.
Endymion, X. **8**, 7
Epicharmus, IX. **7**, 1
Equality and justice, V.; and friendship, VIII. **13**
Equity, V. **10**
Eudoxus, I. **12**, 5; X. **2**
Euenus, VII. **10**, 4
Euripides, III. **1**, 8; V. **9**, 1; VI. **8**, 4; VIII. **1**, 6; IX. **6**, 2
Euripus, IX. **6**, 3
Exact reasoning impossible here, I. **3**; II. **2**, 3
Excellence. See *Virtue*
Excess, II. **2**, 6 f. and *passim*
Exchange, justice in, V. **5**
Expedient, II. **3**, 7; III. **1**, 15; V. **1**, 13; VI. **5** f.; VIII. **9**, 4 f.
External goods, I. **8**, 2, 15 f.; I. **9–11**; IX. **9**; X. **8**, 4 f.

Faculties, division of, I. **13**; opp. passions and habits, II. **5**; faculty and trained faculty or habit, II. **1** f.; VI. **1** f.; exercise of faculty, I. **1**, 2; I. **7**, 13; I. **8**, 9; I. **10**, 10; II. **1**, 4; VII. **12–14**; IX. **9**, 7; X. **4–8**
Feeling, II.; IX. **9**, 7
Friendship, VIII., IX.; and justice, IX. **1–2**
Function of man, I. **7**, 10 f.; VI. **12–13**; X. **6–8**

Gentleness, II. **7**, 10; IV. **5**
Glaucus, V. **9**, 7
God, I. **6**, 3; I. **9**, 2; I. **12**, 3–4; VII. **14**, 8; VIII. **7**, 5; IX. **4**, 4; X. **8**, 7
Good, I.; III. **4**; III. **5**, 17 f.; VII. **11–14**; X.; Plato's idea of good, I. **6**; good in itself, VII. **12**
Goods, division of, I. **8**, 2
Graces, V. **5**, 7

Habit and nature, II. **1** f.; III. **5**, 17 f.; X. **9**, 6 f.
Happiness the end, I. **4**; defined, I. **7**, 15; how got, I. **9**; absolute, I. **12**; = the good, I. **7**; = life, X. **6–8**
Hector, III. **8**, 2. 4; VII. **1**, 1
Helen, II. **9**, 6
Heraclitus, II. **3**, 10; VII. **3**, 4; VIII. **1**, 6; X. **5**, 8
Hermes, III. **8**, 9
Hesiod, I. **4**, 7; VIII. **1**, 6; IX. **1**, 5
High-mindedness, II. **7**, 7; IV. **3**
Homer, III. **3**, 18; III. **8**, 2. 10; III. **11**, 1; V. **9**, 7; VI. **7**, 2; VII. **1**, 1; VII. **6**, 3; VIII. **10**, 4; VIII. **11**, 1
Honour, II. **7**, 7–8; IV. **3-4**

Ideas, Plato's doctrine of, I. **6**
Ignorance and wrong-doing, III. **1–5**; V. **8**, 3 f.; VI. **5**, 6; VI. **12**, 10; VII. **1–10**
Incontinence, I. **13**, 15; III. **2**, 4; VII. **1–10**
Individual and state, I. **2**, 8; I. **7**, 6; V. **2**, 11; VI. **8**; X. **9**

Insensibility, II. **8**, 6; III. **11**, 7
Instruction and morality, I. **3**, 5 f.; I. **9**; II. **4**, 6; X. **9**, 6
Intellectual. See *Virtue*
Intelligence, VI. **10**
Intuitive reason, VI. **6**. **7**. **11**
Involuntary defined, III. **1**; transactions, V. **2**, 13
Irony, II. **7**, 12; IV. **7**, 14 f.
Irrational part of soul, I. **13**, 9 f.; III. **10**, 1; IX. **8**, 4; passions, III. **1**, 27; beings, III. **2**, 3; X. **2**, 1

Judgment, VI. **11**
Just, uncertainty about what is, I. **3**, 2; conditions of just action, V. **8**
Justice, V.; implies the state, V. **6**, 4; part natural, part conventional, V. **7**; and friendship, IX. **1-2**

Knowledge and action, II. **4**; III. **1**, f.; VI.; can a man act against? VII. **1-10**

Law and justice, V.
Legislation, II. **1**, 5; III. **5**, 7; V. **1**, 13; VI. **8**; X. **9**
Lesbian building, V. **10**, 7
Liberality, II. **7**, 4; IV. **1**
Life man's function or end, I. **7**, 13 f.; I. **13**; IX. **4**, 3 f.; X. **5-8**

Magnificence, II. **7**, 6; IV. **2**
Man naturally social, I. **7**, 6; IX. **9**, 3; *cf.* V. **6**, 4; man's nature compound, X. **6-8**; philosophy of man, X. **9**, 22
Mankind, opinion of, appealed to, X. **2**, 4
Margites of Homer, VI. **7**, 2
Mean, the, II. **2**, 6 f.; II. **6**; hard to hit, II. **9**
Means. See *End*
Megara, IV. **2**, 20
Merope, III. **1**, 17
Method, I. **3**; I. **4**, 4 f.; I. **7**, 17; VII. **1**, 5; VII. **2**, 12; X. **2**, 4; X. **9**
Milesians, VII. **8**, 3
Milo, II. **6**, 7
Moderation, II.
Money, V. **5**, 10-11
Moral. See *Virtue*
Motion and activity, VII. **14**, 8; and becoming, X. **3**, 4; X. **4**, 4
Motives, II. **3**, 7; the virtuous man's motive, III. **7**, 2. 13; IV. **2**, 7
Mysteries, III. **1**, 17.

Nature dist. from other modes of causation, I. **9**; III. **3**, 4; and habit, II. **1** f.; III. **5**, 15; VII. **5**; X. **9**, 6 f.
Necessity, III. **3**, 4
Neoptolemus, VII. **2**, 7; VII. **9**, 4
Niobe, VII. **4**, 5

Olympic games, I. **8**, 9; VII. **4**, 2
Opinion, III. **2**, 10 f.; VII. **2**, 4; VII. **3**, 3; current opinions referred to, *passim*, *e.g.* I. **4**; I. **5**; VII. **1**, 5 f.

Pain. See *Pleasure*
Perception, I. **7**, 21; II. **9**, 8; III. **3**, 16; VI. **8**, 9; VI. **11**, 5; VII. **3**, 9
Pericles, VI. **5**, 5
Persia, VIII. **10**, 4; V. **7**, 2
Phalaris, VII. **5**, 2. 7
Phidias, VI. **7**, 1
Philoctetes, VII. **7**, 6; VII. **9**, 4
Philosophy man's highest activity, X. **7**; of human life, X. **9**, 22
Phœnissæ of Euripides, IX. **6**, 2
Pittacus, IX. **6**, 2
Plato, I. **4**, 5; II. **3**, 2; X. **2**, 3; Plato's ideas examined, I. **6**
Pleasure goes with happiness, I. **8**, 10-14; a test of character, II. **3**, 1; moral virtue specially concerned with pleasure and pain, II. **3**, 1 f.; II. **9**, 6; sources of,

VII. **4**, 2; VII. **14**; X. **3**, 8; how related to activity, VII. **13–14**; X. **4–5**
Pleasure, first account of, VII. **11–14**
——, second account of, X. **1–5**
Poets and their works, IX. **7**, 3
Politics, I. **2**, 5 f.; I. **3**, 5; I. **4**, 1. 6; I. **13**, 2–4; VI. **7**, 3 f.; VI. **8**; X. **7**, 6 f.; X. **9**
Polyclitus, VI. **7**, 1
Polydamas, III. **8**, 2
Pontus, VII. **5**, 2
Practical life = happiness in lower sense, X. **8**; philosophy, X. **9**, 22; politicians unable to teach, X. **9**, 18; reason, VI.; VII. **1–10**; syllogism, VI. **11**, 4; VI. **12**, 10; VII. **3**, 6 f.
Priam, I. **9**, 11; I. **10**, 14; VII. **1**, 1
Principles, how got, I. **4**, 5 f.; I. **7**, 21 f.; VI. **3**, 3; VI. **5**, 6; VI. **6**, 1 f.; VI. **11**, 4; X. **8**, 3 f.
Profligacy, II. **7**, 3; III. **12**; VII. **8**.
Proportion in justice, V. **3–5**; in friendship, VIII. **7**, 3; IX. **1**
Prosperity, how far necessary to happiness, I. **9**, 11; I. **10**; X. **8**, **4**. 9 f.
Protagoras, IX. **1**, 5
Prudence, VI. **5** f.; its use, VI. **12**; prudence and virtue, VI. **13**; VII. **10**; X. **8**, 3
Purpose, III. **2**; VI. 2
Pythagoreans, I. **6**, **7**; II. **6**, 14; V. **5**, 1

Quantity, II. **6**, 4 f.; V. **3**, f.

Rational and irrational part of soul, I. **7**, 12 f.; I. **13**, 9 f.; faculties divided, VI. **1**, 5
Real and apparent, III. **4–5**; VII. **12**, 1; VIII. **2**, 2
Reason, VI.; X. **7** f.; and morality, II. **2**, 2 f.; III. **1–5**; VI. *passim*; VII. **1–10**; in narrower sense (= faculty of universals), VI. **6** f.; VI. **11**
Requital, V. **5**
Responsibility, III. **1–5**
Rhadamanthus, V. **5**, 3

Sardanapalus, I. **5**, 3
Satyrus Philopator, VII. **4**, **5**
Scythia, III. **3**, 6; VII. **7**, 6
Science, VI. **1** f.
Self, IX. **4**. **7**; X. **7**, 9
Self-love, IX. **8**
Sense, I. **7**, 12; VI. **2**, 1; VI. **8**, 9; VI. **11**, 5; VII. **3**, 9; VII. **6**, 1; X. **4–5**.
Shame, II. **7**, 14; IV. **9**
Sicyonians, III. **8**, 16
Simonides, IV. **1**, 27
Slaves, VIII. **11**, 6
Social intercourse, IV. **6–8**
Society, VIII. **9** f.
Socrates, III. **8**, 6; IV. **7**, 14; VI. **13**, 5; VII. **2–3**
Solon, I. **10**, 1 f.; X. **8**, 11
Sophists, IX. **1**, 7; X. **9**, 18. 20
Sophocles, VII. **2**, 7; VII. **9**, 4
Soul, or faculty of life, I. **7**, 12 f.; I. **13**; II. 5; VI. **1**, 5 f.
Spartans, I. **13**, 3; III. **3**, 6; III. **8**, 16; IV. **3**, 25; IV. **7**, 15; VII. **1**, 3; IX. **6**, 2; X. **9**, 13
Speculative life the highest, I. **7**, 15; X. **7**; X. **8**, 7 f.
Speusippus, I. **6**, 7; VII. **13**, 1
Starting-point or principle can't be demonstrated, I. **4**, 6; I. **7**, 20
State and individual, I. **2**, 4 f.; II. **1**, 5; V. **2**, 11; VI. **8**; VIII. **9**; X. **9**
Statesmanship, VI. **8**; X. **9**
Suicide a crime, V. **11**, 2
Syllogism, VI. **3**, 3; VI. **9**, 5; VI. **11**, 4; VI. **12**, 10; VII. **3**, 6 f.

Tact, IV. **8**, 5
Temper, IV. **5**
Temperance, II. **7**, 3; III. **10–12**
Thales, VI. **7**, 5
Theodectes, VII. **7**, 6
Theognis, IX. **9**, 7; X. **9**, 3
Thetis, IV. **3**, 25

Troy, I. **9**, 11; VI. **2**, 6
Truth, faculties by which it is apprehended, VI. **2-3**
Truthfulness, II. **7**, 12; IV. **7**
Tydeus, III. **8**, 2

Ultimate truths, VI. **8**. **11**
Ulysses, II. **9**, 3; VII. **2**, 7; VII. **9**, 4
Universals, I. **6**; VI.

Vice. See *Virtue*
Virtue and happiness, I. **5 f.**; X. **6 f.**; moral and intellectual, distinguished, I. **13**; moral virtue, II.; list of moral virtues, II. **7**; account of the several moral virtues, III. **6**–end of V.; of the intellectual virtues, VI.; X. **7**; virtue and vice equally voluntary, III. **5**
Voluntary and involuntary defined, III. **1**

Wealth, V. **5**
Will, III. **1-5**
Wisdom, VI. **7**; VI. **12**
Wish, III. **2**, 7 f.; III. **4**
Wit, IV. **8**
Wrong, can a man wrong himself? V. **11**

Xenophantus, VII. **7**, 6

Zeus, IV. **3**. 25; VIII. **10**, **4**; IX. **2**, **6**

Printed in Great Britain by Butler & Tanner Ltd., *Frome and London*

www.ingramcontent.com/pod-product-compliance
Lightning Source LLC
Chambersburg PA
CBHW030908270326
41929CB00008B/613

* 9 7 8 3 3 3 7 0 4 2 8 9 9 *